JOURNALISTS
IN ACTION

JOURNALISTS IN ACTION

Compiled by
DEAN EDWARD W. BARRETT
in honor of the fiftieth anniversary
of the Columbia University
Graduate School of Journalism

Assistant editor, Robert F. Hewes

Published by Channel Press, Manhasset, New York

Library of Congress Catalog Card Number: 63-17530

Printed in the United States of America

Introduction

Carl W. Ackerman, Dean Emeritus of Columbia University's Graduate School of Journalism, recalls in his contribution to this book the beginnings of the School in September, 1912. "Our greatest liability," he writes, "was the skepticism of the press toward education in journalism, an attitude shared by educational institutions throughout the United States." By now, Dean Ackerman continues, "education in journalism is as firmly established as is education in other professions, and our alumni are pioneering throughout the world."

In the pages of this book the story of such pioneering is, in effect, told by a number of the pioneers. All the articles are original, written especially for this volume, and were contributed by these journalists in acknowledgment of a debt to a small but great institution.

When Joseph Pulitzer, publisher of *The St. Louis Post-Dispatch* and *The New York World,* first approached Nicholas Murray Butler, president of Columbia University, to discuss the setting up of a school of journalism, he declared that journalism should be "one of the great and intellectual professions." Its practitioners, he said, should "have knowledge of politics, literature, government, constitutional principles and traditions, history, political economy; also the history and the power of public opinion and public service."

Ever since, Columbia's School of Journalism has grown and developed in this direction, emphasizing broad professional training based on an ever-broader liberal education. From the start its faculty included men of national distinction—Talcott Williams, Charles A. Beard, James T. Shotwell, and John W. Cunliffe; and, later, Carlton J. H. Hayes, Brander Matthews, Douglas Southall Freeman. Columbia's School was the first in the country to become a graduate school, and it is still the only school of journalism in the nation that is completely a graduate institution. And from the outset, it pioneered in service to the profession—through the Pulitzer Prizes and later the Cabot prizes, through its part in founding the American Press Institute and its role in the creation of the International Press Institute.

Today the School and its alumni find themselves in the midst of an exciting revolution in news communication. The news magazines have become an established part of our society; news is transmitted by radio and television; trans-Atlantic television has become a reality; long-overdue improvements in printing processes are taking place at an explosive pace.

The news itself has multiplied in complexity. The trend is illustrated by today's news vocabulary—Ghana and Togo, nose-cones and silicones, computers and programers, masers and lasers—plus countless other items, concepts and places never before in the public consciousness. To an extent that dwarfs all that has previously been required of him, it is vital for the average citizen of today to comprehend the world about him. While there is no doubt that the nation today is as well informed as any in the world, and while the country's news organs are serving it at least as well as ever before, a central question remains: Are the means of communications improving rapidly enough to meet the enormous needs of an atomic age democracy? To this question the candid answer is No.

Against this background, Columbia's Graduate School of Journalism strives toward two goals:

First, to help singularly promising young Americans progress toward becoming truly superior communicators—with the breadth of knowledge required to understand today's events, the skill to record and interpret them with polish and deftness, the integrity to do so with ruthless fairness, and the vision ultimately to seek and perhaps to find better ways to do the job.

Second, to help in every appropriate way to spur rapid improvement in the journalism-communications system—through honoring the deserving and decent and dealing forthrightly with the shoddy and irresponsible; through supporting leaders of the profession in raising both the standards of practice and the rewards of excellence; through fighting suppression and distortion of news, and through research and experiments that may provide improved ways of dealing with the information glut.

The body of alumni from whom this book was drawn is small. The School has averaged only some 65 graduates a year. The classes will continue to be small, for journalism is not an enormous profession, and, above all, does not lend itself to mass-production education. The work in general assignment reporting, in television laboratories, in production of the experimental *Columbia News,* in reporting at the United Nations and at City Hall—all require a continuing, personal dialogue between the individual student and those who guide him. The approximately 100,000 words written by each student each year must be painstakingly criticized by experienced instructors—and often rewritten and criticized again. In the "Basic Issues in the News" program, leading members of other Columbia faculties teach and work with the students, criticizing the major papers done by each. The School's advanced programs for mid-career training—in International Reporting, in Advanced Science Writing and soon in other fields—also demand intense student-faculty cooperation.

Happily, the size of the School does not limit the distinction of its alumni or the range of the institution's influence. Among those represented in these pages are the former president of the Canadian Press, David Rogers; a former president of the American Newspaper Publishers Association, William Dwight; a recent president of the influential Associated Press Managing Editors Association, representing the many newspapers that belong to the Associated Press, Michael Ogden; and the president for 1963-64 of the American Society of Newspaper Editors, Herbert Brucker. Sixteen heads of other journalism schools and more than a score of distinguished journalism professors are numbered among the alumni, and are represented in this symposium by John Hulteng, Everest Derthick, Ralph Lowenstein, John Tebbel, and others. There are magazine editors among the contributors, too, and broadcasters and figures from the book world.

Represented also are some of those whose writings brought to the new "Columbia Journalism Review" a paid circulation of 7,000 within its first year. The mission of the Review is, "To assess the performance of journalism in all its forms, to call attention to its shortcomings and strengths, and to help define—or redefine—standards of honest responsible service . . . to help stimulate continuing improvement in the profession and to speak out for what is right, fair and decent." Significantly, the magazine has won praise from both James S. Hagerty and Pierre Salinger; Mr. Salinger called it "the one organization in the country that takes a really penetrating look" at American journalism.

JOURNALISTS IN ACTION is itself a reflection of the reach and potential influence of a small educational institution devoted to excellence. It was first suggested by Theodore M. Bernstein, an outstanding graduate and for twenty-five years a teacher in the School, and now assistant managing editor of *The New York Times*. He and the editors have hoped that the book could serve as a constructive guide and inspiration to both students and professionals—and as at least interesting reading to the public at large. We who edited the book will always be deeply grateful to the loyal and distinguished alumni who made it possible through their contributions of articles. At the same time it is regretted that tight deadlines plus major breaking news stories made it impossible to await the contributions of other equally distinguished and loyal alumni.

JOURNALISTS IN ACTION is planned as if it were an informal conversation among notable journalists. It reflects what actually occurs when such journalists meet and chat throughout the world.

When journalists talk among themselves, they trade memories—of the big or unforgettable stories, of the problems of their craft, of the teachers who guided them, of lessons learned.

They reflect, tell anecdotes, sum up. In moments of frustration, some dream of getting out of the big city. Some others determine from the start to choose a small town, to edit a country weekly or to write.

All speak of people they have met. They recall new ventures, first jobs and turning points. They discuss the widening scope of the profession—in radio and television, in industry, internationally.

The editors have endeavored to encompass all of these in this book. They have tried to do so in a way that will make the book long useful to the student journalist and the experienced journalist and that will be in keeping with the School's 50th Anniversary theme: "That the People Shall Know."

EDWARD W. BARRETT

New York
August 15, 1963

Table of Contents

The Big or Unforgettable Stories

The Problems of Their Craft

Teachers Who Guided Them, and Lessons Learned

They Reflect, Tell Anecdotes, Sum Up

Getting Out of The Big City

People They Have Met

New Ventures, First Jobs, Turning Points

The Widening Scope of
The Profession

When journalists talk among themselves, they trade memories---of the big or unforgettable stories...

When Robert Elegant went to the Far East in 1951, he did so with a uniquely appropriate educational background. After graduation from college, he studied at the Yale Institute of Far Eastern Languages and Literature and then received a master's degree in Chinese and Japanese from Columbia. His year at the School of Journalism in 1951 gave him a second master's degree along with a Pulitzer Traveling Scholarship.

Mr. Elegant, who is now chief of the Central Europe bureau for Newsweek, *is the author of several books on the Far East and of articles in* The Reporter *and* The New Leader. *He won the Overseas Press Club citation in 1961 for best magazine reporting from abroad. He is married, has two children, and lives in Bonn, Germany.*

ROBERT S. ELEGANT:
The Night We Ended the War

Foreign reporting, like most reporting, is usually a matter of waiting around until someone is ready to tell you just what he wants you to know. Occasionally there is a great, world-shaking "beat." One to a career is remarkable, two fantastic, and three are unassailable proof of the incredible beneficence of the gods.

Would it be churlish to suggest that these arduous accomplishments are often—indeed, almost always—the result of sheer chance, really demonstrating less about the reporter's real worth than would a competently handled account of an automobile accident? Let us consider, as an example, the night the International News Service was the first by ten hours to bring the good news from Seoul to New York that the Korean War was at an end.

It was the middle of June, 1953, and the pathetically battered city of Seoul was as uncomfortably hot as it had been depressingly cold a few months earlier. Except for the regulars, few reporters were in residence at the Press Billets—the structure in which we lived, worked and

3

squabbled, five men to a two-room "apartment" about the size of a small suburban bedroom. Nonetheless, it was obvious that the peace talks between the Communists and the United Nations Command were approaching a new moment of crisis. Something big was sure to happen soon at the bleak spot between the lines that had once been the village of Panmunjom, but by 1953 was a complex of shacks and tents erected by the negotiators. The only relic of the past was half an adobe-and-timber inn, where the correspondents attached to the two sides held their own conferences.

But it was hot in Seoul, and there remained only a handful of the senior correspondents who had descended upon the city when the peace talks had begun again in earnest two months earlier. Among them was the American columnist who was later to be awarded one of the more prestigious professional prizes for his unique ability to describe stirring, if imaginary, night actions from the comfort of his bed. (It was, incidentally, a crying injustice that no prize was awarded to the distillers who provided the fuel for his flights of fancy.) Next to him, in an outlying wing of the Billets, hibernated an English correspondent with flowing blond hair and fine white hands, attributes he preserved by refusing to venture even into the minor dangers of Seoul; he avoided the front as if the soldiers were all hawks and he a plump partridge. Except for such dedicated eccentrics, we juniors had been left to brood over the peace talks while our betters enjoyed the pleasures of family life —or temporary bachelorhood—in Japan.

It seemed certain that the current round of talks would either result in agreement upon an armistice or, by their failure, would produce a major U.N. drive. Although the stakes were high, the old hands had every justification for their feeling that they could get back in more-than-sufficient time if it appeared that the climax was imminent. We had only two normal sources of information on the progress of the negotiations—the Communist radio, supplemented by rumors planted by our Communist colleagues; and the American briefing officer of the UN Command, who often saw his function as disseminating propaganda rather than information. Thus it scarcely seemed possible that anyone could get a jump on the story.

Three disparate factors, however, upset these calculations and gave the INS one of the few authentic beats of the Korean War. Most important was the fact that Howard Handleman, chief of the INS operation in the Far East until a year earlier, had returned to direct our coverage of the closing days of the war and had chosen to remain in Seoul rather than to retreat to Tokyo. The second was the unlikely but honest friendship that had sprung up between our John Casserly and Captain Oh, aide to Major General Choi Duk Shin, the Korean delegate to the peace talks. Although Choi's government had ordered him to boycott the talks in protest against any agreement which would prevent the nation's reunification, the general was still informed of their progress from hour to hour. Finally, I had developed a close relationship with Pyun Yong Tai, Foreign Minister of Korea and Acting Prime Minister, whom the resentful UP had taken to calling "the INS stringer."

None of these relationships seemed terribly important at about midnight on that stifling June night. Since it was too hot to sleep, Handleman was next door playing poker, while I was tapping away at an uninteresting feature. Casserly had disappeared.

I looked up from the typewriter, eager for distraction, when Jack's 190 pounds lurched into the room, almost smashing the glass door en route. Since it was obvious that he was blind drunk and no fit conversational partner, I contented myself with a glance to see that he had subsided safely into a chair despite his surprising state of drunkenness.

Jack sat quietly for about five minutes before enigmatically informing the bathroom door, "Well, it's over!" No reaction from the alert reporter at the typewriter.

Five minutes later, Jack roused himself again. "DidjahearwhatIsaid?" he asked, managing to sound aggrieved though all his words ran together. "I said it's all over. Captain Oh told me." ← *AIDE TO KOREAN DELEGATE.*

I finally awoke from my lethargy. After three cups of coffee and a half hour of patient questioning, Casserly told me a fragmented story. He had been drinking with Oh. "Sdrinking a lot," he said unnecessarily. Captain Oh was in despair. The Communists had just agreed to accept American assurances that the troops of the Republic of Korea would engage in no independent adventures after the signing of the armistice. Since that was the only point of difference outstanding, it should have been clear that the war was indeed over. It should have been clear—if I could have been sure that I understood Casserly's slurred syllables correctly, and if I could have been sure that Captain Oh himself had gotten the story straight before seeking solace in companionable drinking.

We'd be embracing a hell of a big limb if we filed a flat report that the war was over on the basis of one man's half-coherent report of an infinitely complex situation, no matter how good a reporter he ordinarily was.

I trotted next door to fetch Handleman, carefully contriving a story that would not alarm the competition. Poor Jack, who should have had all the credit, was vilified that night. Casserly, I announced to Handleman, was "fighting drunk" and was "threatening to smash the furniture, the typewriters and the windows." Perhaps he'd listen to the voice of authority.

After another half hour of questioning and three more cups of coffee, we got a repetition out of Casserly before he slumped into bed. Handleman and I then shared an anxious ten minutes. Was the story solid enough to file? How far would our necks be out if it were wrong? Could we bear to sit on it? And if we did not file, how would we feel if it turned out to be right?

We had no real basis for our anxious deliberations. It was true that the report was logical, yet there were three nagging elements of doubt: Had we really understood Casserly's alcoholic ramblings correctly? How much did Oh know? Was it a plant?

We finally made the right decision, I pressing Handleman, who really carried the responsibility. It could just as well have been the wrong decision, but when all is said, it was not. As Howard sat at the typewriter, I got through to the INS office in Tokyo and began reading his first take for transmission "urgent press."

But there were other difficulties to be overcome. INS was in the midst of one of its periodic cable "hold-downs." A small voice from Tokyo asked plaintively if the story could not wait for the regular transmission scheduled three-quarters of an hour later.

"No," I said.

"Does it really have to go urgent?" asked the voice.

"Yes," I said.

Then we hit the roadblock. The voice absolutely refused to send the story until the cast—the regular, leased transmission period—and we could not file directly to New York. Finally Handleman himself got on the phone and, after five minutes of bullying that, quite understandably, brought him near to hysteria, he dictated his own flash: "Communists and United Nations Command today agreed on terms which would end war in Korea."

The next take attributed the information to "authoritative sources." I continued to read as Handleman produced the story. All activity had to cease at one point as a couple of UP men wandered in to help deplete our cellar. But the story was finally on the wire. I sat down to have a drink, while Handleman returned to his poker game to lull the opposition.

It was about two-thirty, and we needed a full story for the regular cast. When Howard returned to smooth off the rough edges, a radioman appeared in a state of high excitement. "What are you guys up to?" he demanded, echoing the question in our own hearts. "New York just called to tell me INS was saying the war was over. What gives?"

Handleman silently handed over the carbons. After vainly trying to induce us to name our source, the radioman stamped out to deliver a broadcast which repeated our beat and won him congratulations from his office for "quick and excellent reporting."

As Casserly, the man who got the big story, snored oblivious in the corner, Bob Tuckman of the AP came through the door. He was wearing that half-defiant, half-sheepish expression which indicated that he had received what we called a "rocket," but what the dignified AP insisted upon calling an "advisory." The gist was the same: "INS says war's over. What's your story?"

We assured Bob that the story was true, though we could not, obviously, tell him our source. He wandered out even more unhappily to make a quick check of his own sources. Since none would tell him we were right, he was forced to report, quite properly, that his "authoritative sources" knew nothing of any agreement.

As our second story went out over the Teletype to Tokyo, Howard and I paused for a moment of reflection. Although we were both in a state of high excitement, neither one of us was happy. In fact, our beat had made us desperately unhappy. We simply couldn't relax while the world read an INS report, attributed only to "authoritative sources," that the war was over.

Howard looked at me quizzically without saying a word. "Okay," I replied, "I'll try to find him."

A couple of phone calls to puzzled Korean friends revealed that Acting Prime Minister Pyun, having returned from Pusan that afternoon, was staying with distant cousins in a building identified as "an old bakery, the only big building still standing in that area." Inevitably, it had no telephone.

After half an hour of driving through the blacked-out streets of Seoul with only the jeep's "cats' eyes" on (there had recently been a spate of nuisance air raids), I found the building. Although we had also had a spate of jeep-stealing, I decided that the story was worth leaving the jeep unguarded in the street, though I wondered how I'd get back if it were stolen. I hammered on the doors of the bakery and finally roused the proprietor. After a ten-minute conversation in Japanese, he admitted that Pyun was present, and he let me in.

At four in the morning, I knocked on the door of the simple bedroom where the Prime Minister of Korea slept. A sleepy voice asked, "Who's there?" "It's Elegant of INS," I said. "I'm terribly sorry to disturb you, but I have an urgent question to ask you."

The door opened on Pyun, who was wearing a dark-brown sweater over his pyjamas. His face alone told me that our story was right. The

Koreans, moved by their own national interest, were absolutely opposed to an armistice. Although I felt a stab of pity for the man in the midst of my own elation, I asked the question I'd prepared, "Sir, we understand that the UN and the Communists have agreed upon peace terms. What will your government do?"

Pyun replied slowly: "Yes, your information is correct. We will try to fight alone."

I stayed for another five minutes to fill in details and then rushed to my jeep, which, providentially, was still there. Back in the Billets, I found the radioman sitting glumly in front of my typewriter. "They want more," he said. "But I'm beginning to worry about this story. Nobody else has it. I think I'll do a rowback." He did not get the confirmation.

When he left, I could sit down to write the story which got us off the hook. It began: "Acting Prime Minister of Korea today said two sides had agreed upon peace terms . . ."

Except for Casserly, the INS staff did not sleep that night. There was too much work to be done cleaning up the details of the story. About seven that morning, Handleman and I were having a drink and exchanging congratulations when Casserly finally began to stir.

Bob Tuckman of the AP, one of the most magnanimous men who ever lived, appeared once more. Solemnly he shook first Howard's and then my hand.

"Well," he said, "you skunked us. Maybe UP started this war, but the INS ended it. I feel the AP kept up its end pretty well too, but this time you beat the pants off us. I'll have a drink."

Jack Casserly, the author of all the excitement, sat up in bed, looking with obvious bewilderment and evident disapproval at our 7 A.M. drinking party.

Ralph L. Lowenstein served in two wars and with two armies. He was an American volunteer with the Israeli Army in the Arab-Israeli war of 1948-49, and he served overseas with the U. S. Army during the Korean War.

Mr. Lowenstein, who was graduated from the School of Journalism in 1952, was a reporter for The El Paso Times *before his appointment as associate professor of journalism and business administration at Texas Western College. He won the Columbia Journalism Alumni Award for Distinguished Service to Journalism in 1956, and a Pall Mall Big Story award in 1957. He lives with his wife and two children in El Paso.*

RALPH L. LOWENSTEIN:
Mother's Day Feature

The news story is the journalist's bread and butter. But for me, at least, the feature story has always been the dessert. It provides an opportunity for the newspaperman to break away from the cold, analytical, objective jurisdiction of the news report and put his heart into his work. It allows him to be subjective, emotional, warm and, above all, creative.

I believe the newspaper reader has a similar fondness for the feature story. Into the thick rain forest of politics, finance, mayhem and the like, the feature story peeks like a golden shaft of sunlight.

My fondness for the feature story began in the feature seminar taught by Allan Keller at the Columbia University Graduate School of Journalism. At almost every class session, Mr. Keller would give us information for a feature assignment. There were two basic rules: We could not tamper with the background facts Mr. Keller gave us, and we had to write our stories under pressure of a deadline.

These two conditions were extremely important for our training. We learned from the beginning to be as creative as possible, but only under the limitations of truth and time—the boundaries for any good re-

9

porter, whether writing news or features for any responsible newspaper. We learned that we were not fiction writers, but simply the means whereby another human could share his humor, express his philosophy or write his epitaph. Rare is the newspaper that keeps a man on the staff as a feature writer only. Editors expect, properly, that every reporter be able to recognize and write a feature story when one comes along.

In an experience that was to prove the most interesting of my career, I turned to the feature story not because it was what I did best, but because the situation I had to describe was so cold and heartless that only a feature story could put it into proper contrast.

The story was brought to *The El Paso Times* by a Catholic priest serving one of the poorest sections of the city. It was about a family that was separated by the Mexican-American border. The family, consisting of a mother, father and seven daughters, was split by a strict application of a severe law, the McCarran-Walter Immigration Act of 1952.

Mrs. Juan Valadez, a native of Mexico married to an American citizen, had been deported to Mexico four years earlier. A special hearing officer of the U.S. Immigration and Naturalization Service had ruled that Mrs. Valadez had committed perjury when, in applying for a local crossing pass, she had declared that she had no intention of living in the United States permanently.

Mrs. Valadez was a simple, uneducated woman who could hardly comprehend the meaning of perjury. Yet without giving her benefit of attorney, the U.S. Immigration and Naturalization Service had been prosecutor, judge and jury in her case. Perjury is a felony. According to the McCarran-Walter Immigration Act, any alien convicted of a felony must be deported and can never again be admitted to the United States. In the four years since she had been deported, the case had been appealed three times. Each time the appeal was heard and rejected by the same hearing officer who had first found her guilty of perjury.

Her husband, a $48-a-week laborer, remained in a one-room apartment in El Paso with the couple's four oldest daughters. Thus he could be near his work and the girls could attend American public schools. His wife lived in a one-room apartment in Juarez, Mexico, with their three youngest daughters. The family was fortunate if it could get together in Juarez once a week on Sunday.

It was difficult to believe that any such unbending law could or would be applied in the United States. But officials of the U.S. Immigration and Naturalization Service confirmed the story. Mrs. Valadez, they said, admitted that she had lied when she had signed the crossing pass oath (she did, indeed, hope someday to live permanently in the U.S.). A lie under oath was perjury. Perjury was a felony. And felony called for her permanent removal from the United States. It was a pity that a family had been broken up, they said. The McCarran-Walter Act was a harsh and unforgiving law, they agreed. But it was their duty to administer it.

The Catholic priest told us the story a few days before Mother's Day. For maximum impact, *The El Paso Times* ran my story on page one on Mother's Day. It was accompanied by two pictures, one showing the El Paso half of the family, the other the Juarez half. The story began:

"Mother's Day will be the same as almost every other Sunday in the year for Mr. and Mrs. Juan Valadez and their seven young daughters.

"The family will be together in a little one-room apartment at 1118 Calle Azucenas, just across the river over in Juarez.

"But as nightfall approaches Sunday, the unity of the Valadez family will come to an end and another week of separation will begin."

The story had a shocking effect on many El Pasoans. Among the calls we received, the most important were from attorneys who stepped forward to report that the Valadezes were not the only separated families. There were many more, perhaps hundreds, in the El Paso area alone, they said, and they offered to open their files and give me the actual names and case histories.

The El Paso Times ran a series of four more articles on separated families. An El Paso attorney drafted a new appeal for Mrs. Valadez, this time directed to the Board of Immigration Appeals in Washington, D.C. The U.S. Congressman from our West Texas district volunteered to appear in person before the Board and support Mrs. Valadez' plea.

Hours before the appeal was to come before the Board, the Commissioner of the U.S. Immigration and Naturalization Service ordered that Mrs. Valadez be granted an "indefinite parole" into the United States. He credited the articles in the *Times* with bringing to his attention the compassionate aspects of the Valadez case. He also opened the way for other families to be reunited under the same "indefinite paroles," a method never before used to bypass the technicalities of the McCarran-Walter Act.

In the first year following the solution of the Valadez case, more than 300 families were reunited under the "indefinite parole" provision. Toward the end of 1956, the "indefinite parole" rule was used to admit 15,000 otherwise ineligible Hungarian refugees to the United States.

Since then, hundreds of other "separated" families have been reunited under the method first used in the Valadez case. But more important by far, the U.S. Immigration and Naturalization Service has since been reluctant to rend a family. Compassion is now used in the administration of what remains a very severe law.

As a result of the Valadez stories, I received several awards. One, the Pall Mall Big Story Award, showed me how a story could be transformed once the bars of truth were removed. ("Remember," Allan Keller used to tell us, "don't tamper with the facts.") In the TV show, telecast nationwide, there were a number of startling changes. The seven children were reduced to two. The mother became a singer of plaintive Mexican ballads, accompanying herself all the while on a guitar. The priest was all but forgotten. And the reporter virtually lived with the Valadezes, advising, exhorting, encouraging them constantly. (As undramatic as it sounds, I never once saw the Valadezes or any of the other separated families.)

I don't criticize the television writers and producers. They did the best they could within the limits of their medium. Seven children would no more fit conveniently into a 21-inch screen than would the details of a rather complicated case fit into a half-hour program. The very brevity of time in radio-television, and of space in news magazines, I have found, tends to distort truth much more than the possible desire to slant it. The space available in a newspaper day after day allows a more accurate reflection of life as it really is.

Without false modesty, I can say that my winning the awards for the Valadez stories was also a reflection of unreality. I felt then, and I feel now, that Father James Loeffler was more deserving of the awards than I. My feature story simply gave volume to his compassion and outrage, and image to the families that had been separated.

The great excitement and satisfaction for me was hearing that the Valadezes would be reunited, and later that hundreds of other families would be brought together again. And along with this satisfaction came the realization that the feature story can be more than a cream puff in the newspaper business—that because it is bound by truth, it can be a powerful weapon in behalf of truth.

Peter Kihss, who won a Pulitzer Traveling Scholarship from the School of Journalism in 1933, started his newspaper career with the Associated Press in Washington and shortly thereafter spent a year in Latin America, part of that time for The New York Times.

Between 1934 and 1952, when he returned to The Times, *Mr. Kihss was a reporter with* The Washington Post, The New York World-Telegram *and* The New York Herald Tribune. *A specialist in United Nations affairs, he has written a number of pamphlets and articles about the organization. Among the many awards Mr. Kihss has received are the Order of Merit from Chile, the Citizens Budget Commission medal and the Meyer Berger Award. He lives with his wife and two children in Jamaica Estates, Long Island, New York.*

PETER KIHSS:

The World's Best Assignment

Covering the United Nations for the first six years of its life was the greatest privilege I've had as a newspaper reporter.

The U. N. has its faults, grave ones. But it remains the greatest cause, the greatest opportunity, we have for a better world. It's also the most interesting assignment I know—foreign corresponding, but with American plumbing.

In January, 1946, L. L. Engelking, city editor of *The New York Herald Tribune,* assigned me to cover the U. N.'s quest for a headquarters. It was because other New York newspapers had beaten us on a story that the site-hunting committee was going to select for a permanent headquarters Franklin D. Roosevelt's home community of Hyde Park.

It was a good story for us not to have had, I found out. For it wasn't so. A day later, we got a story that New York City would be recom-

mended as the home of the U. N. for the five years or so that it
would take to build a permanent headquarters. I was amazed next
morning to find it was an exclusive story. The story in the other papers
was that the recommendation would be a triple one—for New York,
Boston and Atlantic City, pick one.

How did we happen to have a beat? In an open news conference I
had asked the Yugoslav chairman, Stoyan Gavrilovic, whether New
York would get the recommendation. He said it would. He wasn't
supposed to be quoted at that point. The other reporters had been
working with the site committee for weeks. They knew without asking
that he was also supposed to have in mind the other two cities. The
only trouble, it turned out—and the break for me—was that he meant
what he said.

Sometimes it's good to be a believer.

The U. N. offers many things.

Opportunity? For one thing, I remember how, in December of 1948,
I learned exclusively from both Netherlands and Indonesian sources
that the Dutch were going to reopen warfare in their then East Indies
colony despite a U. N. truce. Diplomats from both sides gave me the
story in the hope that publication would be a preventive. It wasn't. The
story didn't get published. One editor remonstrated that "Indonesia is
10,000 miles away." The war did break out again, for nobody at U. N.
or in journalism was then caring much about averting it.

Missed opportunities at the U. N. have been all too common.

Interest as an assignment? Consider the people you meet. It may be
impolitic to say, but I liked Andrei Gromyko, the often glum Soviet
delegate. He came in on the liner *Queen Mary* once when I was
covering him. A photographer asked if he could smile for a picture. "I
could," Mr. Gromyko replied, "but it would be artificial."

He did have his humor. In early 1948, the Soviet Union was be-
laboring the United States in U. N. meetings for not doing anything to
enforce the General Assembly's plan for partition of Palestine. Without enforcement, the plan was obviously going to lead to Arab-Israeli
warfare. I asked Mr. Gromyko what the Soviet Union would do to
enforce the plan, adding—in the words of an old radio program—
"that's a $64 question, Mr. Ambassador." "I have lost the $64," he
announced.

The U. N. has its non-official decent human beings. Raphael Lemkin
was a Polish refugee who had fought bravely against the 1939 Nazi
invasion, escaping with a bullet in his leg. In the war and persecution,
he lost 45 members of his family. Just about singlehandly, Dr. Lemkin

lobbied through the General Assembly—and then got ratified—a U. N. convention to make mass extermination of peoples an international crime, genocide. The convention remains unenforced; the crime goes on.

One day I got around to scanning a week-old copy of the *United Nations Weekly Bulletin*. In the middle of a dullish story, I found a line that a moving firm had offered to do all the moving of the U. N.'s effects from the temporary headquarters at Hunter College in the Bronx to Lake Success and Flushing Meadow for $1. Tracking down the facts, I discovered that this had been a gesture made four months earlier by a moving man who lived in Lake Success. He believed in the U. N., and he did go ahead and do a $12,000 job for a token $1. James O'Neill shied from publicity, but I got the story from U. N. officials, and I wrote it, in the hope that his moving effort might move some hearts as well.

But the U. N. has its dangers for a reporter.

The risk is that a reporter can lose his objectivity.

For months I knew about continuing United States interference with the legally international secretariat during the Communist-hunting heyday here. With some exceptions, I wasn't sending out the story.

My thinking was that it would hurt individuals to have it known that they were under suspicion as domestic left-wingers. Nobody was accusing them of doing anything wrong in their U. N. jobs. My thinking also was that it would hurt the United States to have it known that it was in fact violating the Charter injunction against interference with the staff. And further, I thought it would hurt the U. N. to have it known that the world organization was buckling under to pressure from the United States, even though it had withstood such efforts from the Communist bloc.

Whether these thoughts had any merit or not, the fact is that the story did break. It broke wholesale instead of piecemeal, when the Senate internal security subcommittee called hearings and paraded in public the suspected American secretariat members and the responsible State Department officials.

Suppressing the story had done no good. Printing it earlier might have helped hold down the eventual damage. Faith in the people's right to know is the thinking that has built up a free press. That faith is indispensable in a democracy. But it's sometimes not always recognized, even by reporters.

The longer a man stays at the U. N., the more he is likely to believe in its cause, and the more—probably unfortunately for him journalistically—he is likely to get drawn into its crusade. Many a delegate asked me for advice during my years as a U. N. reporter and after.

This didn't always help the paper in stories. When the Soviet Union in 1949 exploded its first nuclear weapons device and then renewed its call for a census of all atomic weapons and conventional armaments, the Western powers opposed the Soviet resolution in the Security Council. They saw it as an effort to ferret out details of the still stronger Western atomic arsenal.

A United States delegate expressed concern to me.

I suggested an amendment that would make the Soviet Union veto its own resolution. This would simply provide that the censuses should be in accordance with the then Soviet-blocked plans of the U. N. Atomic Energy Commission and the Commission for Conventional Armaments. The United States delegation relayed the idea to the French, who then offered such an amendment.

The story of the move ran in every paper except ours. I had the day off when a U. N. press officer brought the amendment around; nobody happened to be in our bureau at the moment, and neither the American delegation nor the U. N. press office thought of protecting the *Herald Tribune*.

For a Western delegate with a sincere anxiety to get agreement on atomic energy, I drafted a General Assembly resolution that might embody a minimum area of agreement. In it also was a new proposal to pledge all members against use of atomic weapons except in case of aggression, as defined by a majority of the Security Council, or except in case of self-defense, the right reserved under Article 51 of the Charter. The resolution did not get introduced. The delegate found himself upbraided by the major Western powers as falling into a Soviet trap. Some years afterward, Western delegates finally got started talking in such terms.

One foreign delegate made a front-paged General Assembly speech, largely of my authorship, which offered a new idea on atomic cooperation. A senior United States delegate scoffed. The next day, the idea became a United States proposal, and later some very constructive results ensued. My friend was told he must have had advance information on the United States proposal. He didn't. But fortunately, sometimes at the U. N. somebody's listening.

One problem in weighing what to do about U. N. stories is that far too many newspapers have far too little interest in U. N. affairs, anyway. They print only the minimum they have to. Take a look at what U. N. news, if any, is printed on any non-crisis day in United States newspapers other than *The New York Times* and *The Christian Science Monitor,* despite the availability of excellent press service reporters.

No one can think seriously about the cause of peace and a better world in this overwhelming age of the atom without realizing the value of the U. N. concept. There are alternatives, and they have to be explored and followed.

But the U. N. opportunity is potentially the best.

My experience was that the U. N. worked best—the governments who make it up tried hardest—when the public eye was upon the doings. That eye has to be the eye of the newspapers.

One day I got gloomy about a story I couldn't get in the paper. Herbert V. Evatt, then Australian Minister of External Affairs, sent me a message. It could be a slogan for the U. N.:

"In the words of an old Siberian motto, if at first you don't escape, try, try again."

In the mid-Twenties, after a year on The Brooklyn Eagle *and another on* The Oregon Statesman, *Robert C. Notson joined* The Portland Oregonian *and began the editorial climb to managing editor. From general reporting he went to real estate and then to political assignments before becoming, successively, assistant city editor, night city editor and city editor. He has been managing editor since 1941.*

Mr. Notson was a member of the Class of 1926 at Columbia School of Journalism, and has taught news writing at Lewis and Clark College. He is an officer of the American Society of Newspaper Editors and the Associated Press Managing Editors Association, and served as a Pulitzer Prize juror in 1962.

ROBERT C. NOTSON:

The Day After the Big Game

It was Sunday morning, December 7, 1941.

The staff of the *Oregonian* had held a party the night before. Although I had preceded the majority in excusing myself, I was still in bed when the phone rang insistently.

"Office calling," said my wife, watching me come alive reluctantly. Such calls are no novelty in the life of a managing editor.

It was Hollis Goodrich, acting assistant city editor and now head of a Portland public relations firm.

"The radio has done it again," he announced.

"Done what?" I asked, yawning.

"Another Orson Welles invasion from Mars, or something," said Holly. "A little while ago Virgil Smith [then wire editor for KGW and now night city editor of the *Oregonian*] ran across the hall and said there was a bulletin being broadcast that the Japanese were bombing Pearl Harbor."

"That's screwball," I said. Holly readily agreed. Everyone knew that Pearl Harbor, our great naval bastion, was impregnable.

"But," he continued, "they're still broadcasting the bulletin on NBC at intervals, and we're getting a flood of calls."

"How about the Associated Press?"

"The AP wire isn't open yet—it's Sunday and they open late," Holly replied. "I've called the bureau chief and they're sending a man down to open the wire."

"Okay," I decided, "let's get this straightened out right away. It's either the biggest story of our time or the biggest hoax, and we'd better get the answer fast. Keep me informed."

The children returned from Sunday School with their grandfather. I switched on the radio. A song ended and on came the cryptic bulletin. It had been reported that Japanese bombers had attacked the fleet at Pearl Harbor. Nothing more. It was incredible.

I dialed Palmer Hoyt, then publisher of our paper and now head of *The Denver Post*. There was no answer. I switched to M. J. Frey, then business manager of the *Oregonian* and now publisher. He was golfing at a Lake Oswego club. The club pro verified that he was on the course.

"This may be important," I said. "We may have a war on our hands." The pro agreed to send a caddy out to intercept Frey.

Goodrich called back. The Associated Press had the same bulletin but no details, no confirmation.

The minutes ticked away. Should a young managing editor stick his neck far, far out? Quickly I called the composing room superintendent and the production manager, telling them both to summon crews to put out an early edition. I was dressing when the phone rang again. It was Frey. I told him about the bulletins.

"Sounds like a phony!" he exclaimed.

I told him I was not so sure. It had now been nearly an hour since the first report, and there had been no denial from either Honolulu or Washington. It began to look as though something was going on. Frey said he'd finish his game, get a bite to eat and meet me at the office.

When I informed him that I had ordered crews in for an early start—on overtime—he did not sound enthusiastic. "All right, I'll dress and see you as soon as I can get to the plant. Go ahead."

The men were straggling in when I arrived. The newsmen, many with a few hours' sleep at best, looked particularly sad. There was much nervous jocularity, much incredulity. Still no real news. Talk centered intermittently on the football game the day before between the Uni-

versity of Oregon and the University of Texas. Dana Bible and his
Texas boys had poured it on, angered because they had been passed
over for the Rose Bowl. Oregon was a convenient target, since it was
from the Pacific Coast Conference. The score: 71 to 7.

Office wags decided to needle L. H. Gregory, sports editor, on his
return. They had gone to the Fred Meyer store across Sixth Avenue and
picked up a long sheet of butcher paper. Frank Sterrett, loquacious
photographer and a great practical joker, rolled it out on the floor and
painted a message in huge black letters: "REMEMBER THE ALAMO!" The
plan was to hang it over Greg's desk.

But Holly Goodrich, facing the sudden emergency, had to interrupt
Sterrett's efforts; Frank was needed to phone other members of the
staff and summon them to the office. As Holly stepped over the still
wet sign, he read "Remember the Alamo."

"Sterrett," he called back over his shoulder, "better change that to
Remember Pearl Harbor!"

Later, someone at the *Oregonian* wrote a little feature on the incident. The Associated Press picked it up. The slogan blossomed over
the nation: "Remember Pearl Harbor!" It was, of course, a natural.
The idea may have erupted spontaneously, but the men who were in the
newsroom that day still believe the famous World War II slogan was
born of an incipient joke.

Soon the Japanese radio confirmed the attack, making elaborate
claims of great damage to the Pacific fleet—battleships capsized, others
resting on the bottom with superstructures battered and aflame. We
didn't believe it.

We had decided not to go to press until the story was confirmed.
We had also decided that we would "roll" only with a complete newspaper. Different counsels prevailed at *The Oregon Journal,* our competition. They decided to pick up a few pages from the Monday edition, then in preparation, and some Sunday type, and go with a large
banner over the original flash bulletin.

Pressure by our street circulators for papers became heavy. Mr.
Frey, naturally conservative, had recollections of newspaper experience
with the "false armistice" in 1918. He wanted no such fiasco. He held
out for confirmation. When we got it, the flood gates of news suddenly
opened. Japan declared war. Germany prepared to declare war. The
President called Congress into extraordinary session to hear his message
on the "day that will live in infamy."

Reactions internationally were electric. Stories could not be set in
type before they were overtaken, revised. Clayton (Barney) Bernhard,

then as now a member of the news desk team, sweated to get into production.

Finally the first edition rolled. It was a complete paper. It had the confirmation, the detailed claims, the war declaration. When *The Portland Oregonian* hit the street the public discarded the early incomplete extra, and papers sold as fast as newsboys could hand them out. Many people failed to claim their change.

On through the evening the presses rolled with only a pause for replating. Carloads of papers were rushed out of the city to points as far as The Dalles and Salem. The appetite of the public was insatiable. America was at war!

The next few days were hectic. American officials were tight-lipped regarding the debacle at Pearl Harbor, but angry denunciations by President Roosevelt of the sneak attack, which took place while negotiations were in progress with the Japanese in Washington, suggested that we had suffered a damaging blow.

Blackout curtains went up. Automobile headlights were reduced to slits. Curfews were declared. Civil patrols roamed the streets. A lighted window brought a knock on the door. Mayor Earl Riley advised the people repeatedly over the air to be calm, but there was tension in his voice.

A fog curtain hung off the Pacific coast. What did it conceal? Would the Japanese attack our coast? Would they try to land while we were reeling and stunned, and without naval cover? No one knew.

A cadre of *Oregonian* executives and workers lived in a downtown hotel for several days because of interruptions in normal travel. Almost overnight the lives of our people were altered, never to be the same. *The Portland Oregonian* geared itself to print the story of World War II and the comeback of the United States from the brink of military chaos to the decisive force in winning the war in two hemispheres.

It was the greatest story of our times.

William Kreger, who was a "semi-pro newspaper-man" from the age of twelve, worked as a reporter for three years after graduating from Cornell College in Iowa and before entering the Graduate School of Journalism. A member of the Class of 1952, he joined The Wall Street Journal *immediately after leaving Columbia and has been with that newspaper ever since. In 1960 he was made a news editor.*

Mr. Kreger, who is married to the former Anita Sackrison, is the father of two children, Thomas and Laurie. During World War II he served with the Army Air Force.

WILLIAM C. KREGER:

Clash of Steel

President Kennedy was understood to be shocked, dismayed and personally disillusioned by the U.S. Steel announcement. At his news conference this afternoon the President is almost certain to have a statement sternly critical of the big steel maker's decision and its impact on the economy.

That paragraph was supplied by *The Wall Street Journal*'s Washington bureau shortly before midnight on Tuesday, April 10, 1962, just as the night people at our central news desk in New York were ready to close up shop.

It was obtained by chance. But it filled a frustrating news gap that had existed for nearly six hours: What was President Kennedy's actual reaction to the announcement by the United States Steel Corporation that it was raising prices across the board at a time when the White House obviously neither wanted nor expected a rise?

The paragraph was the last insert moved by the New York desk for a story that ran nearly three columns in the final April 11 editions of the *Journal* across the country. I'd like to describe some of the things that happened that Tuesday night because such occasions are one of the

22

big reasons I'm in the newspaper business and not out selling shoes or sickles or soft soap.

I had charge of the *Journal*'s national news desk. This, of course, isn't a "desk" at all, but rather a collection of them staffed by two news editors besides myself, a couple of rewrite men, a clerk, and the head of the copy desk and his copy editors. At the *Journal,* the national desk gets practically all the spot news copy from the paper's reporters in the U.S. and elsewhere, along with the daily file from the press associations and an avalanche of so-called news releases and other mail. Stories selected to be printed get their final editing at the copy desk, and then —through a maze of electronic and other equipment—are set in type in the *Journal*'s printing plants across the country.

Probably 98 percent of the chosen stories are significant enough to publish, yet differ little from those of yesterday or tomorrow. A news editor agrees to apply whatever talents he has to that vast percentage so that he can get a chance to work on the other two per cent—the stories he knows will really grab the attention of the readers.

For the *Journal,* as for many other newspapers, U.S. Steel's attempt to raise prices was THE story that night.

My part in its evolution was less than unique. Other news editors were doing the same things I did that Tuesday night, I'm sure.

But I had advantages over many of them.

For one thing, *The Wall Street Journal,* as the "national business daily," has a large staff of reporters—fine ones—so located as to cover the country. Their day-to-day activities keep them extraordinarily close to the chief sources of information in commerce and industry. Within less than five hours that night, more than two dozen of these men provided eminently usable material for the story; one of my problems was what to omit. That's why I'm not going to single out any of them by name in recounting what they did.

Furthermore, the *Journal* has a vehicle for packaging such a story—a "round-up" that carries no dateline but in appropriate paragraphs makes clear the sources of the information. Continual contact with these wrap-ups has trained *Journal* reporters to provide memos that are often finished newspaper prose. That night I wrote the top of the story in New York and then just tacked sections onto it from other cities.

But I had disadvantages, too.

The main one was that U.S. Steel disseminated its announcement at a remarkably inconvenient time for us—about 6 P.M. in the East. Six o'clock is our normal copy-desk deadline for the first edition.

That Tuesday had been a relatively dull news day at the *Journal.*

Things were so slow at deadline that I was chinning at his desk with one of the few reporters left in the New York office. Most of the bureaus had got "good night" on the Teletype wires.

At about 6:10 I ambled back to my desk. In the in-basket was a large brown envelope with U.S. Steel's insignia in the upper left-hand corner.

I opened it routinely. In the early evening U.S. Steel's public relations department customarily delivers advance texts of speeches the corporation's executives will make in the next day or two.

This handout had the heft of a speech. I glanced at the first page:

"Pittsburgh, Pa. April 10—For the first time in nearly four years, United States Steel today announced an increase in the general level of its steel prices. This 'catch-up' adjustment . . ."

The release ran four pages, followed by eight pages of tabular matter. I skimmed along, confidently looking for some indication that the rise was limited to one class of products or to certain exports. And I wondered why they hadn't serviced the Pittsburgh bureau before it closed for the night.

Then I read the announcement a second time—minutely. It sank in that the company was raising prices across the board.

To nobody in particular I proclaimed, "U.S. Steel just raised prices $6 a ton!" My chief associate gave me a look that showed he was as astounded as I was, and both of us like to think we're difficult to astonish.

I read the announcement a third time, trying to see how the corporation explained the increase.

My interpretation was this: U.S. Steel needed to raise prices in order to get more money so that it could modernize its plants and make steel cheaper. Then it would be able to cut prices and compete more effectively with other materials and with lower-priced foreign steel. It conceded that a first result would be to make its competitive position worse. And it denied that the increase reflected a new steel labor contract effective July 1 that was reached under Government prodding.

I had a hard time visualizing the American people's understanding this position or divorcing the price increase and the union contract. I was even more doubtful that the President of the United States would stand for it. I didn't know that Roger M. Blough, chairman of the board of U.S. Steel, had visited the White House to tell Mr. Kennedy about the announcement before it was released, and that the President was infuriated already. And I didn't envision how that fury would be translated into a massive attack on the steel industry by "troops" ranging from Mr. Kennedy and his Cabinet to FBI agents and a grand jury.

Anyway, mental numbness began to dissolve with the realization that we had to compile some sort of account of this unusual event for the *Journal*'s readers. I set the night news editor to informing the bureaus by phone or by Teletype that we needed reaction—from other steel producers and from anybody else they thought worthy.

He started with Washington, the center of government. I started with Pittsburgh, the center of steel. Both of us ran into similar receptions there and elsewhere—either stunned silence or outright disbelief.

Just one day earlier, the paper's weekly steel review had reported that steel producers expected neither a rise in business nor in prices before autumn. Customers had stocked up in anticipation of a possible strike. Settlement with the union meant no big strike, and heavy inventories made a spurt in sales unlikely. Company after company had echoed this conclusion.

I reached the Pittsburgh bureau chief—the man responsible for this weekly review—just as he entered the door of his home. He blurted, "You're kidding . . . you must be!"

His wife shoved a sandwich and a Thermos of milk at him, and he started back to his office.

I looked at the clock; it was 6:25. About half of our 800,000 readers were going to get the first edition the next morning, and yet the first edition still didn't contain a word about a price increase that could easily be the biggest business news of the year.

I considered what we had up to then, and decided that everything significant could really be said in a few sentences. Luckily, the *Journal* has a place where you can say something big in one paragraph—the "What's News" summaries on page one that are labeled "Business and Finance" and "World Wide." These highly-concentrated items, tricky to write, are composed by two extremely competent men, but I figured it would just slow things down to ask the business-column man to perform the routine of mental gymnastics I had just been through with the U.S. Steel handout.

So I wrote this paragraph, which was slapped in at the top of the page-one column in 400,000 papers:

STEEL PRICES were increased an average of 3.5%, or $6 a ton, by United States Steel Corp., the largest producer. The boost, first across-the-board rise since 1958, comes despite heavy public pressure from the White House to avoid a price increase. The Kennedy Administration has contended the steel labor agreement reached last week by U.S. Steel and 10 other major producers with the Steelworkers Union is non-inflationary. Leslie B. Worthington, U.S. Steel

President, said the increase is only a "partial catch-up" for past rises in costs and doesn't take into consideration the added expenses that will start July 1 under the new labor agreement. Steel producers calculate they have absorbed cost increases amounting to 40 cents hourly under the labor pact expiring June 30. They have held off from price rises because of competition from foreign steel and substitute materials.

I hoped the first-edition readers would get the message: Competition or the White House, or both, just might torpedo this price increase, although we hadn't got anybody to say so yet.

I made two more calls before beginning to sort out a story for the final edition that would start to be printed a short four hours later. I phoned my boss, the managing editor, who had gone home at his normal time. He had several suggestions of things to incorporate in the story.

And I called my wife and told her not to wait up for me. She's used to that, although the word usually is passed later in the evening.

Meanwhile, reporters were making the phone company happy with toll calls.

In New York, all attempts to pump U.S. Steel encountered a genial but firm reply. The company had told all in its release. Sorry, but top officials were definitely unavailable.

In Philadelphia, the bureau manager had come home from Wilmington, Delaware, after the annual stockholder meeting of Bethlehem Steel, the nation's second largest producer. He and other newspapermen had interviewed E. F. Martin, president of the corporation, after the meeting; our man reported that Mr. Martin declined to discuss prices until July 1, when the new labor contract would go into effect.

But the Philadelphia bureau chief noticed a story in a local paper that differed somewhat from what he was sure he had heard. He called New York to tell us that he was sticking by his version—and ran smack into U.S. Steel's rise. Bethlehem's reply that night was a uniform "no comment" to repeated queries.

(The differences in published accounts of Mr. Martin's remarks led to an FBI agent's seeking to question the Philadelphia bureau manager before daylight on Thursday morning; our man quite logically told the agent to talk to him at a more normal time.)

The Detroit bureau chief had been asked to get the auto manufacturers' viewpoint; he was pessimistic about his chances. But at a country club he reached a man involved at close to the top levels in the pricing of one company's cars. This informant doubted that a price increase would be made in the midst of a production run, and he pointed out that one manufacturer couldn't raise prices if his chief competitors did not do the same. But he did foresee a price rise in the fall if the steel boost stuck.

(The Detroit bureau had to file another piece of major business news that night. The Ford Motor Company had just proclaimed that it was dropping U.S. assembly of the Volkswagen-sized Cardinal shortly before it was supposed to get under way. So another Detroit hand supplied that story, one which would have led the paper on many other nights of the year. Everything in the news business is relative.)

The Cleveland office learned that Republic Steel Corporation, third largest in the industry, would review its prices "immediately"—a corporate way of saying "Call us tomorrow, we'll probably be going up." But Armco Steel would say only that it was "watching the situation."

Our Chicago news room fired in reinforcing reactions of surprise, joy and relief from smaller steel makers, but drew a blank from its prime target, Inland Steel Company. Non-committal that night, Inland speeded the cancellation of the price increase later in the week by renouncing it.

The San Francisco office had been urged to get at least two things: The reaction of Kaiser Steel, a non-conformist in the industry, and the impact of the increase on steel warehouses on the West Coast. Warehouses get steel from mills and generally fill small, difficult or special orders. Kaiser Steel would study U.S. Steel's move. Warehouse owners said they would pass any price increase on to their customers.

Pittsburgh, meanwhile, was supplying a good part of the story. It provided much of the information from steel executives (most of it not for attribution to them or their companies) indicating that they were pleasantly surprised by the price increase and would probably raise their own prices shortly.

A Steelworker source told the Pittsburgh bureau that the union felt double-crossed because steel company negotiators, led by a U.S. Steel official, had pleaded the horrors of their competitive position in the recent contract talks. And the Pittsburgh operatives also came up with a table of a few prices before and after the increase.

The Washington bureau was just about ready to close down when the SOS came that U.S. Steel appeared to be assaulting the White House. The White House correspondent, the economics reporter and the labor specialist quickly provided the basis for an accurate appraisal that U.S. Steel had, knowingly or unknowingly, sandpapered at least three sensitive spots in the Kennedy Administration:

The President's broad design to prevent inflation by keeping price and wage increases within limits keyed (by him and his advisers) to rises in workers' productivity;

The Treasury's efforts to preserve an image of U.S. fiscal and economic stability, particularly for some European doubters;

And the prestige of Arthur Goldberg, then the Secretary of Labor, who had prodded large steel companies and the Steelworkers to agreement on new labor contracts an unusual three months before the old ones expired. The agreement raised fringe benefits but not pay rates, and the Administration thought it had made clear that this meant prices weren't going to rise, either.

A Washington desk man dashed off a provocative column of copy hinging on the idea that a chief Administration aim would be to isolate U.S. Steel by pressuring other steel makers not to raise prices. If enough big companies refused to follow, U.S. Steel would have to back down.

All this made dandy paragraphs, but just how disturbed was the President himself? The answer unexpectedly came from a stag dinner on Embassy Row for a visiting foreign dignitary. The *Journal*'s diplomatic correspondent was one of several newspapermen at the dinner; he wasn't expecting to get a story out of it.

The seat next to the guest of honor was reserved for Walter W. Heller, chairman of President Kennedy's Council of Economic Advisers. But not until two hours after the dinner started did Mr. Heller arrive— obviously agitated. A friend twitted him: "You're late."

Mr. Heller exploded: "U.S. Steel has just raised the price of steel $6 a ton. This is the worst sandbagging this Administration has ever taken." He made it clear that a sense of crisis permeated the White House, and that the President was determined to rally any steel industry holdouts to his side to cancel the price rise.

As soon as he could, the diplomatic correspondent got to a phone to call the Washington office. He made it just in time for the last insert in the last replate on the final edition.

Flora Lewis, London correspondent for The
Washington Post, *has been a regular contributor to*
The New York Times *Magazine and other publications. She has been a foreign correspondent during most of the years since her graduation from
the School of Journalism in 1942.*

*Miss Lewis, who won the Overseas Press Club
magazine reporting award in 1956 and the
Foreign Affairs interpretation award in 1952, is
the author of "Case History of Hope," the story
of the Polish revolution. She is married to Sydney
Gruson, London correspondent for* The New York
Times. *They have three children—Kerry, Sheila
and Lindsey.*

FLORA LEWIS:

Polish Surprise

There was a good deal of uneasy anticipation involved in my arrival
in Warsaw in early March, 1956. It was a return, since I had lived
in Poland from 1946 to 1949, but it was a return to an unknown
quantity. In the Warsaw I first knew right after the war, everything
was in ruins but spirits were lively. Three years later, when I left,
physical reconstruction had begun but the atmosphere had sunk to
unrelieved grimness. The likelihood was that if I had stayed on much
longer, I would have been arrested or expelled; that was the way the
countries of Eastern Europe were getting rid of Western correspondents
in those days. We were not wanted, and there was really nothing we
could do about it. Once we had gone it was unwise to write to personal
friends; even a Christmas card might have been enough to get them
into trouble. Thus there was no way of knowing what I was now
going to find.

It turned out to be the most unexpected and one of the most
important and exciting stories I have ever covered. Perhaps my husband,
Sydney Gruson of *The New York Times,* and I stumbled on it a
little sooner than would have been the case if we hadn't already known

people in Warsaw. But I can't pretend to special foresight or intuition. From that first cold spring day in 1956, the evidence kept piling up insistently that some drastic change was working beneath the opaque surface of this Communist state.

The notion of a monolithic Soviet bloc was then still widespread, and except for the defection of Tito's Yugoslavia, there had been nothing visible to the West contradicting the idea. It is true that just about this time the first reports of Khrushchev's secret de-Stalinization speech to the Soviet Union's Twentieth Party Congress were seeping out. But they were uncertain reports, in no way reflected in the official behavior of the Communist government, and Western officials were dubious about their accuracy and significance. The assumption to be taken on any assignment behind the Iron Curtain was still a simple paraphrase of Gertrude Stein, "A Communist state is a Communist state is a Communist state. . . ."

The signs that this might no longer be quite valid were all over Warsaw, but they were small at the beginning, and you had to consider them carefully. The first clue I had was when I hesitantly began to look up people I had known, not sure whether they would be pleased or discomforted to see me again. The reaction was startling. Not only old friends, but slight acquaintances as well—among them people who had preferred not to be seen with foreigners in the years just after the war—came pouring out of heaven knows where. I had a few addresses, but word got around and people turned up, as though they had been waiting breathlessly all this time just for the chance to talk to an American reporter.

The food at the Polish Journalists' Club had not improved, but the atmosphere was unrecognizable. Communist newspapermen were glad to talk and to be seen talking with us; one even took it upon himself to be sure that I was up to date on all the anti-Communist jokes (these, it turned out, had become Warsaw's major daily product). Another Communist journalist made a point of racing me through a tour of artists' cafés, writers' clubs and actors' clubs, to listen to some strange talk and to look at some crazy, definitely non-socialist and non-realist paintings splashed on the walls. Conversations were guarded at first, either reserved or trivial, but a willingness to talk at all did not fit either the old or the current pattern in the rest of Eastern Europe.

Day by day, as there was more chance to see people informally and in small groups, the reserve dropped away.

A Central Committee member agreed to talk with me, and made an appointment to meet me in the café of our hotel. I had asked for the appointment because a reporter must ask to see people who know what the government is up to. But I didn't really expect him to show up. He did, and we sat for nearly two hours over endless glasses of tea while he explained views that no Communist propaganda record had played before. "We went wrong somewhere back in the Twenties," he said. "We've got to trace everything and figure out just what it was. It's not good enough to blame one dead man or another, Beria or even Stalin. We've got to see where the system broke down. It will take time to make the drastic repairs we need, we can't get too far ahead of the other [Communist] countries, but we can't move backwards and we can't stay still. Our people won't stand for it . . ."

That was certainly a brand new line for a leading Communist. What was behind it?

On the Sunday after my arrival in Warsaw, the weather suddenly turned spring bright. A Polish newspaper friend suggested a picnic in the country, and we drove out with his girl friend, an ardent Communist. They were too full of their thoughts for small talk, and after some polite questions about life in the West, the emotional dam broke. She was a party activist, but not a high-ranking one, and there could be no doubt from her quivering voice that she truly said what she believed. She told how she had become a Communist, a young girl cowering before the Nazis at the wall of Warsaw's ghetto, and she told how fervent was her faith. That was to prepare me for a surprising little personal confession—Khrushchev's secret anti-Stalin speech had been read aloud at her party cell meeting not long before, and she had fainted on the spot. Now, she said, she no longer knew what to believe about anything.

Somehow the conversation turned to the war in Korea, not one of the subjects mentioned in the Khrushchev speech. She dealt with the question by parroting the familiar line about aggressive American imperialists and South Korean reactionaries. "An aggression that began with a backwards march until nothing but a beachhead remained?" I asked her. "Isn't that just what Hitler was saying about Poland in 1939? An 'aggression' that began with a backwards cavalry march until nothing was left?" It was an obvious response, one that had been ducked or rejected by Communists since the Korean war began in 1950, but for the first time I heard a different Communist reaction.

"My God," she said, nearly weeping, "do you mean to tell me that Korea was a lie too? That all those purges and the terrible shortages for the Korean war were all because of lies?"

The next evening I went to see an old friend, a witty and sharp-tongued Polish woman who was anti-Communist but who had nevertheless retained a number of Communist acquaintances from the prewar coterie of intellectuals.

"It's wonderful," she said gleefully. "I'm driving them mad, and it's the simplest thing in the world. I used to taunt them about their boasts of how perfect a state they had created—and that was all I could dare say. But now they're beating their breasts and moaning about mistakes, and I just reply, with syrup in my voice, that it really wasn't all that bad. They can't stand that. It's all they can do not to break down and blubber."

An eminent Polish scientist, a man of the far left who visited her regularly for a dip in her intellectual acid bath, nodded ruefully in confirmation. He went on to say he was reading a fascinating book that revealed a good deal. It was Alex Weissberg's *Conspiracy of Silence,* a disclosure of cooperation between the Gestapo and the Soviet NKVD.

I told him, in some amazement, that it was by no means a new book—that it had been published shortly after the war, and that he was reading it ten years too late to put its warnings about the Soviet police to use.

"Ah," he said with a candid smile, "but if I had read it sooner, I wouldn't have believed it. Now I see what truth is."

There were many conversations like that, but there were other things, too. Poles were reading Western newspapers. A few such publications were even on sale in Warsaw. Suddenly people were no longer afraid to ask relatives abroad to send them foreign periodicals; and they weren't afraid to take these publications into public places, reading them in the cafés, where anyone could see.

In front of the American Embassy, on what had once been Aleja Ujazdowska and was at that time Aleja Stalina, there had always been a glass display case where photographs of American scenes and personalities were posted. All through the day, knots of people now stood there staring. A taxi driver gestured toward them as we drove by, and said, "A year ago, the police would have swept them away in a twinkling. The police don't show themselves so much any more. Things really seem a lot better. But for heaven's sake, please don't tell anybody I said so. Who knows how long it will last?"

And then, traveling into the country, I picked up hitchhikers. It is an ideal way to sample ordinary peoples' opinion in a frightened country. They know you are a foreigner by your car; they know they cannot be overheard by a compatriot; they know you have no idea of their name and address, and that you are most unlikely ever to meet again—and so they are glad enough to talk.

The hitchhikers, like the Warsaw taxi drivers and waiters and shop clerks—the people outside of political life with whom one can exchange a few words inconspicuously—said they were still afraid. Things were a bit better, there were small signs on the grocery shelves and the dry-goods counters of a little easing in life, but they did not believe the regime could be anything but harsh. They hated, and kept still, except for such snatches of talk with a rare foreigner.

It did not take very long to collect all this evidence—the talk among Communists about a "second revolution" that was coming, and the cold disbelief of the rest of the country. The obvious conclusion was that deep, widespread rumblings inside the party were gathering explosive force, but that the population at large had not yet begun to play a part in the growing unrest. Even the Polish newspapers reflected some of the turmoil inside the party, but only in the devious, coded way that Communists use to talk to each other in public so that only those who already know what is happening can understand.

From time to time during this initial period of our discovery that a very big story was brewing in the Poland of 1956, I took what I was learning to the American and other Western embassies in Warsaw to get the diplomats' view. Their response was flat disbelief. Even people who had been living there for several years simply rejected the idea that anything had changed at all. And they insisted that if some things did change, there could be no significance in it because the pattern was immutably fixed.

Once I asked an American Embassy official, who had a good many more personal contacts with Poles than most of the isolated diplomats, what he would consider a real sign that the pattern was fraying.

"When the secret police stop following me wherever I go," he said, and he launched into a long anecdote about the game of hide and seek he had played with his familiar escort on a drive to the countryside a few days before. Yet it seemed obvious enough that surveillance of foreign diplomats would be the last item on the list of police renunciations, not the first, if there were a priority list for relaxation. But he was adamant. "I know those fellows very well," he said, "they are always with me. Look at their brute faces, in those two cars across the street. They haven't changed a bit, so how can you say anything is different in this country?"

There were indeed grounds for skepticism, but not for ignoring so many evident facts. It was a question of delicate judgment and of delicate handling when it came to writing day by day, and it was a vital help that the two of us were there together, so that Sydney and I could test the sturdiness of our impressions by bouncing them off each other's minds.

Eventually, in October of that year, when Wladyslaw Gomulka returned to power in defiance of Soviet tanks, and when Hungary flamed in revolt, no one continued to doubt that there had been a development of great historical importance. The cracks in the Soviet empire and in the monolith of Communist ideology had opened into bloody breaches for all to see. By then, the reporting job changed from a painstaking task of weighing clues and piecing them together to a frenzied chase after rapid developments. It was a great satisfaction, when the huge quake came, to have been able to watch and to gauge the approaching tremors.

Before Wilfrid Fleisher was graduated from the School of Journalism in 1921, he had been educated in France, England and Japan, and had served with the A.E.F. in Siberia. It is hardly surprising that foreign correspondence was his choice for a career.

Before World War II, Mr. Fleisher worked in Japan as editor of an American newspaper, The Japan Advertiser, *and as correspondent, at different periods, for* The New York Times *and the* Herald Tribune. *After the war, his interests turned to the Scandinavian countries, where he is currently serving as correspondent for CBS and* Newsweek. *The author of books on Japan and Sweden, he received the Order of the North Star from the King of Sweden. Mr. Fleisher is married, has three children, and lives in Stockholm.*

WILFRID FLEISHER:

F. D. R. Supplied the Story

In November of 1940, the Japanese could no longer tolerate the presence in their country of the American newspaper I edited, *The Japan Advertiser*. The paper was confiscated ("sold"), and I was forced to leave the land in which I had lived and worked for eighteen years.

Deeply certain of impending conflict, I returned to the United States, baffled to find my countrymen in no way conscious of the sizzling fuse in Asia. Thus it was that I could witness in Washington the events leading to Pearl Harbor, share in a potentially momentous conversation (unrevealed until now) with President Roosevelt, and, eventually, speak into a microphone for the most meaningful sixty seconds of my life.

I was assigned, immediately after my return, to serve as correspondent at the State Department for *The New York Herald Tribune*. Many of the participants in the Japanese-American negotiations were men I knew well: Admiral Kichisaburo Nomura, for example, and Saburo

35

Kurusu, who was sent as a special envoy to assist Ambassador Nomura shortly before Pearl Harbor; and I had a host of friends in State who had served, at one time or another, in the Far East.

I was soon to realize that the State Department was sharply divided regarding our policy toward Japan. There were those who favored a "soft" policy, arguing that the United States should avoid being drawn into a war in two oceans simultaneously. Since the Nazi menace was the greater, they said, it should be dealt with first; meanwhile a truce should be made with Japan—even at the expense of China, if necessary. They contended that if Germany were defeated, Japan would probably yield to pressure without a fight.

The other group, those considered the "rebels"—junior officers, for the most part, who had served in the Far East—believed that Japan, as an ally of Germany and Italy, would play the Axis game, and that Japanese militarists would not be stopped by warnings or by sermons but only by force if need be. They were bitterly opposed to any accord with Japan at the sacrifice of China.

As a newspaperman, I was to profit by this split. Both sides wanted an outlet for their views. The hard-line group was quite ready to use publicity to discredit the "appeasers" if it could. In this situation I was constantly fed information by militant junior officials who, to my amazement, knew every facet of the top-level talks then going on between Secretary Hull and Ambassador Nomura. Hull was frequently surprised to read in *The New York Herald Tribune* details which he erroneously suspected had been leaked to me at a high level, whereas they had come from members of his own staff ready to take policy into their own hands.

By July of 1941, Japanese forces were penetrating into Indo-China. The United States retaliated by freezing Japanese assets and imposing an oil embargo. Under pressure of this embargo, the Japanese secretly proposed a meeting between Premier Fumimaro Konoye of Japan and President Roosevelt. This proposal was contained in a note delivered by Ambassador Nomura to the President on August 28, as I was able to reveal in an exclusive report in *The New York Herald Tribune* a few days later.

I can now disclose that this information came to me directly from the President.

My first meeting with Franklin Roosevelt had taken place in the early summer of 1935. Although the President's day had been filled with congressional matters, we nevertheless discussed the Japanese situation for more than an hour. I had been impressed by the fact that

Roosevelt was remarkably well informed about Japan. He summarized his own policy then in these words: "I want to avoid rocking the boat."

Four years later I again had a private meeting with the President. By then our relations with Japan had further deteriorated, and Mr. Roosevelt was gravely concerned. He still retained the hope, however, that somehow a settlement could be worked out.

Now, in September of 1941, a few days after Nomura had secretly proposed the top-level conference, I again found myself in private conversation with the President. An advance copy of "Volcanic Isle," a book I had written about my experiences in Japan, had just arrived from the publisher. At the end of a White House press conference I lingered behind to present the book to Mr. Roosevelt.

The President turned its pages with interest and remarked: "Japan is a country I have always wanted to visit."

"I'm afraid, Mr. President, you have waited too long," I replied.

"No," said Roosevelt, looking at me directly and seriously. "I don't think so. I have a mind to go and talk to those Japs."

"But surely not now," I said.

"Why not?" asked Roosevelt, as he closed the book and placed it on his desk.

I was stunned. The President of the United States, just back from a meeting with Winston Churchill aboard a warship in the Atlantic, was now considering going to meet the Japanese. This was news indeed. The President knew I was a *Herald Tribune* correspondent, yet he imposed no bans or limitations on the information he gave me that afternoon.

I felt that ethics demanded that I conceal the source of the news, while journalistic standards required that the story be fleshed out. I spent two feverish days pumping my usually voluble sources in the State Department. Then, inadvertently, I learned the final details, those enabling me to break the story, from a State Department acquaintance who was in no way connected with Far Eastern affairs. This junior official told me that the President planned to meet Premier Konoye of Japan aboard a Japanese warship "somewhere in the Pacific" in a final attempt to placate Japan.

My dispatch, dated Washington, Sept. 3, 1941, appeared in the *Herald Tribune* under a four-column headline on page 1, and in *The Washington Post* (which subscribed to our service) under a streamer headline across the front page. The lead read as follows:

> Prince Fumimaro Konoye, the Japanese Premier, proposed to
> President Roosevelt last week that they meet aboard a Japanese war-

ship somewhere in the Pacific for a personal discussion of Japanese-American relations in an attempt to reach a settlement of Pacific affairs, it was learned authoritatively here today.

Konoye's proposal for a conference modeled on the Roosevelt-Churchill meeting in the Atlantic is understood to have been submitted to the President early last week, even before the Japanese Premier's note was delivered to the White House last Thursday by Admiral Kichisaburo Nomura, the Japanese Ambassador.

President Roosevelt is said to have made acceptance of the Japanese Premier's invitation contingent on Japan's acquiescence to certain basic principles which, it is understood, Japanese authorities have failed, at least so far, to meet.

Further in this dispatch, I added: "While President Roosevelt was understood to have been pleased by the Japanese suggestion for a conference, there are indications that the negotiations subsequently have not developed in a manner which would lead to the hope that such a parley can be brought about."

Not until January of 1943 was the story fully confirmed. The day after its appearance it was laughingly dismissed by Stephen T. Early, the President's press secretary—a friend of mine, incidentally, and a former colleague. He said that the President had received "no invitation," and that the only plan he had for a trip on the water was a cruise on the Potomac. He added that "if the *Herald Tribune* cares to follow the President to Annapolis, they will readily see the falsity of this story."

(One week after Pearl Harbor, President Roosevelt declared in a message to Congress: "I should have been happy to travel thousands of miles to meet the Premier of Japan . . . but I felt it desirable, before doing so, to obtain some assurance that there could be some agreement on basic principles. This Government tried hard—but without success —to obtain such assurance from the Japanese Government.")

For his part, Cordell Hull would neither confirm nor deny my story on the day of its appearance; I consider it a measure of his integrity that he refused to issue a denial. A White Paper, released on January 2, 1943, made it plain that Hull had promised American Ambassador Joseph C. Grew in Tokyo to keep the proposal confidential, at the request of the Japanese government. When my story appeared nonetheless, the chief of the American Bureau of the Japanese Foreign Office, Mr. Terasaki, had called to protest my disclosure of the proposed meeting. "The result," he said, "would be to increase the opposition to the Japanese Government on the part of rightist elements, since it would be alleged that the Government was yielding to American pressure."

Premier Konoye had wanted to confront these pro-Axis elements with a "fait accompli," said Mr. Terasaki, and he urged that an official announcement of the meeting be issued as soon as possible.

Could war have been averted? We now know differently; we know that Japan's plans for sudden attack and simultaneous "peaceful negotiation" were made with time-table accuracy. Yet only a few days before Pearl Harbor, Ambassador Nomura came up to me in the corridor of the State Department and called me a "war monger," because I had reported how perilously close the two nations were to conflict.

On December 7, when I heard the unconfirmed radio reports of the attack at Pearl Harbor, I rushed to the State Department, arriving just in time to see the Japanese envoys, Nomura and Kurusu, emerging from their last meeting with Secretary of State Hull.

Three years, eight months and seven days later, I stood again in almost the same place—the outer office of the Secretary of State—carrying a microphone. The Secretary was no longer Cordell Hull, but Jimmy Byrnes. A young foreign diplomat with a briefcase came running in. He was the Swiss chargé d'affaires, bringing with him Japan's formal note of surrender.

The American Broadcasting Company cut in on its network for one precious minute. I made the announcement.

It was not only the end of the war, but the end of an era, one I had followed closely and long. The United States had won the war, but Asia had asserted itself and would never again be the same.

*When Everest P. Derthick describes an episode
that took place in the news room of* The Cleveland Plain Dealer, *he is writing about one of the
subjects he knows most intimately. After he
studied at the Columbia School of Journalism in
1923, Mr. Derthick went right to the* Plain
Dealer, *where he served, successively, as reporter,
copy reader, chief of the copy desk, day city
editor, executive assistant to the editor and managing editor.*

*In October of 1962 he resigned to join the
faculty of the Ohio University School of Journalism. Mr. Derthick is married and has two
daughters, and resides in Chagrin Falls, Ohio.*

EVEREST P. DERTHICK:

Quiet Afternoon in Cleveland

The afternoon in the *Plain Dealer* city room had settled into routine
and waiting.

Nothing on the local assignment sheet on that afternoon of October
20, 1944, would merit page one play. National and international
news would fill the page. MacArthur was invading Leyte, the allies
were driving against Hitler, and Dewey was masterminding his campaign for the Presidency.

The afternoon had that nothing feel. Nothing to heckle the city hall
reporter about. He hadn't called in and he wasn't answering his phone.
Nothing to hash over with the politics reporter when and if he called.
The man on the police beat called in to report nothing without even
being asked. Maybe we could do a weather short for page one about
one more bright day of mild Indian summer.

The minute hand of the Western Union clock was counting down to
forty after two. Moments later tension that would wind tight through
the night snapped up the slack in the city room.

The blank glass eyes on the phone cabinets winked to life to signal
the first of hundreds of calls asking or telling about the East Ohio Gas

Company explosion that took 130 lives and burned out a square mile of homes and small stores.

"The air is on fire."

No reporter ever phoned words better chosen to command city room action. The politics man who hadn't checked in, who should have been following a candidate for something or other, was on the edge of an inferno where sewers were feeding geysers of flame and blasting man-hole covers skyward.

"Some tanks exploded. Gas ran down the streets like water. There's fire from St. Clair to the shoreway and from 60th maybe to East 55th. Send everybody."

You need staff. All the guys on beats. All the guys at home. But in-coming calls have jammed the PBX. Damn the phones. You can't get them answered, you can't get a line out. Your Girl Friday at the information desk is swamped.

Get this thing under control.

You head for the sanctum of the editor-in-chief. He's headed for the city room. Collision in the corridor puts you in business. Take anybody from editorial writers to test-kitchen cooks.

You put the society editor, the club editor and the P.T.A. editor on city room phones and tell the chief operator to switch the "what happened" questions to them.

Grab a cub from sports, the church editor and a general assignment man just in from a convention. Put them at three more phones to take whatever information can be sorted out.

"And now, Girl Friday, let's get some people in here. Take your staff list, get the girl sorting the wire copy to help you. Call everybody who's off. Let me talk to the beat men as soon as they call in or when you reach them. Tell the slot man to come in early with a couple of copy-readers."

Two photographers have been on the scene long since. They heard a radio flash and steered for the pillars of fire overhung by smoke.

The chief police reporter calls from a church on the perimeter of the fire. How many dead? Who knows? How do you find bodies when firemen can't go in among the burning houses?

(All through the night the same question will bring the same an-swer.)

You send three or four more men for your police reporter to deploy.

"I've got city hall on line five," says Friday as you're telling the man-aging editor he'd better take on extra pages, put a paper out early, whether there are ten dead or a hundred.

"Where the hell have you been?"

"Out with the law director for a milk shake," the city hall man says. "Look, in case you don't know it you've got a story on your hands. The radio in his car . . ."

Disaster control is being organized at city hall. Military police, the Coast Guard, civil defense forces, half the city's fire companies and most of its uniformed police are mobilized around the stricken area. War plants on the outskirts are in danger.

"Stay there for now," you say. "You're where there'll be most for the lead. Then come in and start writing. We'll get someone to feed you the rest of the story."

The mayor, downstate in his campaign for governor, is flying back to take charge at the hall.

An hour and another have gone, and you recheck the notes on three spindles.

Production manager alerted for composing room load. Engraving and press room alerted. Circulation knows a selling story's in the works. Advertising will clear off a couple of inside pages.

The political reporter has called in again and is set to do an inspired color story.

The veteran city editor who works the night side should be on hand, but it's his day off and he doesn't answer his phone. Send a telegram that will hit him when he gets home.

And where have you sent your regular reporters and the score of departmental specialists who are available and eager? To the city morgue, of course, where lines of those who fear the worst are forming. A couple of men start compiling the lead list, the roll of the dead that won't be fully known for days. And two more men work on the list of injured.

And a reporter is at each of the six hospitals where the injured arrive in increasing numbers. Photographers are making the rounds there.

A rewrite man is assembling bits and pieces from the phone staff. . . . explosion heard in suburban area 16 miles away, birds fell dead from utility wires, heat so intense workers closed windows in factory three miles away, paint on autos parked near fire area blistered and broke into flames.

It's getting dark outside and Friday puts coffee and a sandwich in front of you as the city hall man comes in. He tells you there have been five major explosions and that 30 of the city's 40 fire companies are fighting to contain the disaster. He'll start writing a 20th add—and before he's through, the additions to the story will be triple that.

He has phrases such as "flames shooting 1,000 feet in the air" and "houses that kindled like orange crates under a blowtorch."

You have a man working on a history story of other disasters. A sidebar, on the rescue efforts and the fire-fighting role of Navy, Army and Coast Guard forces is coming. There's an assignment on the Red Cross: It will be coping with the needs of an estimated 10,000, including some who escaped the fire and many more who were ordered evacuated from the perimeter danger zone.

A reporter is calling East Ohio Gas Company officials and scientists for opinions on the cause of the explosions. Like the number of dead, the answer must wait. One of four tanks holding 400,000 cubic feet of liquified gas, expansible to 240,000,000 cubic feet when released, exploded. Why? No one knew.

What about war production? We're checking on plants presumed destroyed, damaged or out of production because gas will be cut off. And a financial man has come in with a note on insurance adjustments.

The drama critic, back from the Italian front as a war correspondent, is doing a story that pictures the home front devastation in terms of battle.

The city editor got his telegram and is now guiding the flow of copy.

Out on St. Clair Avenue a block-long section of pavement is sinking. And nearby is the church where the chief police reporter and his legmen are still working the eye-witness angles. Power lines are down. They've phoned for a lantern, for food and for coffee.

The most dependable office boy is ordered to round up the supplies and go to the rescue. Lantern and sandwiches in hand, he comes hesitantly to the desk and says, "Radio reports the church is going to blow up. No use taking sandwiches to bodies you probably can't find." But he went, and the church stood until a freeway demolished it years later.

And so the night wore on. And the city hall reporter wrote:

"Thirty-four persons were known to be dead, scores were missing and 175 were under medical treatment last night as the most devastating fire in Cleveland's history raged through a district bounded by St. Clair Avenue, E. 55th Street, E. 67th Street and Memorial Shoreway.

"Twelve hours after an initial explosion at 2:40 P.M. that converted the liquid storage plant of the East Ohio Gas Co. into a gigantic flamethrower which consumed hundreds of homes and small stores within a square mile, Fire Chief James E. Granger said the conflagration would continue at least through the night."

Two eight-column streamers bannered the story. And MacArthur invaded Leyte under a one-column head at the bottom of the page.

In books, magazine articles, on television and, above all, through his reporting for The New York Times, *Richard Witkin has helped this country understand the daily developments of aviation and space technology.*

A 1940 graduate of the School of Journalism, Mr. Witkin served as commander of a B-24 bomber during World War II. He covered the United Nations for UP from 1947 until 1954 before joining The Times, *where he is now aviation editor. Winner of the Newspaper Guild's Page One Award, Mr. Witkin has written for* Saturday Evening Post, Reader's Digest *and other magazines, and has contributed essays to two books,* "The Challenge of the Sputniks" *and* "America's Race to the Moon," *the first of which he edited.*

RICHARD WITKIN:

Crash Detection

Microscopic clues, surprise witnesses, astonishing laboratory discoveries, courtroom revelations—these are some of the mystery-story aspects of air-crash inquiries. But while detective fiction seeks only to entertain, investigations of air disasters represent an intensive effort to prevent the multiplication of tragedy. It was the account of one such successful inquiry that started me writing professionally about aviation.

On June 17, 1948, a DC-6 crashed at Mt. Carmel, Pennsylvania. The plane was carrying 39 passengers—among them Earl Carroll, the producer-showman—and a crew of four. For several miles before the impact point, the plane staggered, at uncommonly low altitude, down a valley pocked with mine shafts. Just before it was about to smash into a wooden, 11-story coal breaker, it went into a steep right bank and struck the hillside, ripping a 66,000-volt power line in the process.

I learned many tricks of the crash detective's trade in reconstructing the Mt. Carmel case. The most impressive discovery was that, no matter how badly mangled the wreckage of a plane, clues to what did or did

44

not happen can always be found. For instance, propeller blades will shatter into many more fragments when the engine is generating power than when it is idling or is feathered. Again, there are several techniques for deciding whether a plane was afire in the air or burned only after impact; one is to examine a piece of fuselage smashed into a pleated accordion shape and charred on the outside by fire. If, when the accordion is opened, the pleats are also found to be burned on the inside, that area must have been ablaze while the plane was still airborne.

The best positive clue in the Mt. Carmel case was not in the wreckage but in tape recordings of messages from plane to ground. Although the recordings were so garbled by static that much of what had been said was lost, one significant message from the plane came through clearly: "We released the fire extinguisher in the forward cargo pit."

Five weeks earlier the crew of another airliner had responded to a fire warning by setting off an extinguisher in the baggage compartment. The pilots soon noted fumes in the cockpit, and made an emergency landing at the nearest airport. When they alighted, according to the ground crewmen present, they appeared to be "slightly groggy."

This incident suggested that the pilots on the Mt. Carmel plane might have been overcome by fumes. But how to prove it?

The most direct line of inquiry was to try to ferret more meaning out of the static-ridden recordings. The Civil Aeronautics Board team sent the discs to a laboratory, where filters were used to remove some of the static. Portions of the most unintelligible sections were recorded as many as 100 times on individual discs. A panel of experts then set to work listening to the repetitions of individual phrases. They listened with earphones, over loudspeakers, through additional filters and at different speeds and volumes.

The main result: Several were certain they heard a pilot refer to fumes in the cockpit.

Finally, a physiologist specializing in aviation medicine, Dr. Ludwig G. Lederer, was called in—not to listen to content but to the inflections of the voice from the plane.

He determined that the pilot's tone strayed more and more from normal speech. Several words, he found, indicated "gasping and agony." And the final message, "emergency descent," was "typical of thick, torqued enunciation."

Summing up, Dr. Lederer said he believed the "abnormal transmissions" could be attributed to "physiological impairment" caused by carbon dioxide.

Mt. Carmel was a thorough freshman course in crash detection. But it was taken in the lecture hall, so to speak, not in the laboratory; I did not follow the inquiry while it was going on, but reviewed it only after it had been completed. Not until I joined *The New York Times* in 1954, to cover aviation and space activities, did I follow an accident investigation from the start.

There have been many of them since, unhappily. The one with by far the most ramifications was the investigation of the mid-air collision of a jetliner and a piston airliner over Staten Island at about 10:30 A.M. on December 16, 1960.

My personal pursuit of the facts began only a few minutes later, when I was called to a phone in the Visiting Officers Quarters at Randolph Air Force Base in San Antonio. I had been asleep for less than an hour after a sleepless all-night flight to the base.

Hal Faber on the *Times* national desk filled me in briefly on what had happened. I told him I would head back to New York immediately. A spirited cab driver sped me, with about five minutes to spare, to the airport, and I caught a plane for Dallas. En route to Dallas, I woke up sufficiently to realize that I wasn't going to do the paper's first-day coverage much good if I were airborne most of the day.

So, at the Dallas airport, I prevailed on one of the airlines to lend me a desk, a typewriter and a phone, and I notified the paper that I would try to think up a "think" piece.

The Associated Press office in Dallas read me the latest dispatches. The piston-engine Super Constellation had come down at the edge of Miller's Field on Staten Island. The DC-8 jetliner had crashed eight and a half miles to the northeast in a thickly settled section of Brooklyn. There had been 128 aboard the two planes (all died, although an 11-year-old boy aboard the jet survived for a day). Others had died on the ground (the final toll on the ground was six). It seemed obvious that no matter what mistakes the pilots may have made, a prime focus of the inquiry was going to be the role of the air-traffic controllers and their radar sets.

I knew that many of my best sources in the Civil Aeronautics Board (which investigates crashes) and the Federal Aviation Agency (which writes flight rules and operates the traffic-control system) could not possibly be reached by phone; they would be at the scene or en route to the scene or closeted in meetings. But I did get through to two or three specialists on traffic control who had been left in Washington to mind the store. And we developed enough ideas for a "news analysis" piece, which I phoned to the *Times*' dictation room in time for the first edition.

The jump-off point for the article was that, while there had been a dozen or more mid-air collisions involving one or more airliners, this was the first in which both planes had been operating under direction of the traffic-control system. (A congressman later wrote to remind me— correctly—that I had forgotten the collision of a Brazilian airliner with a U.S. military plane carrying a Navy band.)

It was the first such crash in the United States, anyway. And the point was that the excellent record had made for dangerous complacency about the ability of the traffic-control system to guarantee safe separation of planes under its jurisdiction. This despite surveys that showed four near-collisions involving airliners every day. The Staten Island accident was certain to dispel whatever complacency remained.

The specific issue could be simply put: Why had not the controllers seen the impending collision on their radar scopes and radioed one or both pilots to change course?

In partial explanation, I told how traffic controllers used radar when guiding planes in and out of a metropolitan area. The planes appeared on radar scopes as "blips" of light about the size and shape of rice kernels. "Blips" and planes could be matched up by radio messages between pilots and controllers, and the controllers could follow and supervise the courses the planes flew. But there was one big deficiency to this system, I emphasized: A blip indicated only the plane's position in its course over the ground; it revealed nothing at all about the craft's altitude.

Another deficiency was to become startlingly apparent as the investigation developed. Now, however, having filed my first-day story, I caught a plane to Kansas City, only to be pinned there for the night because of the crowds of college kids going home for the Christmas holidays. I reached the office by noon the next day, a Saturday.

During the next two days I concentrated on two things: learning the instructions that had been given the two planes as they entered the control area; and finding out what deviations (or which combination of deviations) from those instructions could have brought about the collision.

It was not long before large gaps in the sequence of events leading up to the tragedy began to be filled. Two officials I phoned told me that traffic controllers had actually seen the slow-moving blip of the piston plane and the fast-moving blip of the jet come together. One said that the piston pilot had been warned of a blip approaching his, although there was no telling what altitude it was at.

The next thing I learned was that one of the jet's four engines had been found on the edge of the small Army air field where the piston plane had crashed. Since jet pods do not have aerodynamic characteristics enabling them to glide very far once detached from their wing, the collision had evidently occurred over Miller Field.

Once this was established, it followed that the jet crew had failed to follow instructions given by traffic control. The crew had been told to "hold" over the Preston, N.J., holding area used by planes waiting to land either at Idlewild (where the jet was headed) or at Newark Airport. But the collision had occurred 11 miles northeast of Preston, outside the holding area. And the jet had finally crashed eight and one-half miles still farther to the northeast.

It was a high-level F.A.A. official who pointed out a significant pattern: Four key points in the probable flight path of the jet lay in a straight line. Point A was the point where the plane would normally have made a left turn onto the airway headed northeast to Preston. Point B was Preston itself, where the plane would normally have turned right to start flying a racetrack-shaped "holding" course. Point C was the collision point over Miller's Field. Point D was the Brooklyn section where the jet came down.

The implication was that for some reason—a malfunction in radio navigation aids on the ground, a malfunction aboard the plane, or error by the jet's crew—the plane had simply overshot Preston.

The vice-president of an airline not involved in the crash called me a few days after the crash. There was speculation in the trade, he said, that the pilot of the jet might have mistaken the radio aid at Stroudsberg for the Solberg station—the one he was supposed to use. Not only did the names sound alike, but the code identification signals were also similar and the radio frequencies were not far apart.

Soon afterwards, the name of the Stroudsberg station was changed to Tannersville, and there were changes in identification signal and frequency.

The biggest news break in the case came six days after the crash when the C.A.B. released a voluminous transcript of messages between ground controllers and the two planes.

The copy boy did not arrive at the office from Idlewild with the transcript until about an hour and a half before first-edition deadline. I managed to pull out a few highlights and dash off a story. There would be time to make more sense of it all for later editions.

Dick Haitch, who is a private pilot and was reading copy on my contributions for the city desk, came up with the angle that "made" the later-edition stories.

Alongside each air-ground message was the time that message had been radioed.

One vital message was the last from the area controller to the jet. It repeated previous instructions: That the plane was to "hold" at Preston. The controller said that he was discontinuing radar service and that the pilot should contact the local Idlewild controller for further instructions. The message was sent at 10:33:15.

A second vital message was the call from the jet to the local Idlewild controller. It was sent at 10:33:28 (just 13 seconds later).

The third vital message was a longish reply from the controller.

It was followed by silence from the jet.

Similarly, exchanges between the piston plane and the local controller at LaGuardia Airport were abruptly interrupted by silence from the plane.

Dick Haitch took the times of the messages and did some interesting calculations. They showed that at 10:33:15, when the area controller told the jet for the last time to "hold" at Preston, the jet must already have been well past Preston.

Otherwise, in order to cover a minimum of 11 miles (the distance from Preston to the collison point) by about 10:33:42, the jet would have had to have been going well over a thousand miles an hour—an impossibility.

Was the area controller looking at the wrong blip when he gave the jet pilot his final instructions to hold at Preston? Or was he not even bothering about the jet's blip?

The answer came as a surprise to me and a shock to many in the industry; pilots who had flown in and out of the area with routine regularity were dismayed by the revelation. If they had previously been a little casual about following instructions to the letter, relying on radar to back them up, they were unlikely to be casual any more.

The answer was that traffic controllers physically were not able to keep constant watch on the blips of every plane they were handling. They were not required to do so. They were allowed to stop following a particular blip once the plane had been "cleared" to an assigned "holding" area, as had the DC-8 in the Staten Island collision.

The theory was that a plane so cleared could not collide with any other controlled plane because no two planes were cleared to the same holding area at the same altitude. But what if one of the planes did not, for some reason, follow instructions?

Later, at the official hearing on the crash, F.A.A. officials stressed time and again that the controller was not required to be looking at the jet's blip when the jet pilot was given his final instructions to hold at Preston. The F.A.A. emphasized that the controller had already given the plane instructions which, if followed, would have kept it safely separated from other known traffic.

The transcripts also verified what I had learned from informants some days earlier—that the LaGuardia controller handling the piston plane had twice told the pilot of another blip about to merge with his.

That no evasive action was taken was not unusual. The traffic system, the pilot knew, was not supposed to allow two planes flying blind in the clouds to enter the same area at the same altitude. Since he was in the clouds, he reasoned, the other plane must be at another altitude.

Why had the radar controller not changed the piston plane's course, just to play safe? Because blips of planes at different altitudes were constantly crossing, particularly in good weather when private pilots not under control of the traffic system were flying about. It would be impractical to keep steering blips around one another.

What is more—and observers were surprised to learn this—controllers were instructed not to provide course changes to steer a plane around an unidentified blip unless the pilot, warned of a blip approaching, requested an evasive maneuver.

For about two months I did little else but cover the crash inquiry. By the time the reasons for the disaster had become apparent, the story was no longer front-page news. By the time steps were taken to put new patches in the obsolescent traffic control system, reports from the Brooklyn hearings had been relegated to the back pages of the newspapers, flanked by shipping news and weather statistics.

Investigations often end off the front page—not in an action-packed last chapter in which everything is neatly tied up, with justice done and broken hearts mended and the butler sent off to the pen. Nonetheless, the reporter has already had his reward: Partly as a result of his stories and the spotlight of the press, the planes that arrive and depart thereafter are likely to be safer.

When journalists talk among themselves, they trade
memories---of the big or unforgettable stories,
of the problems of their craft...

*A former Marine Corps combat correspondent,
Henry Giniger has been a* New York Times *foreign correspondent since 1946, stationed mainly
in Paris.*

*Born in Brooklyn in 1922, Mr. Giniger received
his B. A. at the City College of New York in 1942
and was graduated from the School of Journalism
in 1943, the recipient of a Pulitzer Traveling
Scholarship. He then enlisted with the Marines,
serving with the Corps until 1946. He and his
wife, Janine, and their daughter, Marianne, reside in Paris—where (see article by Theodore
M. Bernstein) he interprets the news of France for
American readers, and the needs of American
editors to French printers.*

HENRY GINIGER:

Silent in Hungary

The best story in the world is no good if you cannot get it to your
paper. This is true whether a reporter is one mile or 5,000 miles away
from his editors. Foreign correspondents, however, are most often
afflicted with communications problems, and anyone who has ever
been abroad as a journalist knows that one of his first duties is to make
sure that he has a way of getting his story out. Occasionally he may be
reduced to running the communications himself, as correspondents in
Leopoldville who had to tap out their stories on a Telex machine after
long hours of waiting will attest with absolutely no nostalgia.

But the worst thing of all is to have the means of communication at
hand and not be able to use them. For ten days in November, 1956, I
was among several score of correspondents who watched and heard a
country in the act of losing a bid for freedom, yet could say nothing
about it until the bid was lost. The country was, of course, Hungary,
which amazed the world and probably herself by suddenly rising up
against a despotic Communist regime and actually casting it out of
power.

53

The rebellion began with a student demonstration in Budapest on October 23. Only a handful of correspondents were on hand for that. By October 31, when I crossed the border from Austria, the Revolution was in full swing, with a sort of cheery chaos reigning as the whole repressive structure of the Stalinist state tumbled at every level of political life.

To report all this one had only to make a reasonably easy telephone connection with Prague, where a Press Wireless office was providentially functioning. The copy was dictated onto recording machines to be transcribed later and filed by radio.

Vienna, too, could serve as a relay point for reports, although here one needed a friend or colleague to take the story down, since Press Wireless does not operate in Austria.

Finally, the Austro-Hungarian frontier was a sieve through which the whole world seemed to pass on foot or on bicycles or in cars during the first exciting days of the Revolution when nobody seemed to be in charge of anything.

In other words, the paths of communication were open. Then suddenly they were closed. They were to stay closed while the vast might of the Soviet Union desolated the country and smashed the hopes of its people. Few moments in contemporary history have produced such complete frustration at two ends of the spectrum—for a people that thought it had freedom in its grasp, and for correspondents who were there to tell the tragic story but had to keep it to themselves until it was all over.

The Duna Hotel lies on the right bank of the Danube, from which it takes its name. It was there that the vast majority of newspaper, radio and television correspondents and photographers were living and working. It was there that they were sleeping when Russian tanks came roaring down the Danube's embankments well before dawn on Sunday morning, November 4. The Russians had withdrawn from Budapest a few days earlier, as if bowing before the virtually unanimous opinion of the people. Now, with fresh troops and equipment, they had come back, and everybody knew it was to stay. A few newsmen may have been able to get some bulletins out by telephone, but the central exchange came quickly under Soviet control and that was the end of filing.

It was the beginning of our prison.

Just as there was no way to get copy out, neither was there any way to get oneself out. The borders had been tightly sealed by the Russians for the ugly work that lay ahead.

Within the Duna Hotel the correspondents hurriedly packed their bags and then went down to the lobby to mill around. Firing could be heard in various parts of the city. The hotel seemed to be in what newspapermen call an "exposed position." Besides, it would be only a matter of time before the hotel ran out of food and coal. With the exception of a few correspondents who resolved to stick it out, we decided to go to our respective legations. This does not sound very heroic, but at the time it seemed to almost everyone that the situation was hopeless, and that it would be best for us to seek safety first.

I had brought a bed roll from Vienna on the romantic notion that I might have to sleep in the fields while seeking out the Revolution. The roll was now used to make the floor of the United States Legation a little less hard. The Legation personnel, from the minister on down, were wonderfully kind and cooperative, but the building and its facilities were not designed for a hundred or more "permanent" residents.

One of the peculiar things about the chaos in Budapest was that electricity and telephone service continued with only very occasional lapses. I am referring, of course, to the automatic telephone system within Budapest. For the first few days this was to be our main link with the outside. Calls were made from legation to legation to exchange information; Hungarian friends and contacts phoned in during the day to report how things were going.

The reports added up to the sure, progressive extinction of a resistance that could not make up in bravery what it lacked in strength.

Along with two other correspondents I ventured out on the streets of the city. We walked back to the Duna, where the hold-outs of the first day were still holding out. There were great holes in the back wall; windows were smashed, and plaster from the walls and ceilings littered the beds and floor. Hungarian fighters had posted themselves in rooms overlooking the Danube and had fired down at Soviet tanks along the river embankment. The tanks had replied—and now the nicest part of the Duna Hotel had become unusable.

Fantastically, the hotel was still able to heat water. I bathed in someone's unused bathroom, and then we walked back through the sinister streets to the Legation, trying to maintain the casual air of strollers while Soviet armored cars and tanks patrolled the streets.

We walked out another day on to a main boulevard, and immediately a crowd collected around us. We were the West, the representatives of freedom; and we were made answerable for the fact that Hungarians were fighting alone when they had a right to expect help. Radio Free Europe, the voice of refugees from the Iron Curtain countries, was partially responsible for the impression the Hungarians had that they were going to get help. But we knew that no help was coming from either the West, which did not seek to risk war, or from the United Nations, whose effectiveness was blocked by Soviet vetoes in the Security Council.

Detachment is a wonderful thing, and every newspaperman should have it if he is to maintain balance and objectivity in his judgments. But there is probably at least one moment in every reporter's career when he is sucked into events despite himself. While he can look detached, he cannot feel detached.

That November day on a streetcorner in Budapest with a crowd of desperate Hungarians around me was my moment for losing detachment. I became merely the helpless citizen of the strongest free nation in the world who had nothing, absolutely nothing to offer in answer to their appeals. I tried to explain that I was a mere newspaperman who was more than willing to tell the story of their fight to the outside world, but that I could not do even this for the moment. The crowd grew—while my two colleagues and I grew more and more nervous. The Russians could easily start shooting if they came upon our group. To our Hungarian friends we could give only our sympathy, which was embarrassingly inadequate to the circumstances, and then we quickly made our way back to the Legation. The episode—indeed, the whole Hungarian affair—was a lesson in humility.

Here was a story where the correspondents' hands were completely tied. Yet supposing that all that week we had been able to report daily on how this country was being raped—we knew very well that even then our information would not have brought one soldier or one bullet to Hungary's side, nor would it have stayed the Russians. Toward the end of the week the Russians had Budapest in hand, although defiance continued in such forms as a general strike. On Friday we made the mistake of applying to the Hungarian Foreign Ministry for exit visas; obtaining them, we set out in a long convoy of cars on the road to Vienna. The convoy did not get much beyond the outskirts of the city before we were subjected to the further humiliation of being turned back by a Soviet road block. It was the price we had to pay for naively thinking the Hungarian Foreign Ministry was free.

Back we went to Budapest, where a large number of Hungarians mistook us for a United Nations delegation and cheered us under the noses of stolid Soviet soldiers. There would have been humor in the situation if we'd been in the mood for it.

Two days later we forgot our pride and went to the Soviet commandant for the only effective exit visa available. It is difficult to say whether it was by design or through inefficiency, but hours passed before the necessary papers were drawn up. Meanwhile we stood and fidgeted, with stories already written and ready to be filed in our pockets. Those who got their visas first did not wait for a convoy to form but took off for Vienna immediately. I gave my story to one of the early birds, asking him to pass it on to the Austrian communications people in Vienna, and suddenly felt better about things.

But not for long. I suddenly remembered after my story had roared off that I had written it with ordinary punctuation, as if I were going to telephone it. Official transmission agencies never take account of punctuation. So to the end, my part in the Hungarian story was to be a depressing business. Sure enough, the copy desk in New York received a sentence 1,200 words long. It all came out readable the next day, however, for all that it mattered.

Voted the outstanding journalism graduate at Cornell University in 1954 by Sigma Delta Chi, Stuart H. Loory worked as a general assignment reporter for The Newark News *and for the Fairchild publications before entering the Columbia Graduate School of Journalism, where he was a member of the Class of 1958. Again he was honored as an outstanding student, this time with the award of a Pulitzer Traveling Fellowship.*

At present Mr. Loory is Washington science reporter for The New York Herald Tribune, *and also serves as special science editor for the New York radio station, WNEW. A contributor to* The Reporter, This Week, Saturday Evening Post *and other magazines, Mr. Loory and his wife, Marjorie, are the parents of three children.*

STUART H. LOORY:

May, '61: Reporter's Education

In the month of May, 1961, I learned to my own shock that I endure the same reaction whether I'm watching a crazed crowd beating a group of Negroes, or an astronaut reaching out into space for the first time.

It's a physical reaction. It starts deep down in the gut and works its way upward and outward, producing a quick, prickly, shivery sensation as it goes. In an instant it's all over, perhaps because the reporter realizes he's not supposed to be reacting to the events around him. He's only supposed to be noting them down and reporting them at deadline time.

Should this be so? Should a reporter be only a catch-and-carry-forward tape recorder? I think not. In explanation, let me tell you about two days in my life.

May 5, 1961: I remember the date of Lt. Cmdr. Alan Bartlett Shepard's ride into space easily because it also happens to be my wife's birthday. (I find that my job compels me to miss many of the family's commemorative days because I'm holed up in a hotel room in Jackson, Miss., or a tent in Tezpur, India, or an airplane en route to El Paso.)

Arc lights cast the fuming rocket against the black predawn sky, and just above the eastern horizon Venus hung like a beckoning siren. Did Shepard see Venus through the thick glass window of the capsule he called "Freedom Seven"? Did he, as he waited for fire in the tail of his Redstone rocket, rhapsodize about someday setting foot on Venus (unlikely) or Mars (more likely) or the moon (a distinct possibility)?

Purple, orange, reds and blues played across the thick cloud banks that always seem to hang over the Gulf Stream at dawn; a Cape Canaveral sunrise must be among the most beautiful in the world. Shepard waited in his capsule and we waited on the beach, noting the trivialities we thought should be set down to fill in the story of this historic moment. We interviewed one another on the species of birds witnessing this event (Jerry Greene, the hardnosed military editor of *The New York Daily News,* is also a birdwatcher of good repute, it turned out); we noted one another's reactions in case anyone wanted to read about them the next day.

Then the blastoff at mid-morning. Fire in the tail. The black and white rocket, its checkerboard pattern standing out against the deep cloudless blue, rose slowly at first and then ever faster. Most of the reporters shouted and helped the rocket with all the body English they could summon.

Many of us who had waited so long could not believe it was really going to happen—that the United States would finally send its first man into space—and then suddenly there he was, cutting a vapor trail through the stratosphere and rising rapidly out of sight.

Here in these few minutes under the hot Florida sun, surrounded by the forbidding palmetto scrub, we witnessed man at his best. A rocket rose into space carrying an explorer. Man was breaking free of his gravitational restraints. He was finding the true New Frontier. Having all but conquered as much of the earth as he could digest, he was now setting his toe into the black, three-dimensional sea of space. What strange demons awaited him?

This was a story that called for poetry. This was a story that would go unsatisfied with the mere answer of the newsman's traditional five "w's." This was a story that begged to be told in such a way that the reader would experience the same prickly sensation in his gut the reporter felt when the rocket's roar raced in across the palmetto.

If Alan Shepard's ride was such a story, maybe there are other happenings which demand that a reporter try to outdo himself—that he be

as much a writer as a reporter. Where and what are these stories? If the
admirable in man deserves paeans, then those things which are disgusting deserve exposé. Such a disgusting story was not long in coming after
Shepard's flight.

May 19, 1961: I stood waiting on the loading platform of the Grey-
hound Bus Terminal in Birmingham, Alabama, for another dawn. A
group of young Negroes huddled together in front of the stainless-steel-
plated bus. They prayed and chanted and sang "Freedom, give us
freedom." After much confusion, officials hurriedly loaded the bus and
it set off for Montgomery with careful police protection.

We reporters followed across the Black Belt countryside in a caravan
of rented cars, and one hour and fifty-two minutes after we left the bus
station in Birmingham we arrived at the bus station in Montgomery,
Cradle of the Confederacy. We were there in plenty of time to watch
the Freedom Riders step down from their bus.

Before I knew it I was in the midst of a bloody riot, a kind of event
I had never before witnessed. I didn't know which way to turn, what to
do as my less fortunate colleagues—the ones who use cameras and
microphones and tape recorders to earn their living—were set upon by
the mob and beaten. I had enough sense to put my notebook away.

Then I saw two Birmingham reporters running. Suddenly I realized
I was alone and afraid in this strange city, where mobs appeared to
pounce upon strangers and break open heads on a whim.

"Where are you going?" I shouted.

"Come on and climb in the car with us," one of the Birmingham reporters replied. "Get in the car and take off that necktie quick, and if
anyone asks you you're a Ku Kluxer and don't you forget that."

The comedy of the situation struck me immediately: An obvious
Northerner in a buttondown collar and horn-rimmed glasses saying, as
the mobster lifted his brickbat, something that sounded as foreign to
him as "Pardon me, my good man, but I'm a Ku Kluxer, you see!" would
sound to me in New York.

I did take off the tie, and I kept my notebook concealed, and then I
climbed out of the car to witness the continuing riot from the fringe of
the crowd. While I watched, the mobsters began picking the Negroes up
and throwing them over a pipe railing into the parking lot of the post
office adjoining the bus terminal.

Next to me a little white girl, about three years old, tugged repeatedly
at her father's hand and yelled, "Daddy, daddy, what are they doing?"
The father watched like one transfixed and ignored the child's question. But a tall man, dressed in the uniform of a short-order cook,
looked down at the little girl. A leer crossed his face.

"They sure are giving those niggers what for," he said.

That's when the shivery sensation hit me all over again—just as it had two weeks before at Cape Canaveral.

Covering man at his best and man at his worst, with both stories producing the same reaction . . . maybe it's just the magnitude of the story, not its quality, that generates the feeling.

Whatever the reason, I am growing increasingly proud of my ability to react. I don't think it's enough for a reporter to be only objective in his work. And not only is objectivity undesirable, it's unsalable.

It is a cliché of our profession that no one cares about the reporter—who he is, what he does or what he thinks. I believe there is no validity in that cliché, and that the point is proved by the fatuous questions posed by people who ask a reporter, in private, for the "real" story of some event.

I wish to avoid a discussion here of the range of services a newspaper should provide to its readers. Suffice it to say that I do not think newspaper stories alone can supply enough information to allow men to take intelligent actions. For example, a doctor can't perform an open-heart operation after reading about one in the morning paper; nor can a physicist build an atom bomb, nor a general wage war, nor a politician win an election, nor a citizen vote intelligently. About the only thing that can be accomplished on the basis of a newspaper story alone is that a housewife can bake a soufflé or roast a turkey; and sometimes, my wife says, even these things don't work out too well.

If newspapers do not inform satisfactorily, then there must be another rationale for their existence. I think it is adventure. Newspaper readers want to share the adventures of the mountaineer climbing Everest, the astronaut exploring space, the Indian infantryman in the Himalayas, the politician on the campaign trail, the cop on the beat—and the reporter after the story. This is a lesson Sir Henry Stanley taught us a long time ago and one, I think, many publishers have forgotten.

I have two reasons for saying all this:

1. The reporter who thinks of himself primarily as an adventurer and raconteur has, I think, a better chance of coming to grips with his job and enjoying it than does the one who too altruistically thinks that what he writes might have some effect on the world's events, or that it is his mission in life to educate the masses and save the Republic.

2. The reporter who shares with his readers not only the dry facts but the color, the meaning (as he sees it), and the life of a story does a greater service to his readers. He brings them into contact with strangers and with strange events. By making these events seem true-to-life prob-

lems (and not a series of tortured parliamentary debates), he may
stimulate the reader to learn more about a subject from more complete
sources. Perhaps the reader may even learn enough to form an "intelligent opinion"—that chimerical goal of the communications industry's
responsible editorial segment.

All of this is a long way from those two strangely contradictory
events in my life during May, 1961, but, on the other hand, to share my
adventures must be to share my thoughts—and this is what I think about
my job.

*William Dwight's career has been intimately bound
to Holyoke, Massachusetts, the town in which he
was born and where he is the publisher of a daily
newspaper, the* Transcript. *A graduate of Prince-
ton University and the Columbia School of Journalism (Class of 1926), Mr. Dwight is a former
director and president of the American Newspaper
Publishers' Association. He is the American vice
president of the Fédération Internationale des
Editeurs des Journaux et Publications.*

*Mr. Dwight has been a member of the Holyoke
Board of Aldermen and a commissioner of Hamp-
den County. He is married and has four children.*

WILLIAM DWIGHT:

An Untold Story

This is about a news story I could have written and did not write. And
it will always haunt me.

It concerned a bank defalcation. The time was March, 1930, six
months after the stock market crash that triggered the great depression.

We didn't know then what was to come in the area of financial and
economic distress. The stock market was rocking along, struggling to regain strength and resume the forward march that, during the late 1920's,
had made it reach dizzy heights. A hope prevailed that the worst was behind us.

That is the background to the story I didn't write.

On March 17, 1930, the Massachusetts state bank examiners found
that a bank teller had been stealing money from the Hampshire County
Trust Company of Northampton over a period of time. He was a principal teller at the bank and, during off-duty hours, was a prominent band
leader, one of the favorites of the day in New England. He had several
bands and they played in the best ballrooms and for the finest social
functions.

The community was shocked by the discovery. The bank officials announced that the defalcation totaled $15,000. The court set bail at

$30,000; it was customary for a bail to be established at twice the amount of the theft.

The public was aware of this custom. They knew, also, that any bank, especially one of the standing of the Hampshire County Trust Company, could absorb such a loss. They further knew that all banks were bonded against thefts up to certain limits, and that a $15,000 defalcation was well within the range of insurance protection. What surprised some people was that the $30,000 bail money was not provided; the embezzler had many friends and a thriving business. His containment in jail also puzzled me. I asked some of his intimate friends why they didn't go to his rescue. One person confided that the theft was far greater than had been publicized; that it was "astronomical." The court had deliberately set a low bail with the understanding that none would be offered. My informant knew this because he had raised the $30,000 bail money and had been told not to present it. If he insisted, he had been told, the bail would be raised out of sight. I believed him.

I then proceeded to question some of the bank officials. They shuddered at my information. They implored me not to print the story. A news story would cause a run on the bank that would force its closing. They said they believed that the bank could work its way out of its difficulties if given time, but that a stampede by frightened depositors would wreck the institution.

I pondered deeply over this responsibility. Were the bank officials telling me the truth? Could they save the bank? Would I break the bank by revealing the facts? Was I being honest with the public by withholding the full story?

These were some of the harrowing questions I had to answer for myself.

We were sorely wounded by the stock market crash. The closing of the bank would aggravate the situation and the entire community would suffer. Did I want to close the bank and cause more suffering?

I did not write the story.

For the next few days the area churned with concern. But the general public, the little depositor, continued to believe that the theft amounted to $15,000.

The bank closed within a fortnight. Several of the large depositors in the meantime had reduced or withdrawn their accounts. The little depositor, the trusting depositor, had not.

The defalcation amounted to $285,000. The insurance coverage was trivial compared to the loss.

It was several years before the affairs of the bank were concluded.

During that time many people had their deposits frozen; eventually they received dollar for dollar, but during the liquidation process they lost the use of their money. The depression steadily gathered impetus, engulfing us and adding bitter burdens for many of the trusting depositors.

I have never quite forgiven myself for not writing the story in time to close the bank and prevent privileged insiders from making use of their information.

If I knew then what I know today, I would have been certain that the bank could not have weathered the storm. I would have written the story.

The most recent Journalism School graduate to have contributed to this book, Kim Willenson is currently a reporter and rewrite man on The Washington Post. *Before attending graduate school, he worked for two years for* The Wisconsin State Journal. *Mr. Willenson was born in Wisconsin and received his B. S. in history at the University of Wisconsin.*

He was an International Fellow at Columbia, from which he received his degree in 1962. Mr. Willenson was also the winner of a Pulitzer Traveling Fellowship.

KIM WILLENSON:

Stop, Look, Listen

Of the thousands who have been graduated from Columbia's School of Journalism since 1913, I am one of the most recent. Class of '62. This will be, then, no recollection of things long past; it is merely an account of three incidents that taught me lessons one does not learn as a student.

The first occurred while I was working in the Midwest for the newspaper that gave me my first job. Quite by chance I was assigned to cover a series of meetings of a group of 200 "leading citizens" in the community. This group had decided that something was wrong with the juveniles in their town. Too many young people loitering on streetcorners, cluttering the streets at night with their cars, drinking beer, occasionally vandalizing a construction project for lack of anything better to do. The leading citizens, being conscientious, moral and upstanding, had arrogated to themselves the job of studying the problem and deciding what to do about it.

As will any group of self-anointed crusaders, this assemblage made some crucial mistakes. Foremost among them was the *a priori* decision that there really *was* a problem with delinquency. Second, the committee of 200 had hooked up with a gang of real, live do-gooder social workers from the state welfare department, who talked them into proposing a plan of massive psychological treatment for the children of the local proletariat, the ones who were "causing all the trouble." The

66

meetings culminated in a two-part report—a dramatic picture of juvenile criminality, a series of recommendations to combat the scourge.

After studying the document I went to my city editor and said something on the order of, "Looka here, boss. I'm no expert in the field, but this so-called report doesn't look so hot. In the first place this is a rich little town. It doesn't have slums like Detroit or Chicago. It doesn't really have a large population of poor people. It is mostly full of middle-class and upper-middle-class white-collar workers whose kiddies go off to college and come home to become pillars of the community. They raise a little hell, sure, but they aren't the first generation of kids to do that . . . or the last. You and I know that crime isn't important here. How come these people think 'our youth' are going to hell in a handbasket? Another thing—you take a look at this report and count up how much money these people want to spend. With all the psychiatrists, psychologists, social workers, recreation therapists, guidance counselors and everything else they want, it'll cost a couple of million a year. Who's going to spend that kind of money? Let me take this report around to some people who know what they're talking about."

"Go ahead," he said.

So I did. I took it to the police and checked the statistics. It turned out that delinquency in the area had been going down steadily for four years, and that about 90 per cent of the arrests were for traffic violations. I took it to three psychiatrists, two of whom had advised the committee. They said that the report, as it stood, went too far; the independent called it ridiculous. I took it to two sociologists, specialists in urban problems. They said it would treat symptoms without getting at causes. I took it to the head of the department of social work at the local university. He refused to comment. "I have to work with those people," he said. I took it to the head of social services in the public school system. "They want to put *this* on the schools too?" he asked, shaking his head. "Schools are a place for learning, not for solving social problems." I took it to an expert on recreation. He said they wanted to spend more money at one fell swoop than the entire town had put into recreation since World War II. "What's *their* problem?" he asked me.

So I went back to the office and wrote an eight-part series in which I went through the report paragraph by paragraph, applying the specific criticisms I had gathered. It was published. Three days after the last piece appeared, a deputation of ten of the leading citizens appeared at the office, took the publisher in tow and converged on the managing editor, the city editor and me.

"What's the matter with our report?" one of them demanded.

"If you read our series, you already know," was the answer.

"Well, people in this town put their heads together to decide upon the answer to this problem," said another.

"We arrived at our report by a democratic vote," said a third. "Two hundred people all working together, compromising, thinking, planning. That's how democracy works."

The conversation went on and on. It ended, finally, with the publisher's promising them half a page for their point of view. On the way out the city editor asked me to meet him for a beer after work. I did. He was a nice guy. I like him to this day. But this is the fatherly advice he gave me:

"Listen, our circulation has been going up, and management thinks we have a good, successful formula. We give them a lot of light stuff and a taste of news, but not too much. We don't want any thousand-word think-pieces. We want nice, light features that the Republican ladies can read over their morning coffee without getting upset. You can write them, I know. But if you don't want to, you had better get yourself another job." Needless to say, I did.

Lesson number one is that too often newspaper management is more interested in producing a profit than in performing a public service.

The second incident took place at *The Washington Post*. Late one night, while I was on rewrite, the House Commerce Committee reported out its version of a new federal law on drugs. The regular (Mort Mintz, who broke the Thalidomide stories in this country) was out of the office, but the desk managed to locate him. He supplied background material obtained from an on-the-scene source. Using this information plus wire copy, I was to put together a story of our own.

The crucial point, it seemed to me, was not the version of the bill that had been sent to the floor (everyone knew that it would be worked and re-worked before passage) but the amount and kinds of influence used by the drug industry to keep out provisions requiring that descriptions of side-effects be included in drug advertising. The drug lobbyists had been present in nearby rooms while the committee was in executive session. When the committee faltered over a technical point or was in disagreement over the wording of a provision, it recessed and sent the draft bill to the lobbyists who, in conference with representatives of the Food and Drug Administration, worked over the portions being questioned. In other words, an industry that had demonstrated a shockingly casual attitude about the effects of its products, but a very warm regard for profits, was able to exert powerful influence on a bill supposed to govern its future actions.

Space was limited. In roughly 400 words I wanted to report that the bill had passed committee; that its half-dozen major provisions would do such-and-so; and that "authoritative sources" had given the following picture of its creation. Finding myself unable to include all these elements, I wrote two versions. In the first I glossed over the less-important aspects of the bill, but included the essential (to me) background. In the second version I left out the on-the-scene report of the lobbyists' influence, but went through the bill provision by provision.

A deskman (who shall remain nameless) read the two stories. He pointed to the first draft. "This happens all the time anyway, doesn't it?" he asked.

"Of course it does," I replied. "But that's the point. It happens all the time, and you and I know it does. But we never tell it to the people who read the newspaper."

For what seemed a long time, he stood there looking at the two pieces of copy. He flushed. He shifted from one foot to the other and back again. He looked off into space. Finally he looked at me.

"It would sound like an editorial," he said, putting the version I would have chosen on the spike.

Lesson number two is that even on good papers many deskmen are either so incompetent that they do not understand the nature and responsibility of the medium, or are so afraid to use its power that they act like civil servants (i.e., they refuse to risk publishing something that might ruffle feathers).

The third story took place during a meeting in Washington of the American Political Science Association. I was assigned as anchor-man to cover it, the first really good assignment I'd been given at *The Post*. It was a massive job—more than a hundred papers were being presented in four days—and I had only a little help. I had to guess by title which papers might be worth a story, then read through the ones I'd picked out. There was a lot of homework involved. One of the titles that caught my eye was a piece called "The Press and the Formulation of Foreign Policy" by Bernard C. Cohen, a professor at the University of Wisconsin. It was an absorbing essay, filled with rare insights that only a trained but independent eye can produce. Essentially, Cohen detailed the process of gathering and publishing the news and then pointed out that the operation of the news-gathering mechanism itself may be having a detrimental effect on the conduct of U.S. foreign policy.

First, said Cohen, foreign news tends to feed on itself. Reporters and editors steep themselves each morning in yesterday's work, then proceed to today's working day by looking for followups to what has already hap-

pened. The resulting repetitive appearance of major stories gives newsmen a self-reinforcing conviction that news has an inherently long life.
Furthermore, when a story looks as though it may last more than a few
days—or when there is physical action involved—resources are mobilized for on-the-scene coverage. When money has been spent to get a
correspondent to the scene to cover a single story, he is obligated to
file daily, and his file must be used. The resulting flood of material often
keeps the situation in the news, whether it belongs there or not.

Second, said Cohen, the monetary pressures of the trade, and the resulting drives for circulation, lend themselves to oversimplification of
stories and to the casting of major events in terms of storm and thunder,
so as to heighten reader interest. Thus foreign news is too often simpli-
fied to the primal struggle between light and dark, between "Com-
munism" and "Democracy"; too often represented as a test of wills between grappling giants when it is in reality only a test of wits between
cautious bargainers.

Third, said the professor, the men who make foreign policy must often
rely on newspapers as the only comprehensive—and comprehensible—
source of information. And they deal daily with reporters themselves.
Facing an intellectual assault from two sources, they are forced subtly to
re-order their thoughts and their priorities to the whims of the newspaperman. The result, Cohen contended, has been a crisis-hopping pattern, both in news and in policy itself, in which events tend to break out
with dramatic suddenness; their antecedent causes are explored only in
the midst of crisis, when it is already too late to rectify the situation.

I was well aware, by the time I had finished reading Cohen's paper,
that I had a major news story on my hands, but one that would take a
bit of selling. So I asked the desk for a column and a half, and sent over
a copy of the paper, figuring it would sell itself. Evidently it did; I got
my space. The reaction, when the story appeared, was startling. I had
beaten everyone by a day, simply because no one had taken the time
to read through the lengthy paper. I enjoyed watching the wires and a
couple of our competitors fall over one another trying to pick up the
story on the second day. Some weeks later, when I wrote to Cohen for
additional copies, he replied that he'd been deluged with requests for
them, including some from high levels at the State Department.

Lesson number three is that no matter how discouraging the business
sometimes gets, around the next corner there is always the chance of
finding a story that will give you the intellectual elation of discovering
and conveying to your readers something genuinely new and significant.

As Dean of the University of Oregon School of Journalism, John Hulteng brings to his post a rich background of practical experience. After a first job as general reporter on a weekly newspaper, he became a sports writer and then night city editor of The Grand Forks (*N.D.*) Herald, *and later editorial writer and editorial page editor of* The Providence Journal and Bulletin. *Mr. Hulteng joined the faculty of the University of Oregon in 1955.*

Mr. Hulteng won a Pulitzer Traveling Scholarship upon his graduation from the School of Journalism in 1947. He was a Nieman Fellow at Harvard in 1949, and in 1961 received the Ersted Award for distinguished teaching. Mr. Hulteng is a frequent contributor to professional publications.

JOHN HULTENG:

Trench Coat for Sale

Talk about turning points—Columbia's School of Journalism provided me with an experience that led not simply to a change of direction, but to an abrupt, tire-screeching U-turn in my journalistic career.

Since high-school days I had been entranced with the glamorous image of the Foreign Correspondent, hat arake, up to his trench-coat belt buckle in international intrigue, at home alike in imperial palace or secret agent's hideout.

The picture floated before me through my years as a college editor, as a reporter for a Midwest weekly, as a sports writer for a small-city daily—even through three years of World War II service. It stayed bright and compelling through my year at Columbia, and when in June I came up with one of the three Pulitzer Traveling Scholarships, the vision was suddenly within reach.

Before I left for Europe I had lined up a full schedule of journalistic obligations. The paper that had hired me out of Columbia—*The Providence Journal and Evening Bulletin*—wanted a regular correspondent's stint from me, of course. And then I had put together a do-it-yourself

71

syndicate of dailies in my home country of Minnesota and North Dakota ready to take weekly dispatches of my filing.

When my wife and I got to Europe, reality matched the long-nurtured dream. There were black-market rings to cover in Paris, and furtive exchanges in a side-street bar. I wrote about the British public's first reactions to the institution of socialized medicine in Great Britain, covered a golf match at St. Andrews, interviewed the foreign minister at Stockholm, and was received in audience at the palace in Oslo while preparing a feature on Haakon VII, Norway's hero-king of World War II. By the time I journeyed down to Italy it was clear to me that this was the only life to live.

My mission in Italy was to develop a series of articles for the Providence papers. The series was to describe postwar conditions in the belt of inland villages from which much of the Italo-American population of Rhode Island had migrated a generation or so earlier.

Some of these stories I got without too much trouble, operating out of a base in Naples. Naples was still full of ugly reminders of war—families camping in the streets, shattered buildings, rusting bottoms of sunken shipping showing above the harbor's gentle blue. But we were reasonably comfortable in our hotel.

Finally, though, to complete the series I had to move inland and operate from a village about a hundred miles from Naples, up on the mountain spine of Italy.

There was only one way at that time to get to Frosolone. A one-vehicle bus line made a trip in and out every few days. So I set off one morning with typewriter, cameras and letters of introduction from Rhode Islanders who still had ties in the home village.

It was a weary, rattling ride, enlivened only by the discovery that the black-mopped lad who sat up next to the driver was actually the owner of the bus. He had made a killing as a black marketeer and through his sensitivity to the various needs of soldiers during the war, and had later invested his all in the transportation industry.

It was late at night when we reached Frosolone. The narrow, stone streets were dark, but the headlights of the bus picked out a small group waiting in the cobbled square. They were a reception committee for me, and among them was the man who was to be my language link. He had visited America 27 years earlier, and was the village expert.

Unhappily for me, his visit had been a brief one, and so it was mostly with gestures and nods that we exchanged greetings and started making our way through the black alleyways of the village.

More of the villagers were waiting at the home where I was to stay. It was a fine home by village standards, built wall-to-wall with its neighbors, as was the case throughout Frosolone. It had three stories, with a room on each floor, and two on the ground floor. The kitchen, where we now gathered, was on the second floor and was thick with smoke from the open fireplace that was the only source of heat in the house. It was, of course, the cooking fire as well.

Though the hour was late, the table was spread for a welcoming feast, and everyone had waited for me. I knew the village was poor, particularly in this post-war year, when life was hard throughout Italy. So I wanted to be careful to accept what was offered with enthusiasm, in order not to cause my hosts any embarrassment.

Once we had all settled down, with many smiles and vaguely unsuccessful efforts to communicate, wide, steaming plates of broth and chunks of bread were brought to the table.

I was hungry after the long ride, and knew that this was probably a principal part of the menu, so I dipped in with gusto. I had two great bowls of the broth and was feeling moderately satisfied when in came platters of spaghetti, accompanied by more bread and pitchers of local red wine, somewhat harsh and gritty.

I buckled down manfully, again anxious not to offend my hosts by a seeming lack of appreciation for their food.

But when, a few moments later, came plates of chicken, swimming in oil and garlic, I faltered momentarily. There was no help for it, though, so I tackled that, too, already becoming aware that I was not entirely well.

In a desperate, mechanical daze I next was confronted with bowls of fat pork, also glistening with oil and fragrant of garlic, to be washed down with an unfortunately sweet white wine of local vintage.

Later, I believe, the feast concluded with some small cakes, quite a few of them, and after them some beer, no doubt procured especially to honor the visiting American. I say I believe, because my recollection of those concluding passages is mercifully clouded.

The night that followed is only too vivid in memory, however. . . .

It was bleak dawn, despite the magnificent view out my window across the mountain valleys. Somehow I staggered sleeplessly out of the quilts, found enough water below the thick ice in the basin by the bed for a rasping shave, turned aside my hostess' proffer of breakfast on the ground that I had picked up some bug in Naples, and went off on my assignment.

Through that day and the next I subsisted on bottled mineral water and oranges, the only available items I felt sure would not be impregnated with garlic and oil. "It's the bug," I explained apologetically. "The bug from Naples."

I got the stories I wanted, traveling from village to village in the only automobile to be found in the vicinity. It was an ancient, wheezing wreck, whose driver-owner was burstingly proud of it. (He had an alarming habit of turning full around to me in the back seat as we rattled along the mountain roads to shout his only phrase of English—"Best damn driver in Frosolone!"—as children, goats and an occasional black-frocked priest scattered frantically from the trail ahead.)

At night I would type my stories in the kitchen, in front of the smoking fire, with a semicircle of villagers sitting quietly watching me work and occasionally asking what I had written. By that time I had augmented my channels of communication through the discovery of a German doctor in the village, a deserter from the Wehrmacht who had settled down to make his home there. Since I could speak some German, a three-way conversation was possible.

By the third evening, after two days of the mineral water and orange diet, it was clear that I was the source of great pain to my host and hostess. The story of the bug from Naples had worn thin, and they had decided that it was their food that had made me ill. Since they and the whole village had been at great pains to make me welcome as an emissary from the great American city to which so many of their own had emigrated, they were crushed by my reaction to their table.

I realized that I had to do something—that while I was still in desperately delicate shape, I had to restore confidence somehow and mend the impression of hospitality rejected.

The memory of that fatal succession of oily, redolent dishes of the first evening was still harsh. Then I thought of a way out. I asked my hostess if she would be good enough to cook me an egg—in the shell. That, I thought, was safe enough. You can't get garlic inside an egg.

But when it was brought to me in smiling triumph, I discovered on cracking the shell that the local notion of cooking an egg was to warm it briefly in the ashes.

My poor, unstable stomach was in no condition to take on a lukewarm, raw egg. But there it was. And there were my anxious host and hostess.

Somehow I gulped it down. Somehow, with great effort, I even managed a tight-lipped, wan smile of thanks. Whereupon they promptly brought me another egg!

There's no point in dwelling on the untidy closing passages of the visit to Frosolone. It's enough to say that from that point on the glamorous image I had nurtured so long began to deterioriate as precipitously as the picture of Dorian Gray.

When, a few months later, I returned from abroad, I was entirely content to embrace the quieter precincts of the editorial room, and to make a career of phrasing judgments and prophecies rather than sending dispatches with exotic datelines.

David Rogers started his journalistic career on his home-town Nova Scotia paper, The Amherst Daily News, *in 1921, a year before he attended the School of Journalism. Upon his graduation he returned to Canada, joining* The Toronto Daily Star *and working as a reporter, news editor and European correspondent. He left* The Star *to become managaging editor of* The Saint John (*N.B.*) Telegraph Journal *and, later, was named assistant managing editor of* The Winnipeg Free Press.*

Since 1940 he has been editor of The Regina (*Sask.*) Leader-Post, *and during World War II was chief of the domestic branch of the Canadian Wartime Information Board. Mr. Rogers has been president of the Canadian Press and of the Canadian Managing Editors Conference. He is married and has two daughters.*

DAVID B. ROGERS:

Uncompleted Assignment

"That one? His name is Trotsky."

It was early 1917, and the lads in my home town of Amherst, Nova Scotia, used to spend long hours watching the prisoners in the exercise yard of an internment camp. By scaling telephone poles overlooking the yard, we could look down at the men, most of them seamen taken from commerce raiders; among them were many fine singers and musicians, and a few remarkable gymnasts. Conspicuous in all the activity was a small, bearded man with bulging forehead and heavy spectacles who sat always by himself, reading and writing.

One of the guards told me that his name was Trotsky, that he had been removed from a Norwegian boat at Halifax, and that he had been a revolutionary leader in Russia, forced to flee before the big uprising. In New York he had been active with radical labor groups and had edited a leftist organ called *The New World*. He remained in the internment camp at Amherst only a few weeks and then was released at the request of the Kerensky group in Russia. He returned to Russia in a round-about way, helped to overthrow the Kerensky regime, and in close association with Lenin rose quickly to the posts of foreign commissar and commander of the Red Army.

It was in this period that I briefly saw Trotsky again, taking the salute from an army detachment in Petrograd.

Now it was 1922; and with the late L. J. Spiker, a top deskman with *The New York Times* when he died a few years ago, I had signed on an ancient American tramp steamer—the *Winnebago*—as an ordinary seaman. We were spending the long summer vacation preceding our 1923 graduation from the Columbia School of Journalism in a search for stories and adventure. The *Winnebago* was carrying a cargo of corn to the starving Russians; after willingly accepting this early American aid, the Russians began to find a multitude of reasons for preventing our departure from Petrograd (now Leningrad). Spiker and I roamed the city, gathering information on the great famine and inflation that followed adoption of the New Economic Policy; we saw Trotsky in his brief time of power and prestige. Then, apparently, the *Winnebago*'s captain at last bribed the right official. We were permitted to sail on.

In 1930, I was based in Berlin as European correspondent for *The Toronto Star*. Reacting to the depression, the paper decided to abandon staff coverage in Europe. They invited me to return and become feature editor. But I was young, eager and curious; I decided instead to try my hand at freelancing in Europe. The old Consolidated Press Association gave me an assignment—interview Trotsky.

After Lenin's death in 1924, Stalin had risen to power. Trotsky and Stalin disagreed on the extension of the Communist revolution; and in any event, Stalin could brook no competition. Leon Trotsky was banished. Yet even in exile he was a marked man. In constant fear of assassination, he moved from country to country. Although he wrote prodigiously, he disliked personal interviews; other than Emil Ludwig, few newspapermen got through to him.

My wife and I thumbed our way by airplane from Berlin to Istanbul, almost coming to grief in a battered pre-war Blériot Spad on the last leg of the journey from Belgrade. Trotsky was then a prisoner in exile on the tiny island of Prinkipo, not far from Istanbul in the Sea of Marmora.

On arrival at Istanbul, I was told by Trotsky's representatives that he was ill and would speak with no one except the members of his small staff. In a carefully prepared letter, put into Russian at consider-

able cost to my dwindling financial resources, I made a friendly appeal
for an interview, dwelling on an interest in him that had begun in 1917
and had been reinforced in 1922. It brought only a polite but firm
reply: Sorry, ill, no interview.

I then decided to transfer operations to the island of Prinkipo itself,
with my wife as a willing collaborator.

Persistent efforts to get through to Trotsky during our week's stay on
the island drew blanks at every point. He was obviously ill, suffering
from, I think, a type of jaundice, but not too ill to leave his secluded
villa for occasional strolls and fishing expeditions. Once I hired a boat
to see whether the brotherhood of Izaak Walton might prevail. Friendly
hails brought quick retreat on the part of his boat. Again, I encountered
him visiting some ancient ruins on the island, but was firmly cold-
shouldered. A visit to the villa with the milkman likewise got me nowhere.

At week's end, not wishing to give up without something to show
for effort and expenditure, I decided to concentrate on getting a picture of Trotsky on the terrace of his villa. There were guards posted
around the grounds, but they did not seem to be too alert. A laneway
gave access through deep shrubbery to a point which commanded the
terrace. I had learned when he usually came out for exercise, and on
the appointed day I avoided the front guard and crept into the grounds
for a close-up while my wife kept watch outside. I got one good picture
of the villa and terrace on the last exposure of a film. I tossed that roll
out to my wife and put in a new one. At this point Trotsky emerged
and I started shooting in earnest. But alas, my actions were observed.
Trotsky quickly withdrew. And before I could flee, a guard dashed in
and grabbed me. The camera and film were confiscated. My wife also
was taken into custody and we were marched off to the small village
lock-up and held there on suspicion of attempted assassination.

We were kept in detention for several hours before, at my insistence,
an interpreter could be found. He was a genial character from Malta,
vacationing on the island, and was fortunately a friend of the police
chief. Following a great deal of arguing, the police finally accepted
my version of the episode. After being severely reprimanded, we were
escorted to our hotel for check-out and thence to a boat which carried
us back to Istanbul. Our orders were never to return to Prinkipo. The
camera was returned but the second roll of film was kept. The original
roll, however, remained in my wife's blouse front. Later the picture of
the villa figured prominently in a large layout which *The Toronto Star*

Weekly used with my story under an eight-column banner headline declaring, "Trotsky Wouldn't Talk."

Why have I selected this abortive experience from forty years of active journalism? It is to demonstrate that even in the face of failure, one of the everyday hazards of our craft, it is possible to salvage something. We sold a story; on the way to and from it, we got good copy about the newly-emancipated Turks and colorful Istanbul; and we perceived that someday someone would again slip past guards who could only delay, but not prevent, an act of vengeance. (It happened, and cruelly, in Mexico, ten years later.)

And finally, we have a memory. The boat trip across the turquoise waters of the Sea of Marmora from Istanbul to Prinkipo is breathtakingly beautiful, and the island itself is a paradise. Some day I would like to return.

Sanche de Gramont won the Pulitzer Prize for re-porting under pressure of editorial deadlines in 1961, just six years after his graduation from the School of Journalism. He was then a reporter for The New York Herald Tribune; *he now serves as correspondent in Rome for that newspaper.*

Mr. de Gramont, the author of "The Secret War" and "The Memoirs of the Duc de Saint-Simon," was born in Switzerland and was gradu-ated from Yale University before attending Co-lumbia.

SANCHE DE GRAMONT:

A Gap in the Curriculum

Self-defeating as this may sound, there should be a course at the Columbia Graduate School of Journalism entitled "What you can't learn in the classroom."

This course would not deal with the kind of exercises that prepare students for professional assignments they are not likely to encounter immediately upon graduating—"Write an editorial about a summit meeting," for example, or "Give a Lippmann-like interpretation of what Russia will do next in 500 words or less."

No, this course would examine the meddlesome, frustrating back-breaking, excruciating mechanics of how to get to the story, how to file it and how to report it without getting too involved in it (like find-ing yourself among your own casualty figures).

For instance . . . you have gone to Bou Saada, an oasis 130 miles south of Algiers, to find a dissident Moslem chief who refuses to join the Algerian rebels. He is so eager to see a reporter that he scours the countryside recruiting volunteers, then holds a ragged parade in your honor at his mountain retreat. All the undelivered speeches he has been hoarding for years are poured into your ears. You have more copy than you can use. His men escort you back to the main road to Algiers, pointing you in the right direction before they depart. Two miles farther, a flat tire. You look in the trunk of your rented car for a spare. The garage neglected to include one.

Hitchhiking in the Sahara is slow work, but you finally catch a ride with an oil truck back to Bou Saada, and you buy a tire. Regrettably, the local rebel chief has been told of your presence and you are taken into custody on suspicion of being a French Secret Army Organization agent. After hours of high-level diplomatic negotiations, the local chief decides that you are after all a reporter, and now he insists on showing you his organization. That takes up the rest of the day.

Another example from Algeria. It is soon after the July, 1962, independence. Enemy Wilayas (or military regions) are fighting for control of the country. And another rented car, this one carrying four newsmen, develops radiator trouble. Let's see—it was August. The temperature was more than 100° in the shade, the water had evaporated while the car climbed into the Atlas mountains, and so the engine stalled. We had to back down the mountain with the engine off to cool it. Even after we found water the car would not go more than twenty miles an hour.

As we chugged back to Algiers we saw one deadline after another vanish before our eyes. At a border between two Wilayas a rebel stopped the car when he saw a cameraman shooting. (One good piece of advice: Never travel with a cameraman.) "Do you have permission to take pictures?" he asked. The cameraman pulled out his press card. "But do you have permission to take pictures at this particular point on this particular day?" the soldier insisted. The cameraman admitted he did not. "Then you are all under arrest," the soldier said, and two of his colleagues proceeded to sit on the car as clear evidence that it was going no further. One of the reporters, fresh in from the Congo, whispered, "Keep quiet, I know how to deal with these gooks." In soothing, respectful tones he told our captors: "Lieutenant Ahmed, the information chief from your Wilaya told us in Algiers this morning that we could go anywhere without special passes. He said in your region there is nothing to hide, and he asked the press to see for itself how the valiant soldiers of your Wilaya are keeping order and preserving independence. He told us that if we had any trouble we should notify him, because he felt certain every soldier in his Wilaya would do what he could to make our work easier. He said we should see for ourselves that in a free Algeria everyone may go where he pleases." Five minutes later, we were released.

Back in Algiers, the phones were dead. The cable office was closed.

Some of us had businessmen friends with Telex machines in their offices which they let us use in emergencies. What use is the greatest exclusive in the world if you can't file it? In Tunis, during the Bizerte crisis, the only way many of us had to file was by telephone to Paris. It was a radio telephone, which wavered in volume so that only one word out of three was clear. What the person on the other end of the line heard was "president . . . of . . . today . . . French . . . murderers," from which he would try to fill in the missing words to make the lead read: "President Habib Bourguiba of Tunisia charged today that the French were mass murderers." You would wait hours for your call, get every third word through, and find that calls were limited to five minutes. By putting in calls through the night, you could sometimes file a coherent story.

In Elizabethville, it was customary to wait eight hours in line to file over the battered commercial Telex machine in the main post office. The wire services had several men who relayed each other. Once a reporter's turn came just as the machine broke down and he slammed his fist into it, breaking several knuckles in impotent rage.

After United Nations troops had bombed the post office out of existence, waiting for the Telex was no longer a problem. Now it was a question of driving out of Katanga into Northern Rhodesia and filing through the Ndola post office, which was remarkably efficient but somewhat harder to reach than a corner phone booth. I once made the mistake of giving a story on the European mercenaries in Katanga to a Belgian couple leaving the beleaguered city to seek refuge in Ndola. I paid them ten pounds to hand the unopened envelope to the telegraph office. I was told by eyewitnesses that the couple opened the envelope in their hotel lobby, read the story, tore it up and stalked off to warn the Katangese gendarmerie about the kind of stories I was sending.

When you see a correspondent who is prematurely gray-haired, vacant-eyed, and has a strange tic or a bad stammer, you can attribute his condition to too many bouts with telephone operators, telegram offices and Telex machines. It's not always the battle.

There is also the delicate matter of personal involvement. The heartlessly professional decision of a news photographer to take a picture of a little girl in a burning automobile before trying to rescue her is not always so clear-cut. A newsmagazine reporter and I once came upon a gang of French teen-agers in Oran about to lynch an elderly Moslem woman. She was on a third-floor terrace, and they were throwing rocks at her and scaling the building to drag her down.

What should we have done? Watched the mob violence dispassionately and reported it faithfully, relying on the power of words to avenge the victim? Or act to save the woman, which in all likelihood would have resulted in three lynchings instead of one? As in the best of cliffhangers, we were saved from the decision by the arrival of firemen (the youths had set fire to several cars to "smoke out the dirty Moslem"). They dispersed the mob.

Adding to the confusion come requests from editors that should help any sane reporter go off the deep end. Among memorable examples is the query from the foreign desk of a New York newspaper (not the *Herald Tribune*) which asked its correspondent in Algiers: "How do you tell a Moslem from a pied-noir (European settler)?" His exasperated reply: The Moslem is the one lying in a pool of blood. The pied-noir is the one holding the smoking pistol."

The curious thing is that despite the difficulties and frustrations involved, many correspondents seem to thrive on so-called hardship assignments. They would rather walk through a mine field than do desk work; they prefer working 12 or 15 hours a day to regular hours. There was one wire service correspondent in Algiers who had just ended a long assignment in the Congo. In his stories he often compared the confusion that followed independence in Algeria to the chaos in the Congo. His recurring theme was that "Algeria is like the Congo." Privately, he fondly recalled the French restaurants and the country clubs in Leopoldville, and contrasted the guilelessness and simple good cheer of the Congolese natives with the subtle perfidy of the Algerians. He would ruefully complain that "This certainly isn't the Congo."

Elements of the course I would like to see taught at the Journalism school: Cars break down, phones don't work, reporters get shot at, high-powered editors should do penance at the scene of the story for every silly question they ask, and Algeria isn't the Congo.

Within five years of his graduation from the School of Journalism in 1956, Larry Jinks was named assistant city editor and then city editor of a major newspaper, The Miami Herald. *He is now assistant managing editor.*

A graduate of the University of Missouri, Mr. Jinks went on to advanced work in literature and creative writing at the University of North Carolina before enrolling at Columbia. He was a recipient of a Pulitzer Traveling Scholarship and next worked as a reporter, editorial writer and city editor for The Charlotte (N.C.) Observer. *Mr. Jinks is married to the former Joan Metzner, a member of the Class of '58 at the Journalism School. They are the parents of a daughter.*

LARRY JINKS:
A Testing of Ideals

In September of 1957, a Negro boy and three Negro girls entered four otherwise white schools in Charlotte, North Carolina. This was one of several modest breaches made in traditional school segregation in the South that fall, and as national news it rated no more than a daily shirttail to the Little Rock story for a week or so. For Charlotte, however, it was a time of uncertainly controlled community crisis; and for the city's two newspapers, it was a testing period of grave, well-recognized significance.

As education writer for *The Charlotte Observer,* I was assigned to the integration story. It stirred me as no other story has; it left impressions I'll always carry with me. These are no road-to-Damascus revelations, but they do have meaning for one man working at an ethically perplexing craft.

I approached the integration assignment with ideals flying. A native Southerner, I had strong feelings about my own role as a newspaper-man and about the need to give Negroes in the South a fair deal.

Quickly, I learned that the two ideals didn't always fit comfortably. My briefing included the information that Charlotte's school board had been meeting privately for some months with the school boards of two other North Carolina cities. The three groups had decided to blunt the inevitable opposition to the first mixing of white and Negro in state schools (below college level) by acting at precisely the same time. Editors of papers in all three cities knew about the plans and, in some particulars, had helped make them.

Of this there had been only bare and uninformative mention in any of the papers. The school boards believed, and the editors agreed, that full coverage of their discussions would rouse opposition that might kill the whole project. I understood their reasoning, but I found it hard to reconcile their policy of secrecy with a general conviction that the press must tell the people what public bodies are doing.

A few days before the Charlotte school board was ready to act in public, it met with press representatives to discuss how desegregation would and would not be covered. This meeting, too, was secret.

At the session I learned that the school board was taking a step for which it had little stomach. The board was made up largely of respected businessmen of basic good will, devoted to progress in a growing and prosperous community. They approached school integration with general reluctance, not a little fear and, in one case, with some personal bitterness. (In contrast the school superintendent, an elderly man for whom I felt great respect and affection, said simply that Negroes should be admitted to white schools because it was right.) They all agreed on one thing—that it was better for them to act than to wait for a federal court to force action.

Mostly I listened, but I did make one point. When board members started suggesting a blueprint for coverage of the first days of integration, I predicted that when the Negroes actually reached the schools, the news story would assume a life of its own and would defy careful planning.

This wasn't true of our coverage of the formal, called meeting a few days later at which the board announced its decision. Not only was coverage planned in detail—but I also wrote the lead story and two sidebars before I went to the meeting. (True, the lead was revised somewhat after the first edition. Although the purpose of the meeting was supposed to have been a secret, a roomful of white supremacists showed up to brandish petitions and denounce the board.)

From then on things began to happen, and we covered them honestly and thoroughly—if a bit cautiously. There were legal actions by Negroes who thought the board hadn't gone far enough, and by white extremist groups who thought it had gone too far. There was a visit from John Kasper, who hoarsely attacked the school board members from the courthouse steps (and who had to look at the words carved in white marble above him to find out what county he was in).

Kasper's visit brought out the Klan types—red-necked, grim and muttering. It also brought out a petite, brunette young mother, one of the many now-familiar, near-hysterical women who have prowled the grounds of integrating schools in a dozen Southern cities, spewing hate. Kasper accepted her invitation to hold an organizational meeting for his own brand of citizens' council at her home after his courthouse harangue. The press was not invited, but an off-duty *Observer* copyreader attended and volunteered to take the minutes. We printed a full account of the meeting and a list of officers the next day. The organization promptly collapsed.

Nobody quite knew what to expect as the first day of school approached. Charlotte, a city of about 200,000 in North Carolina's bustling Piedmont region, had a peaceful record of race relations. City leaders, including the police chief, were determined that community peace be preserved. Tacit support came from Luther Hodges in Raleigh; he was then the governor of the state. There was no Faubus to use an official position as a rallying point for the rednecks. But there were intimations of trouble: Calls and letters to school board members and to newspapers, public agitation by a far-right group called Patriots of North Carolina Inc., and rumblings from South Carolina, just a few miles away.

At the *Observer* offices we planned thorough coverage. The city editor spotted reporters and photographers at all the affected schools. We were instructed not to interfere with orderly school procedures in any way, but to be on top of anything that might happen. Since I would have the job of putting together everything that did happen, I was free to roam from one school to another.

One of the Negro students, a junior high school girl, failed to show up the first day. (She made a peaceful entrance later.) I visited the other three schools. At Piedmont Junior High School, a 12-year-old girl who looked much younger—Girvaud Roberts—walked with her mother past a few catcalls and a lot of stares as she went in to enroll for the eighth grade. At nearby Central High School, her 16-year-old brother Gustavus, accompanied by his father, faced more stares and louder catcalls, but otherwise enrolled without incident. Across town at Harding High School, it was different for Dorothy Geraldine Counts.

Harding, on the wrong side of the Southern Railway tracks, drew its enrollment from sections where income was low and racial prejudice high. Integration there would have been a problem under any circumstances. As it turned out, the problem was complicated by the enrollment arrangements. Returning students registered first, at 9 A.M., with new students, including Dorothy Counts, not due to arrive until 10:30 A.M. Thus there was half a morning for tension to build. At 9 o'clock John Kasper's brunette hostess arrived with her truck-driver husband and began rabble-rousing among pupils on the school grounds. They could keep "the nigger" from enrolling, she told them. By a few minutes after 10 o'clock most of the early enrollees were out. Not many left the grounds, and the truck driver's wife had fresh fodder. Photographers and reporters, plainclothes policemen (who seemed reluctant to do anything) and a few curious adults added to the crowd.

I was standing near the entrance to the school when a car stopped almost two blocks away. The crowd shifted toward it, buzzing. Abruptly the crowd parted, and a tall, deep-tan girl emerged, head high, eyes straight ahead, walking down the street toward the school. A Negro man was with her, but she dominated the scene. Behind her were 300 people, mostly teen-agers shouting insults and gesticulating, but she gave no sign that she heard or saw them. The truck driver's wife ran along, crying, "Spit on her, girls! Spit on her!" Some of them did, and Dorothy Counts was unaware. She walked through open doors into Harding High School Auditorium as if she owned it, leaving a muttering crowd behind.

It was the most magnificent entrance I have ever seen.

From then on, what happened was anti-climax for Dorothy Counts. While she registered, police finally ordered the truck driver and his wife to leave. By the time Dorothy was dismissed, after an uneasy hour or so in school, the drama was gone, but a fourth of the crowd of students remained and the ugliness was still there. A shower of spittle, pebbles, sticks and paper balls fell on her and her escort during their walk to the car. I saw another reporter elbow in behind her. I joined him and we in turn were joined by a third. We formed a protective rear guard during the last 100 yards of her trip. I had always been told not to get involved in stories I was covering, and I give the same advice to others now—but there we were, and I don't regret it.

A week later I sat in the living room of the Counts home, waiting for her father to issue a statement withdrawing her from Harding. Dorothy was on the porch, talking to a Negro minister, a stranger who had come to plead with her to remain. "You don't know what it was like," she said. She had been spat on in the halls. Someone had tossed a pencil eraser and a small piece of tin at her. She was, after all, a 15-year-old girl.

The day after Dorothy withdrew, there was a rumored crisis at Central High School and I was sent there. When I was finally admitted to the principal's office, the school superintendent, my gentle, white-haired, idealistic friend was there. He turned on me and a colleague and castigated us with passion and precision. Stripped of emotion, his message was that if we would go back to our typewriters and give him a chance to run the schools, things would go a lot better.

As a newsman I've been bawled out many times before and since, and I've considered it part of the day's work, but I have never forgotten the shock of that superintendent's attack. It had two permanent effects, one rational and one emotional. I've since been more acutely conscious that newspapers can sometimes exacerbate stress while reporting (and photographing) it. And I've never again allowed myself to grow as fond of a news source as I had been of him.

Gus Roberts and Girvaud Roberts and the other junior high school girl finished the school year, and Gus—a slender boy with an immense reservoir of courage and conviction—went on to become the first Negro to graduate from an integrated high school in Charlotte. By then I had long since moved on to other jobs on the paper, and somebody else was covering education and integration. For me, the assignment was history.

It would be nice to have an uncluttered memory of truth eloquently recorded and right triumphant. Nice, but impossible. In this, as in most other matters in my newspaper experience, truth, right and clutter tend to get all mixed together. The task is to try to untangle them, and you're never quite sure you've done it.

Here was an assignment in which I helped keep the public uninformed for a time about a far-reaching decision by a public body. In which I violated the principle that a reporter should never become involved in a story he is covering. In which I was accused by a man I greatly respected of hampering a cause we both wanted to see succeed.

While these clutter the memory, they also add meaning to it. In the hectic world of daily newspapering, there will always be times when an editor must make a hard decision as to whether the highest public good demands that he temporarily deny the principle of informing the public fully . . . when a reporter will respond first as a human being and then as a newspaperman . . . when we are forced to reconcile our urge to cover a dangerous situation fully with the effect that our physical presence and our reporting might have on the situation itself.

I suppose I knew it already, but the integration assignment brought home to me the bankruptcy of formulae and ringing phrases in guiding newsmen. You can't solve an ethical problem by parroting "freedom of information," "the public's right to know," or any other slogan, no matter how noble the sentiment that originated it.

Where does that leave us? In my book, back on a par with everybody else, as human beings responsible for what we do, with our own sense of right and wrong (unsloganized) to guide us.

When journalists talk among themselves, they trade
memories---of the big or unforgettable stories,
of the problems of their craft, of the teachers who
guided them, of lessons learned.

Dean of the Columbia Graduate School of Journalism from 1931 to 1956—and now Dean Emeritus—Carl W. Ackerman was responsible for a multitude of the innovations that brought the School recognition as a leader in the field of journalism education. In 1934, he initiated the exclusively graduate program at the School, and in 1946 helped found the American Press Institute.

Less well known is the fact that Dean Ackerman (Class of 1913) was a foreign correspondent during World War I, covering first the Central Powers for the United Press and later the Allied Army in Siberia for The New York Times. *He wrote magazine articles from Mexico, Spain, France and Switzerland, and was the author of several books based on his experiences.*

Dean Ackerman was foreign editor of The Philadelphia Public Ledger *and assistant to the president of General Motors before assuming his duties at Columbia.*

CARL W. ACKERMAN

Pioneering in Journalism

In September of 1912, when classes in journalism met for the first time at Columbia University, there were no precedents. The present Joseph Pulitzer building was under construction. Our City Room was in Hamilton Hall and we attended other classes in buildings around the campus. Our assets were Pulitzer's ideals, President Nicholas Murray Butler's confidence and support, and the inspiring instruction of the first director, Dr. Talcott Williams, and his staff of teachers.

Student enthusiasm matched these assets. Our greatest liability was the skepticism of the press toward education in journalism, a doubt shared by educational institutions throughout the United States. As a member of the senior class, a group composed of students who had received A.B. degrees from other colleges, I was one of the pioneer graduates in June, 1913.

Politics and crime dominated the New York City news; we were assigned to cover these stories. My first beat was the National Democratic Headquarters. Woodrow Wilson was making his first campaign for the Presidency. There I met practically all the future members of his Cabinet, future ambassadors and other public officials. Several of these party workers became historic figures: James W. Gerard, Ambassador to Germany; Joseph P. Tumulty, the President's secretary; and Franklin D. Roosevelt.

After the election in 1912 my next big story, as a student, was the "Becker Case," one of the great crime stories of the past half century. Herman Rosenthal, a gambler, was murdered by four gunmen. Police Lieutenant Charles Becker, who had made bank deposits of $70,000 allegedly received for protecting gambling, was accused of having ordered the execution. Hollington K. Tong (a classmate who later became Nationalist China's Ambassador in Washington) and I were assigned to cover the trials. All five of the accused were convicted. Holly and I were ordered by our city editor, Professor Robert E. MacAlarney, to accompany Becker and his guards to Sing Sing prison on his journey to the electric chair. Thus we became the first journalism students to be sent to jail. That was the end of my career as a crime reporter, although Holly and I still enjoy recalling our prison association.

In 1912-1913, few public men or editors thought about or even dreamed of the possibility of a World War, although Dr. Williams forecast it in his lectures. When war did begin in Europe, I was on the staff of the United Press in Washington. I became the first School of Journalism graduate to be assigned to the White House; in 1914, the first to become a war correspondent in London and Berlin.

These opportunities were directly related to my student experiences. And they took me far—to Germany, Switzerland, France, Spain and Cuba. Even farther: In July, 1918, there was a brief item in the newspapers reporting the execution of the Czar and his family in Ekaterinburg, Siberia. Carr V. Van Anda, managing editor of *The New York Times,* asked me to go there and get the story. Because there was no airplane passenger transportation in the world at that time, my wife and I crossed the Pacific by ship to Japan (where she remained), while I proceeded to Vladivostok and then traveled 5,000 miles across Siberia by train. Finally I was able to call upon the American Consul General in Ekaterinburg. He knew a monk who had seen the Imperial family daily. We hired a troika—three horses hitched to a sleigh—and the driver took us to a monastery far from the city. It was cold—40 degrees below zero—but we were bundled in furs.

The monk had kept a notebook in which he recorded the events of the family's last days in the Ipatiff house. I had previously examined this home, room by room, including the basement, where the Czar and his family had been shot. As the monk read, the consul interpreted; then he borrowed the precious document, which he translated afterward at his home while I typed my story.

Since there were no telegraph or wireless communications to and from Ekaterinburg, I had to wait several weeks until a freight-refugee train left for the two-week journey to Vladivostok. There I cabled my story. Six months after I had left New York the story was printed on the front page of the *Times*. It was the first exclusive account of the last days of the Romanoffs, and was reprinted throughout the world.

On our School's fiftieth anniversary I salute the pioneer teachers who inspired me to continue pioneering until University statutes made it necessary for me to retire as Dean in 1956. I served for 25 years; during those years radio and television were introduced in the curriculum, the Maria Moors Cabot prizes and the American Press Institute were established. In World War II Holly and I founded a Graduate School of Journalism in Chungking, China.

Now education in journalism is as firmly established as in other professions. Our alumni are pioneering throughout the world. There is nothing within the realm of news communications that cannot be accomplished by a Journalism graduate.

Ahmed Emin Yalman, an outstanding figure in international journalism, reveals in his article some of the tribulations he has faced. There have been honors as well—among them the "Golden Pen of Liberty" from the International Federation of Publishers, the award of the Time *Magazine World Forum, and medals and citations from Columbia University, the University of California, and the American Newspaper Publishers Association.*

Dr. Yalman, author of a long list of books published in Turkey, England, Germany and the United States (his most recent work for an American audience is "Turkey in My Time," published in 1956), has served his country not only as a journalist but also as a professor at Istanbul University and as a public information officer.

AHMED EMIN YALMAN:
"Never Shrink from Sacrifice"

I am 75 years old, an active journalist in Istanbul. I was sentenced in 1960 to 18 months of imprisonment. An attempt was made on my life in 1952; wounded by five bullets, I was expected by all to die. In 1925 I was charged with revolutionary activities and tried by a political tribunal. In the decade before that I was twice exiled—first by the Sultan to Kutaiah for three months, then to Malta for 21 months by British occupation authorities.

Either compromise or a willingness to look the other way might have enabled me to avoid each of these misadventures.

But in 1914, a great and good man urged me to devote myself to the advancement of Turkey, to be a daring and enterprising journalist, and never to shrink from any sacrifice were it necessary and right.

The man was Dr. Talcott Williams, the first director of the Columbia University School of Journalism. I have tried always to be faithful to his precepts.

I was one of the first Turkish students to study in the United States of America. After the Young Turk revolution in 1908, Columbia University generously offered scholarship aid to Turkey. For this assistance there were 180 applicants; five of us were chosen.

We each signed agreements with the Government in Istanbul, promising to serve as teachers for five years after our return, and for this we received monthly expense allowances of $100 to cover room, board and living expenses.

I had not wanted to teach; my heart turned to journalism. I had entered the field at the age of 19 as the English translator for a daily newspaper, *Sabah*. The year was 1907, and the censorship exercised by Sultan Abdul Hamid was strict. A year later the Young Turk movement achieved notable gains, and in an easier climate for writing I joined the staff of *The Yeni Gazette,* while continuing my studies in the law. In 1909 I became chief editorial writer for the *Gazette.*

Then came America. We began our studies at Columbia in February, 1911. I acquired my degree in sociology and was studying for a Ph.D. when I learned that soon there would be a Pulitzer School of Journalism at the University. Perhaps I could be permitted to take extra work in this division; quickly, anxiously I arranged to meet with the director to plead my case.

What a pleasant surprise was awaiting! After we had chatted for a few minutes, Dr. Williams revealed that he too had been born in Turkey, in the province of Mardin. The son of a missionary family, he had lived in my land for his first 16 years. "I have always wanted to repay the debt I owe your country and your people," he said.

Dr. Williams conducted a class in editorial writing; I was given leave to enroll in it. We met each morning, as if we were an actual editorial board. After we had discussed the general situation, each chose a topic for the day. Our teacher then read our contributions with great care, guiding, criticizing and inspiring us.

His assistance to me went far beyond this, however. His suggestions helped me in the preparation of a draft of my doctoral dissertation, "The development of modern Turkey as measured by its press." And occasionally, when a guest of mark visited him, Dr. Williams invited me to join the group at his home on West 117th Street. Perhaps once each week I met with him in the evening to discuss the old Turkey and the new land that was evolving—invigorating talks that unfailingly ended with the downing of a glass of yogurt.

Just before the summer of 1913, I told Dr. Williams of my plan to spend the school vacation in Turkey with my family.

"You must not do that," he insisted. "It is your duty to spend your vacation becoming familiar with every phase of American life."

This remarkable man had already planned a program for me! First I was to attend the National Editorial Association convention in Colorado Springs as his representative. Next, with a group of small-town journalists, I would embark on a tour of the Midwest, the South and the East. In a number of cities along the way he would make arrangements for me to visit and work with leading newspapers.

And thus a young student from Turkey was enabled to visit Franklin, Indiana . . . and to work for several days on *The Concord* (N.H.) *Patriot,* the house guest of the publisher, Edward Gallagher . . . and to fill assignments on *The Chicago Inter-Ocean* . . . and to write editorials for *The Springfield* (Ill.) *Republican,* explaining the Turkish view of the Second Balkan War, then being waged . . . and to visit an Indian reservation and the Chillocco School in Oklahoma.

Perhaps the wonder of these experiences can be made more vivid through contrast. In the Massachusetts cities of Worcester and Peabody, in Manchester, New Hampshire, and in Providence, Rhode Island, were groups of Turkish immigrants—some 20,000 men, women and children. Between semesters I went to New England to study the conditions in which these working families were living. I did not meet even one who was attempting to learn English; such an effort would have indicated, they feared, that they did not intend to return to their homeland. They thus saw nothing of the United States, learned nothing, felt nothing.

Even this trip to New England had been made possible by Dr. Williams. He purposefully introduced me to a friend of his, a professor who had just returned from Turkey with a rare manuscript, an eyewitness account of the conquest of Rhodes by the Turks early in the 16th century. I was commissioned to translate the work and I was paid so generously that further travels were made possible.

In 1914 I left America—and in the cabin of my steamer a letter from Dr. Talcott Williams awaited me. "Devote yourself to the cause of advancement of Turkey, our common country of birth . . ."

During the years of World War I, there was mismanagement and injustice, betrayal and defeatism to be fought. I allied myself with the National Resistance Movement, and was twice exiled.

Conditions changed—I was invited to head the press and information department of the new government; later I was asked to become Ambassador to Washington. Both invitations, I felt, had to be declined—more could be achieved for my country through journalism.

Sometimes fidelity to the freedom of the press required blunt refusal to write. For more than a decade Turkey had a one-party regime; newspapers that differed with the government were not allowed to appear during the late Twenties and early Thirties. I preferred to remain silent. I could not, after the training in truth I had received at Columbia, do otherwise. Nor did the attempted murder in 1952, nor two months in prison before the revolution of 27 May 1960, as a part of a sentence of 18 months, change the belief I held so proudly that the journalist must try to see what is right, what is wrong, and must tell what he sees.

I have always been in trouble. Yet there has always been a happy, last-minute escape. It has been a life worth living. Were I able to begin again, I would not hesitate to choose the same course.

Thanks to one great man, I hope to live proudly and die proudly as a journalist.

*Now chairman of the Journalism Department at
New York University, John Tebbel has served as
a writer and editor with newspapers, magazines
and book publishers, has taught journalism at the
Columbia Graduate School of Journalism (from
which he was graduated in 1937), and is a regular contributor to the* Saturday Review *communications section.*

*Mr. Tebbel is the author of 20 books, includ-
ing "The Inheritors" and several biographies of
journalism's giant figures: "The Marshall Fields,"
"George Horace Lorimer and the Saturday Evening Post" and "The Life and Good Times of
William Randolph Hearst." Mr. Tebbel is married
and lives in New York City.*

JOHN TEBBEL:

Progress Report to Mr. Rose

Whenever I hear a self-appointed preserver of the nineteenth century
advising a young man not to go to journalism school because he can
learn the same thing in the city room, I think of Douglas Southall
Freeman and a man on the copy desk of *The Richmond News-Leader*
known to me only as Mr. Rose.

At the moment I came into the sphere of influence of these Southern
gentlemen, I thought of myself as one hell of a good newspaperman.
I was only 23, but I had already been working for newspapers for
money for nine years. In the course of this extensive experience I'd
covered everything from forest fires to murders, from violent incidents
in the Michigan oil fields to run-of-the-mill county courthouse stories.
As a stringer for large dailies, I had seen my stories on front pages for
years, and for a full year I had been city editor of the largest weekly in
Michigan. As you can see, an accomplished journalist.

Then I arrived at the School of Journalism and encountered the
late Dr. Freeman. He was teaching a class called "Interpretation of
the News," in which he meant to show us how to digest the previous

100

week's news and reproduce it in the polished style of *The New York Times* Sunday feature, News of the Week In Review. We would, he told us, begin with a few paragraphs a day and work up to ten thousand words a day by semester's end. Our weekly efforts, he said, would be sent down to Richmond, edited by Mr. Rose, and returned to us.

Seven years later, when I was actually helping to write News of the Week, I realized that Dr. Freeman had given us an impossible assignment. No doubt he knew it. It was the technique of research and writing he wanted to impart—that, along with a realization of what good writing is all about.

I finished my first day's copy with time to spare. All of us experienced newspapermen who had tossed those piddling few paragraphs together with the ease that comes with years of practice then retired across the street for a drink.

Next Monday morning we "Christian statesmen," as Dr. Freeman called us with a fine disregard for both our religions and our temperaments, were given the previous week's papers. I glanced at mine with utter disbelief. The original copy was scarcely visible beneath Mr. Rose's corrections. Across the top he had written mildly that the organization was all right, but that the writing was "sloppy."

Sloppy! I was outraged. I planned to go over the piece word for word as soon as I had time that night, disputing Mr. Rose on every point, showing him up for the dull butcher I knew him to be. Already I hated him.

At the end of a long evening of silent argument, followed by a shorter period of acutely painful self-examination, I had to face the humiliating proposition that after nearly ten years in the newspaper business I did not know how to write. State desks had never edited my copy except to shorten it, and on the weekly I'd been my own editor. Now I had fallen into the hands of a master copyreader for the first time, and he was giving me the full treatment.

That night I made up my mind to beat Mr. Rose into submission before the year was over by writing a piece of copy in which he would not be able to find a single mistake. I estimated that three months at the most might pass before I could produce this perfect prose. By the end of the year I had yet to do it. On the final assignment he wrote, "You have improved considerably this year, but, as you will note, I still find a few places which need the pencil." He had, indeed—a dozen of them.

By this time, however, I had learned two things. One was humility, which I discovered years before Arthur Godfrey planted his flag on it. The other was a profound respect for the simple declarative sentence. I realized, too, that learning to write was going to be something that would occupy me the rest of my life.

There was nothing remarkable, of course, about these revelations. Sooner or later every professional writer becomes aware of them if he has any respect for his craft. It might also be argued that a young aspirant could as easily discover what I did by going to work on a newspaper at once. But I wonder. If that is true, why do we see so much newspaper copy that could justifiably have Mr. Rose's verdict of "sloppy" scratched across it?

If a youngster goes to work for one of the few first-class newspapers in this country, or if he is lucky enough to work for one that has a Rose on the copy desk, it may be that he will learn to write well. I submit that a first-class school or department of journalism will do the job better—perhaps saving the newcomer from lost jobs or missed opportunities, and certainly enriching the paper he eventually joins.

The business of a journalism school ought to be to teach recruits how to perform the tasks of newspapering better than they are currently being done. Anyone with reasonable talent can learn to get by on the average daily, but it takes someone with a passion for excellence to lift himself and his publication out of the rut.

The newspaper business has a relatively small cluster of editorial executives who have that passion. On my first metropolitan newspaper job following the year at Columbia, I was fortunate enough to have such a man as city editor. He gave me my second most valuable jolt. Andy Bernhard, now editor of *The Pittsburgh Post-Gazette,* was one of those editorial executives who knew how to get more out of his men than they thought they had. Apparently I disappointed him one day with a story he considered competent but no more.

"It's all right," he said, "but remember—we can always cut you down . . . You're the only one who can build yourself up."

That was, in another sense, what Mr. Rose had been trying to impress upon us with his pencil—that it was essential, always, to try to do better, to strive for excellence with the inner knowledge that there would always be more to strive for. It occurred to me then that this, more than anything else, was what the year at Columbia had taught us. Not to be merely copy editors, if that was our intent, but to reach toward the never-attainable standards set by Messrs. Robert E. Garst and Theodore M. Bernstein, two *Times* editors who taught us. After the first month, I don't think anyone had the temerity to imagine he would ever equal Mr. Rose. Certainly I didn't.

In Dr. Freeman's seminar we learned that there was a great deal more to reporting than covering fires and city hall; we experimented with the kind of investigative reporting that is today becoming more and more the hallmark of good newspapers. In Herbert Brucker's seminar we learned to be dissatisfied with the way newspapers were displaying the news, and in our work with him we developed techniques that were radical then but are standard today. My illustrious classmate, Vance Packard, would perhaps deny it, but it may be that the regularity with which he got his features back from the terrible-tempered Walter Pitkin, with "morgue stuff" lettered across them, had something to do with the fact that he became one of the best magazine feature writers in the country before he turned to producing best-sellers.

So it went through the whole curriculum. I hope no one thinks I am suggesting that the Class of 1937, as a result of this process, became the uplifters of the profession. I do say that we learned not to be satisfied with mediocrity and to make the effort to be better, and that many of us succeeded. This is, I believe, what good schools and departments of journalism accomplish for their students, and it is the reason the best newspapers are liberally staffed with their graduates.

Some of us would have done it anyway, without the School, just as it is entirely possible for talented newspaper people to avoid mediocrity without benefit of professional education, but it is the over-all effect that is important.

For me the lesson has been a lasting one. Twenty-five years and millions of words later, I am still acutely conscious of the imperfections in everything I write. I think I've acquired a good part of Mr. Rose's ability to devastate and reconstruct with the pencil; much of my rewriting in books is done that way. Yet now and then an invisible hand traces across the manuscript: "You have improved considerably. . . . but I still find a few places. . . ." Occasionally it adds succinctly: "Sloppy."

Wherever you are, Mr. Rose, I am still trying to beat you down.

Reporter, rewrite man, night city editor, assistant city editor, assistant regional editor, managing editor and now editor of the editorial page of The Denver Post, *Mort Stern was already an experienced political reporter when he joined* The Post *in 1951.*

Mr. Stern was graduated from Columbia in 1949, where he won a Pulitzer Traveling Scholarship. In 1954 he won a Nieman Fellowship, and in 1963 received the George Washington Honor Medal from the Freedoms Foundation.

Mr. Stern is a member of the admissions panel of the School of Journalism, and has served on both the Sigma Delta Chi and Pulitzer Prize awards committees. He is married and has two children.

MORT STERN:

The Lesson

The chill winds knifing up from Riverside Drive were enough to cut into the consciousness of even an unusually preoccupied student. A glance at the newsstand across from the Columbia campus that fall morning in 1948 showed plainly that Thomas E. Dewey was confidently, perhaps even briskly, walking ("running" wouldn't have been the appropriate word) toward the Presidency of the United States. Only a little ex-haberdasher from Missouri who happened to be President through a fluke of fate, and who was just perverse enough to want to hang on to his job, stood in the way of the formidable governor of New York. Trudging unnoticed around Morningside Heights, overwhelmed by the frustrations of my first month at the Graduate School of Journalism, I felt a kinship with Harry Truman. I remember thinking, "We're going to get snowed under, Harry, both of us, and no one else will give much of a damn."

I had an old brown overcoat that didn't fit very well and a portable Smith-Corona in equally shabby condition. As I got into the school's "city room" and set these aside, Professor Roscoe Ellard had already begun his lecture. He was pacing up and down in front of the students, punctuating his anecdote with great sweeping gestures of his arm, his fingers extended like a baseball pitcher's. Finally he came to the end of his story with a chuckle and a stuttered punch line that had his audience straining forward in suspense and excitement before it slumped back in amused relief. On we went in this way until it was time to pick up our assignments from the pigeon-holes on one side of the large, high-ceilinged room. This was the day of the week when the students were turned loose on an unsuspecting city of New York—to ride ferry boats, interview hobos on park benches, bother cops, haunt the press rooms of municipal office buildings and in general to do what was overgenerously called "competing" with the city's working press. We journalism students approached these assignments with mixed emotions at best. We realized deep down that the experience was valuable, but we were unable to shake the misgivings that go with knowing that wherever we were sent we were likely to be as welcome as wasps in a nudist colony.

I had developed what I considered to be a good stoic front toward this trying experience of drawing assignments, but I wasn't prepared for the one I drew this day. The substance was this: Some New York Democrats had accused Governor Dewey of misappropriating or otherwise misusing several millions of dollars in state funds. My job was simply to find out if the charge were true.

My stoicism—if it ever really existed—evaporated. What did "they" think I was, I asked. A couple of girls who were heading for the zoo seemed sympathetic, but mostly I just got shrugs and grunts and that "tough luck, pal" expression that had become so familiar in the Army. I don't know how long I spent griping or trying to get my thoughts sorted out, but after a while I looked up to see Ellard staring right into my eyes and on up my optic nerve. The message was a very clear, if unspoken, "Get going!" I went.

Outside the wind had abated some, but it was still bracing. Maybe, I thought (and it was good to be thinking again), maybe the Democrats, since they had started it all, might be of some assistance. A pleasant telephone operator helped locate some Democrats who would talk to me. The Democrats I found in a midtown office were cordial, but they didn't know any more about the background of the charge than I did. They were, however, able to dig up press release. I thanked Heaven for verbose press agents. The release went into the charge at considerable length, far more completely than the news stories had. At least some logical questions began to shape up in my mind. Now if I could just find Dewey . . .

The problem was not so difficult as it could have been with a national campaign underway. I picked up a newspaper and saw that Dewey was in fact to be in New York City for an engagement that night. Once again, telephone operators helped find the Republican headquarters where Dewey might be reached. I got to the right office, finally, but the candidate wasn't in. The receptionist, a handsome if aloof woman, invited me to wait.

For a long time nothing happened. It was getting late, and I was growing worried. Then I got a break. The receptionist pulled out a crossword puzzle book and began struggling. As it turned out, I knew a couple of key words. Soon we became friends, and I was sharing my problem with her. Accidentally I had stumbled upon a basic law of journalism and business: Never underestimate the power of a secretary or receptionist. My lovely friend excused herself and went down the hall into the maze of executive offices.

In a few moments she was followed out by a distinguished looking man who offered his hand. "I'm Paul Lockwood, Governor Dewey's assistant. Perhaps I can help you." Lockwood led the way into his office and we sat down. Then he smiled and said, "I'm a Columbia man myself. Now, what do you want to know?"

We must have talked for an hour. The details of his explanation of what had become of the money escape me now, but his account must have been quite plausible because I wrote a long and, I think, convincing story based on it. The part of the episode I do remember clearly was Roscoe Ellard's reaction. Some days later he called me into his office to talk about it.

"You did a good job on the story, young man, once you got going," he said. "But your attitude, your beefing, up to that point was nothing to be proud of. The fact is that if I hadn't thought you could handle the assignment, I wouldn't have given it to you."

He put his large hand on my shoulder and we walked to the door. It was, it turned out, the beginning of a friendship that was to last until his death in 1962.

"One more thing," Ellard said as I was about to leave. "Remember this. Whatever you do, *someone* is always watching."

The lesson was a turning point. The rest of the year at Columbia was different for me. I worked harder, yet somehow it was more fun. I began to feel closer to my fellow students, and there again made some lifelong friendships.

Gradually, over the years, the incident of the assignment began to fade from my mind. Then abruptly it came back, one day in 1956. For five years I had been working for *The Denver Post* as a reporter, re-write man, night city editor, assistant city editor and assistant Empire (regional) editor. I was making fair although not spectacular progress in my career, and I was thinking about a change. I had, in fact, just mailed a letter to a friend inquiring about a particular opening when I got a call from Ed Dooley, the managing editor. Dooley, who is now editor of *The San Francisco Examiner,* was leaving the *Post* to start his own business newspaper in California. There had been considerable speculation among us staffers as to which of the ranking executives would be named to succeed him.

"Come on back to the Old Man's office," Dooley said.

When I got there, the editor and publisher, Palmer Hoyt, was wait-ing for me at the door. Hoyt, whom I barely knew, extended his hand, and with a deep, gravelly voice that I would in time come to know better than my own, said, "You are to be Mr. Dooley's successor."

I don't recall what I said—if anything. I must have looked surprised because Hoyt added: "I know all about you. *I've been watching you for some time.*"

I have since gone on to that Valhalla (or Devil's Island) of all editors who get marked as eggheads somewhere along the line—editing the editorial page. As an executive I have seen my share of promising young men come and go. And when I think it will do some good, I try to get across to them the unscheduled lesson that I was lucky to learn at Columbia not really so very long ago—because I know from experience that it is true. Someone *is* always watching.

The world, quite literally, has been William Mc-Gaffin's beat. From the time he was graduated from the School of Journalism in 1935, until he joined the Washington staff of The Chicago Daily News in 1956, Mr. McGaffin was a foreign correspondent in London, Paris, North Africa, Egypt, Libya, Russia, China, Manchuria and Czechoslovakia. He covered the fall of France, the Battle of Britain and the Battle of Malta.

When the United States entered the war, Mr. McGaffin covered the battles of Saipan, Guam, Iwo Jima and Okinawa. In addition, he has been a U. N. correspondent and has written numerous magazine articles. He lives with his wife and two children in Falls Church, Virginia.

WILLIAM McGAFFIN:

Advice from Dr. Freeman

A Model-A with a Nebraska license plate hit the George Washington Bridge at rush hour one night in early September, 1934.

The young man at the wheel, about a month away from his twenty-fourth birthday, was without any doubt the most nervous driver on the bridge. He had never been in traffic like this before.

As the cars honked and whizzed around him he shuttered his gaze against the staggering spectacle of the New York skyline, and somehow made his way to the campus of Columbia University. To his relief—and astonishment—he reached his destination without accident.

The country was still struggling to emerge from the Depression. The Nebraska he had left behind was aswirl with dust storms and a farm crisis. The cheapest way to cover the 1,500 or so miles to New York was by car; that's why the young man had chosen this method of transportation.

I was that nervous traveler. Soon, only a few years later, I would be as comfortably at home in London as I'd been in Polk, Nebraska (population 500). Not very many years later—after I'd joined *The*

Chicago Daily News for the long-haul stretch of my career—I'd be telling an amusing anecdote about myself: that on this first drive east I had deliberately bypassed Chicago, afraid to face the traffic in the Midwestern metropolis.

But that was all later. In 1934 I was neither comfortable nor amused; I was apprehensive and grateful. I was about to spend a year at Columbia's School of Journalism—a year made possible by a scholarship that honored the late publisher of the newspaper that had just fired me.

When I graduated from Polk High School in 1928, my father wanted me to stay on in town, join him at the weekly paper he edited—*The Polk Progress*—and eventually succeed him. My mother insisted that I first go to college.

I kept all of us happy by majoring in journalism at the University of Nebraska. Jim Lawrence, editor of *The Lincoln* (Nebr.) *Star,* taught there; and as soon as I received my diploma, Jim gave me a job as cub police reporter. The salary was a living wage in those dark days, even after it had been cut from $18 to $16.20 a week during a retrenchment drive. And in 1933 this first job did lead to a place on *The Omaha World-Herald* at a spectacular $30 a week.

But after a year in Omaha, I was dismissed along with eleven other men in an economy move. Only then did it occur to me to apply for the scholarship inaugurated in 1934 by the late Mrs. Martha Hitchcock, widow of the distinguished senator and publisher of the *World-Herald,* Gilbert M. Hitchcock.

I filed my application, and then moved on to take a temporary job on *The Columbus* (Nebr.) *Star,* filling in as a telegraph editor while the regular man was on vacation. The job was nearing an end; no others were in sight. I wondered where next to turn. And then one morning my picture stared out at me from the front page of the *World-Herald.* I was the first recipient of the Hitchcock Scholarship, a $1,000 award "enabling a young Nebraskan newspaperman to spend a year in postgraduate study of journalism at Columbia University."

Carl Ackerman, Douglas Freeman, Robert Garst, Theodore Bernstein, Harold Cross, Howard Jones, Charles Cooper, Herbert Brucker —these were our teachers. They were more than teachers. Brucker was a father confessor. Dean Carl Ackerman talked me into staying on in the School after I'd gotten a mid-year offer of a job. Dr. Freeman gave me twenty-six words of blunt advice that I've carried through all the years that followed.

It hasn't all been one grand and glorious adventure since 1935. Some of it was dull, some of it was disappointing. But most of it was good. I went from Columbia to the AP Feature Service; from there, at twenty-seven, to London as an AP foreign correspondent. For seven incredible years I wrote stories about peace and war from London, Paris, New Delhi, Chungking, Moscow and Cairo. In May of 1944 a telegram from Chicago reached me—and since then I have been a part of *The Chicago Daily News,* working overseas (for nine years), at the United Nations (a little more than two years) and in Washington (over seven years). On this paper I've been associated with some of the most capable men in the business.

Often my mind goes back to the meeting I had with Dr. Freeman at the end of the school year in 1935. This brilliant editor of *The Richmond* (Va.) *News Leader* had just finished his monumental four-volume biography of Robert E. Lee. He was already embarked on further works in the writing tasks he had set himself—and in a hundred and one other activities as well. How he managed to squeeze all this in I'll never know; yet he flew up to Columbia once a week to spend a whole day with us. Often he urged us to write "something more permanent than today's newspaper"; yet at the same time he helped us to be better newspapermen. I shall be forever grateful to him for the knowledge he imparted.

Each of us had one last private meeting with Dr. Freeman at the end of the school year. This was the time when he sized us up on the basis of all he'd observed during the past nine months; the time when he evaluated our chances for future success. And this was the time when we deeply regretted not having worked harder during our year at the School.

"McGaffin," he said, slowly shaking his head, "I don't know. If you will read two good books a week for the rest of your life, there may be some hope for you."

Perhaps that sums up what the School of Journalism gave me. A challenge. A lesson in humility. And very good rules for life.

Fortunately for American journalism, wanderlust is not a prerequisite for a good newspaperman. Walter Pfister, born in Sheboygan and educated at the University of Wisconsin, was already an experienced reporter when he left The Sheboygan Press *to become a member of Columbia Journalism's Class of 1924. Armed with his degree, Mr. Pfister returned to his home town to become city editor of* The Press *and, later, associate editor— the post he holds today.*

He has been a member of Pulitzer Prize juries on local reporting and cartoons. The Pfisters have three children; their son, Walter Jr., is also a graduate of the School of Journalism, and produces network news programs for ABC.

WALTER J. PFISTER:
The Professor Was a Prophet

The private office of Professor Charles Cooper was not really very private. The panels enclosing it did not extend more than half-way-up in the high-ceilinged city room of the School of Journalism at Columbia University.

That is how I happened to overhear most of what was going on in there one bright, sunshiny day in the spring of 1924. Dr. Cooper was my faculty advisor, and I had received notice to appear before him at a certain hour that morning. I was a bit early for the appointment; thus my eavesdropping was accidental, not premeditated.

Whoever was in there was not faring too well. He was really getting his leaves raked over. I could not help but worry and think, "Just what will this man have to say to me?"

When the hapless youth fled, I entered and sat down in the designated chair. While we always addressed this great former editor of *The New York Sun* as Professor Cooper or Dr. Cooper, we nevertheless referred to him as "Charley" or as "Coop" when he was not within earshot.

111

And it was with some trepidation that I now sat in my chair, looking at Charley's back.

Slowly he turned in his swivel chair and scowled, almost glowering at me, his eyes slits under his bushy eyebrows. Suddenly his features reassembled into a broad, engaging smile—a storm cloud giving way to the sun. Then he winked like St. Nick in the Christmas poem.

"Do you know, Pfister," he queried, "that every once in a while you've gotta scare the hell out of these kids to make them find out for themselves whether they'll ever be good newspaper men?"

Then this grand old man, this superb teacher who tried to appear as gruff and tough as the editors depicted on stage and in the movies, continued to smile benevolently and said: "I've checked your record and find it good, I think you could do very well in the big time right here in New York, but you'll probably go back to Milwaukee, marry some girl, and stay there the rest of your life."

(Charley, in all of our meetings, never mentioned Sheboygan or any other Wisconsin city except Milwaukee. As far as his conversation was concerned, the remainder of the Badger state could have been timber, underbrush, and maybe cowboys and Indians.)

I mention the incident to indicate why I am so deeply impressed with Columbia's School of Journalism. Members of the teaching staff gave you real encouragement when you did something the way it should be done. When you did something wrong, they not only told you it was wrong—but why.

William Preston Beazell, then managing editor of *The New York World,* was my instructor in feature writing. You were given your assignment; then you mailed your manuscript to him on or before the established deadline. That gave Mr. Beazell time to go over carefully whatever you had written, and to make notations of errors, missed opportunities and needed improvements. His feature-writing class never met in a group; instead, this very able newspaperman spent every Friday at Columbia with individual students, and, during the allotted ten or fifteen minutes, would diagnose what ailed your story. A very friendly man, he was nevertheless a direct person who pulled no punches in what he had to say.

One rainy Friday morning—it was one of those black Fridays—Mr. Beazell addressed me in words to this effect:

"Pfister, this isn't a bad story, and if you follow my notations I believe you can make it a better one. However, it is the first sloppy copy you have ever turned in, and I want to nip that sort of thing in the bud right now by giving some sound advice from the other side of the desk.

"Try to get into the habit of writing clean copy. It may slow you down a bit at first, but it is amazing how rapidly such a habit can be acquired with the proper application. Clean copy may play an important part in your newspaper career, and I'll tell you why.

"When a big story breaks in the news room shortly before deadline, the desk always turns to the reporter who has been turning in the cleanest copy. Nobody expects him to come up with a perfect story under such urgent circumstances, but the percentages are that a 'clean-copy reporter' will bang out a better, less ragged story than some of his more careless associates. Clean copy, Pfister, could lead you to become a star reporter and to promotions. Incidentally, clean copy put me where I am today."

At the School of Journalism they taught us one more lesson: "If you think you're right, stay with it until they have proved you wrong." One afternoon Henry W. Sackett, an authority on libel law and then legal counsel for *The New York Herald Tribune,* gave us an unusual assignment. We were to take the five o'clock edition of *The New York Journal* and mark all of the instances of libel per se (possibly defensible, but libel on the face of it) on the front page. That would cover news stories, headlines, captions and pictures.

This was the era of the "Broadway Butterfly Murder Case," with which the sensational newspapers were having a grand time. A chorus beauty by the name of Dottie King had been done in by some unknown assailant in her lavish apartment. You can rest assured that *The New York Journal* was doing all right by Dottie.

Fortunately, I had taken careful notes on Mr. Sackett's libel per se lecture, and I had them before me as I started marking the designated issue. It seemed unbelievable that so many examples of libel per se could find their way into a single front page—particularly on a page filled with so many pictures and big headlines. But there they were—more than fifty. I became worried. This just couldn't be right . . . but reference back to the lecture notes said that it was.

So I made my decision and mailed in my libel per se markings—all 57 of them—in time to meet the deadline. The next time Mr. Sackett's class met I was asked by some of my classmates about my total score on libel per se, and I told them. I am sure that more than a few thought me a mental case—until our teacher announced that mine was the first perfect examination paper he had received since he had begun teaching the law of libel.

When I left the School of Journalism, it was with many fine ideas, ideals and traditions. Keep your copy clean—and stay with your idea until they've proved you wrong—were, of course, among them. Beyond that, however, I would like to pay a final tribute to Dr. Charles Cooper, acknowledging more than his abilities as an editor and as a shepherd of budding journalists. As far as I am concerned, the man was positively clairvoyant!

I did go back to Wisconsin, as he had predicted. I did get married and I did stay in Wisconsin. Only in one detail did I cross him up: I planted my roots in Sheboygan, Wis., not in Charley's all-comprehensive Milwaukee. For which, I pray to heaven, that this beloved old gentleman has long since forgiven me. After all, the two cities are only 50 miles apart.

Otto D. Tolischus, winner of the Pulitzer Prize for foreign correspondence in 1939, was graduated from the School of Journalism in 1916. He was reporter, city editor and managing editor of The Cleveland Press *before going overseas for INS; then in 1933 he joined the Berlin bureau of* The New York Times, *and has been with that newspaper since.*

When the United States entered World War II, Mr. Tolischus was in Tokyo as correspondent for both The New York Times *and* The Times *of London. He was jailed and later released in an exchange of prisoners; after his return to the United States, he became a member of* The New York Times' *editorial board. He is the author of three books, "They Wanted War," "Tokyo Record" and "Through Japanese Eyes."*

OTTO D. TOLISCHUS:
Fiduciary Relationships

In the hurly-burly of daily newspaper work—particularly under the pressures of such dictatorial regimes as Hitler's and Tojo's—it was not always easy to apply a rule taught us as students at the Columbia School of Journalism.

"Always be faithful to your readers, your country, and to your sources of information," admonished the first director, Dr. Talcott Williams. We were irreverent students; we joked about his phrase—"you must maintain a fiduciary relationship"—just as we joked about his frequent inability to connect the right name with the right person. But deep down we recognized the validity of what was part of his own professional ethics.

In Nazi Germany and in pre-war Japan, two countries where I was stationed, the line between duty to one's newspaper and the obligation to protect confidential sources of information—not to speak for now of one's own self-preservation—became extremely fine. But the record shows that, with rare exceptions, American newspapermen "maintained their fiduciary relationship" in the face of constant threats of internment, torture, imprisonment and even, in some cases, death.

My first overseas assignment was to cover Hitler's abortive *putsch* in Munich in 1923. Germany was then a really free country. News sources were open and safe, and foreign correspondents working in this environment acquired a sense of freedom and immunity from danger that carried them through the whole Hitler era.

But the dictatorial pressures of the Hitler regime became immediately evident. Curiously enough, in contrast to other countries so ruled, Nazi Germany never imposed a censorship on outgoing news reports, even after it had plunged the world into war. We on *The New York Times* freely telephoned our dispatches to Paris; or, when France entered the war, to Amsterdam; and after the Lowlands were overrun, we cabled the news to New York. To a degree, Nazi Germany under Propaganda Minister Goebbels seemed to welcome full reports of its policy of frightfulness in order to terrify its enemies at home and abroad.

It used other means to keep news from foreign correspondents and to try to intimidate them and bend them to its purposes.

It instituted a censorship at the source in an effort to make the correspondents dependent on handouts. Officials, even those known to be non-Nazis, became closemouthed. Productive contacts with private but knowledgeable persons could be maintained only with circumspection. Sometimes a person disappeared; even if he turned up months later after an evident term in a concentration camp, the reporter could not escape the uneasy feeling that he may have contributed to this tragedy. Finally, there was always the threat of expulsion or worse.

The expulsions started immediately after Hitler came to power and continued until Hitler declared war on the United States. Then the remaining American correspondents were interned. After constant threats and finally a Nazi press campaign against me, I became, in April, 1940, the thirty-second correspondent to be expelled.

Despite these handicaps, the story of the Hitler regime—barring its final savageries toward the end of the war—was, I believe, adequately covered. Every correspondent had his own methods, but I found two factors in Nazi Germany especially helpful. First, the Germans themselves, including some officials, could not quite believe the terror that hovered over them, and often talked freely to trusted friends. Second, a complicated economic and social system such as Germany's could not be run without publication of relevant material, to which were added sometimes indiscreet items in the local press. It then became the correspondent's task to put two and two together, to match snatches of information gleaned here and there and to fill in the missing parts from one's own background in order to solve the puzzle. In actual fact there were few secrets that did not leak to the correspondents sooner or later, and it was just such a combination of odds and ends that enabled me to report in April, 1939, the then-unbelievable news that Hitler and Stalin were negotiating the pact that triggered the Second World War. And the imminent outbreak of war was so patent that I stayed up all night to report Hitler's attack on Poland on that fateful September morn in 1939.

Another technique that enabled me to last as long as I did in Nazi Germany was a device of my own. Being unable to ascribe any but official news to the source, I made it a point to search out relevant items in the press and then to document my news reports with a sprinkling of them. Whenever Goebbel's propaganda machine called me on the carpet, I could point to these items as my source. In one particularly ticklish article I even used copious footnotes, certainly a rare instance in newspaper reports. This device is of no help in some countries, but the Goebbels machine, which kept its own press under strict censorship, had no answer to it, and I stayed.

In fact, aside from the fact that I worked for *The New York Times,* I must have even won some respect from the Nazis. Instead of expelling me outright, as all others, they requested me to take a "leave of absence" with the understanding that I would not return. The irony was that, expecting the same thorough search at the border to which many correspondents had been subjected, I left all my notes behind in Berlin. The border control did not bother to open even one suitcase of mine. Perhaps the fact that I left across the Danish border had something to do with the leniency.

I managed to keep ahead of the Nazi armies during the Scandinavian invasion, leaving Oslo two days before the Germans arrived and helping to cover the invasion itself from Stockholm. I was evacuated later from Petsamo, then a Finnish port, under rather trying conditions. The British ordered our ship to take one route; the Nazis threatened, every hour on the hour over the ship's radio, to sink us unless we took another route. The captain "compromised." He took the British route and we reached New York safely.

After such strenuous experience, I was assigned, ironically enough, to "rest" in a supposedly quiet spot—Tokyo. There was some vague talk about a possible war with Japan, but such talk had been going on for years and nobody took it seriously. In Tokyo in February, 1941, however, there was a war scare (never felt in the United States) so serious and so real that my predecessor and his family decided to leave at once; I had to take over immediately without being able to gratify my wish of first looking around both Japan and China.

Japan, I learned at once, had a hidden but powerful censorship. Telephoned dispatches had to be read to the censor, but cable dispatches were shot into the dark. One never knew what the censor had passed until weeks later, when the papers with the printed dispatches arrived.

And compared with pre-war Japan, even Nazi Germany was an open society. The language barrier was, of course, one reason for the inability of most correspondents to get closer to the Japanese people. But Japan was already under the heel of the militarists and the political police. Except for a few brave souls, most people were afraid to talk. I did not blame them after I noticed that my assistants and I were under constant and close police surveillance. This left as sources of information only the official briefings, a few rather closemouthed officials, the diplomatic corps and the newspapers and magazines. We thus missed some of Japan's secret enterprises. And so did the diplomats. They learned no more about the coming Pearl Harbor than we did.

Apart from available news, we had to depend largely on atmosphere. This thickened perceptibly as the boasts and threats of the militarists grew louder. As in Nazi Germany, I sought to protect myself by citing published reference to the news I was reporting, and in the main I got away with it again. But when Tojo came to power, we realized—at least I did—that we were sitting ducks on a closed island; yet we did not worry too much because the worst we expected in case of war was internment and ultimate exchange.

That was not what was in store for most of us. At dawn on Pearl Harbor day there was an ominous knock on my bedroom door; I was told that Japan and the United States were at war. And then I was hustled off to prison. I could only react with initial incredulity and then with rage to being subjected first to isolated confinement and then to interminable questioning, torture and constant threats of instant execution unless I signed a confession that I was a spy. I don't know what inner resources the others drew upon to avoid breaking under this treatment, but my own fury kept up my courage, even when the prosecutor attempted to brainwash me into working for the Japanese. My "reward" for resistance was a suspended sentence at hard labor. This was a test of fiduciary responsibilities Dr. Williams could not possibly have imagined.

One final test of these responsibilities came, oddly enough, on the Japanese exchange ship that carried me home. Some missionaries and oil men, who were also aboard, expected to go back to Japan and China and resume business as usual after the war. Therefore they violently objected to our "spoiling their public relations" by writing objective stories about the treatment we and many others had received in Japan, Korea, China and the Philippines. Some even threatened to tell the Japanese captain about our "plot" and to demand that he take us back to Japan. But that kind of attempted brainwashing failed as well. The stories were written and sent as soon as we could get to a cable station. They are now part of the record of that time.

Most American newspapers and newspapermen believe in the principle that a free press must be a responsible press. I am proud to belong to their company.

It is typical of the faculty of the Columbia Graduate School of Journalism that they are also working newspapermen. Robert E. Garst, assistant managing editor of The New York Times, *began teaching at the School in 1925, one year after his own graduation, and remained a member of the faculty until 1948. His article reflects his deep interest in the part played by schools of journalism in the development of news writers.*

Mr. Garst is co-author with Theodore M. Bernstein, his colleague on The Times, *of the journalism textbook, "Headlines and Deadlines." Mr. Garst was born in Lexington, Virginia, and received his B. A. at the University of Virginia. He is married to the former Iris Kollmergen, and lives in New York City.*

ROBERT E. GARST:

The Training Ground

In the brief era between the end of World War I and the Depression, the Columbia School of Journalism—its faculty and its courses—met perfectly, it seems to me, the needs of the times.

New York and the world were simpler. The city was sprawling, exciting and adventurous; it had character and direction, and was comprehensible. To chronicle its events day by day required only the application of principles and skills learned in the classroom, plus an inquiring mind and a desire to learn the "why" of the "who, what, when and where." The nation—and its journalists—were then settling back into a pre-war complacency.

The "culture medium," the School of Journalism, was adjusted to the nourishment and growth of the required product. The sincerity and earnestness of the men of the faculty came through to the students and were absorbed as by an osmotic process.

Then came economic collapse, revolutions in economic and social thought, hot wars and cold wars. Relatively simple systems were con-

120

verted into immensely complicated and intricately-meshed systems. So the direction of journalism preparation had to change. The question that should be asked today is whether schools of journalism have changed appropriately in meeting these new conditions.

Great efforts have been made to do so. Training in such specialties as science and linguistics, and background courses in government, history and economics have been provided. But somewhere, in some way, the system has gone amiss. Specialization has reached a point where the reporter is only a specialist, lacking in the broad basic qualifications of a general news gatherer. The ranks of general reporters have been dangerously thinned.

I have the impression that newspapers trying to cope with the new complexities are moving away from the journalism schools to recruit new talent. The new men are college graduates with limited newspaper experience, if any; they are interested in and knowledgeable about specific fields of information or areas of the world. Most aim at foreign service. Few see profitable futures in the domestic field. As one reporter commented recently, they are interested in ideas, not in the story. And few have the experience or maturity to report facts competently. The result is that readers get, not penetrating accounts of situations and events, but atmosphere, description, background and interpretation.

That word "interpretation" is the heart of the dilemma. It has been felt that another dimension must be added to reporting to make today's news intelligible; and this has been done for a number of years, but with an outcome that many regard as less than satisfactory. One result, at least, can be viewed as deplorable: "Interpretation" has tended to introduce opinion or a point of view into the news columns—perhaps the individual's attitude, perhaps that of his newspaper. The principle long held by the pioneers in modern journalism—that the news columns should be strictly factual and objective—has been adulterated. Another device, the interpretive column written to accompany a news story, is currently a staple product. It would be difficult in most cases to distinguish this kind of material from an editorial expression of opinion. As one editor sees it, "We have got the background into the foreground."

The pros and cons of the old methods and the new have been hotly debated by editors. One school holds that if the facts, including background facts, are set forth clearly in accepted news style, the reader is capable of forming his own opinion. The other school contends that in these times the facts alone can be misleading when set forth baldly; that some "interpretation" is essential to give the true picture. This interpretation ordinarily is based on "briefings" by persons involved in the situation; they could be expected to have a point of view that influences reader opinion to one side or the other, and often they do. Or it could reflect an honest bias of the reporter himself. In any case this method of reporting dilutes objectivity and introduces elements of subjectivity that could damage a newspaper's reputation. Once a reporter cuts his mooring to factual reporting, he and his paper are in trouble.

It would seem that the problem of reconciling traditional reporting with the need to give greater service to the reader has not been solved. Continued newspaper progress requires a satisfactory solution; schools of journalism must, I think, address themselves to it.

Another grave difficulty in the profession is the lack of newspapermen sensitive to new areas of coverage or to the need for new depth in covering old ones. One need not look abroad in this connection. The evidence of journalistic sterility is here on our own doorstep. Since the last war, the city of New York has plunged into a sad state of official ineptitude, lack of vision, soaring budgets to meet unforeseen but predictable crises, and general makeshift policies that deepen the city's misfortunes.

Editors have done virtually nothing about it. They have seen great areas of the city leveled for the erection of public housing, one chief aim of which was to take advantage of federal money to build up local bureaucracies. They have seen thousands of New Yorkers displaced. The tragedies involved, the losses in human assets, have never been adequately recorded. They have seen vast apartment and office buildings rise unplanned, entailing untold miseries in traffic congestion and costs; no workable solution has been evolved. New York has become a great slum, East Side, West Side, all around the town. More than that— it has become unpleasant, ugly, crime-ridden.

No newspaper has reported this deterioration comprehensively and comprehensibly on a sustained basis, with an eye to the economic and social implications. This kind of situation, so different from the 1920's, requires new tools and methods of reporting.

Imagination and rededication to public service have got to be engendered somehow. First there must be fundamental knowledge of the routine of government and of party systems, court procedures and the possible venality involved in all of them. The growing secrecy in official places, local and national, has to be taken into account and combatted. Recently a great industrial and housing project on the West Side of Manhattan was disclosed suddenly to the public, with every evidence that it had been long planned and had already won approval in the necessary quarters. The usual community safeguards of public disclosure and debate and hearings had been circumvented, as were proper procedures of urban renewal planning. Alertness on the part of newspapermen with good news sources and investigative ability could have forestalled this accomplished fact.

There are other extensive city projects that have progressed to semifinal stages before the public has been informed. In some cases the citizenry still does not know the origins, backers and real purposes of these plans, so drastically altering the city and the life of its people.

Another quality (always desirable but now becoming essential) that must be cultivated is the ability to see news situations as a whole. Newspapers have treated such vital subjects as urbanization, population growth, taxes, housing, schools, land costs, land use and commuter and automotive traffic as separated subjects and in an incidental or even casual way. Any urban renewal project, for instance, involves some or all of these great public issues.

The unlovely local scene is only a reflection of the national scene. The normal attitude is cynical and political. I find that many reporter and editor "experts" seem to accept this outlook as a matter of course. Yet there is only one agent that can better the dreary picture. It is the newspaper, manned by an alert, experienced and courageous staff.

So we come full circle, back to the training ground—the schools of journalism. What they must review, I think, is the matter of attracting and selecting wisely their raw material. Courses must be reexamined, to make sure that they are designed to train abler general reporters before going on with the training of specialists. The schools may even have to overhaul their faculties to provide seasoned instructors able to encourage and perhaps point the way to the imperative solutions for the newspapers of the future.

When journalists talk among themselves, they trade
memories---of the big or unforgettable stories,
of the problems of their craft, of the teachers who
guided them, of lessons learned.

They reflect, tell anecdotes, sum up.

When he became an editor, says Michael Ogden, he lost forever his chance to achieve the scoop that stops the presses. But then, he ruefully adds, he never quite managed to do so anyway. Mr. Ogden, executive editor of The Providence Journal-Bulletin, *joined* The New York American *immediately after his graduation from Columbia in 1932. From there he went to the old New York City News Association, the slightly seedy enterprise he describes so amusingly here.*

Mr. Ogden was a copy reader for the Bulletin *and news editor of the* Journal *before he became managing editor of the* Journal-Bulletin. *A former captain in the Air Force, he is married and has one son. He lives in Wakefield, Rhode Island.*

MICHAEL J. OGDEN:

The What *Old Days?*

As a newspaperman for more than a quarter of a century, I find it disconcerting to look back and discover that I don't seem to have had a "most interesting experience." What I had could best be described as a pastiche of incidents, any of which had the potential for excitement, but none of which quite made the grade. I'm a big executive editor now, so I don't suppose that I'll ever be given a second chance.

The matters that concern me these days are things like staff morale and how to organize the paper so that we don't wind up with dinky sheets in every section. Additionally, I make speeches and I go to conventions with other editors who are confronted with problems of staff morale and dinky sheets. We exchange views on these subjects and we also pass resolutions favoring freedom of information.

All this despite the fact that I went into newpaper work for the same reasons that moved most of the young men in my class. It was going to be adventuresome and glamorous and the girls would be crazy for us.

Every one of us had read Fowler and Hecht and MacArthur, and I was as ready as the next youth to steal a fire engine, drive a hansom

127

into a hotel lobby, keep an escaped prisoner incommunicado until my paper hit the street, or tie up a telegraph wire by transmitting the Old Testament over it.

I never managed to do anything remotely resembling these ebulliencies. The opportunities may have been there all right, but in my heyday—if that's what it was—I was never the reporter at press conferences who probed with the telling question that made headlines the next day; it was always the man on my right or the one directly ahead of me. Similarly, in the pictures you used to see which were captioned "Newsmen Interview Key Witness," I was the chap on the fringe, the right half of whose face was cropped out for reasons of space.

Many theories could be advanced as to what went wrong in my case. One may be that I wasn't the harum-scarum, hard-drinking, hell-bent type the romantic lore of those days seemed to call for.

Oh, I tried all right. But the single time in the early Thirties when I stepped out of my normally diffident character, it backfired. This was in Tony's, or Luigi's, or some place in Greenwich Village, where a few of us had gone after work of an evening. I had wandered from the group at one point. When I returned, four sturdy, red-faced men appeared to be expressing themselves with unnecessary vigor to one of my fellow-reporters.

I sidled up to the nearest stranger and, neglecting to remove my glasses, growled, "Something the matter, bud?"

Surprisingly, he burst out laughing and nudged the man next to him. "Look who's a tough guy," he said, snorting. Then he pinned my arms to my sides, and he and his companions passed me among them as though I were a totem pole, each planting a noisy kiss on my forehead as I went by. When they put me down, I was still inarticulate, and the friend I had sought to defend introduced me. They were all members of the New York homicide squad.

It took a heap of reporting to obliterate the memory of being kissed by four cops.

That may have been the trauma that set it off. Or it may simply have been the times. We couldn't seem to get out of the depression. In one place where I worked, with relatively few years of reporting and copy desk behind me, I was made managing editor; the pay differential was only $5, but for the $5 I could be taken off the five-day, 40-hour week and be legally permitted to work forever. With the elevation went, I'm afraid, my last chance for adventure.

I had hopes in the beginning, though. After all, I got my start with the legendary New York City News Association. This was as much a part of the legendary New York City scene as the legendary Schwab Mansion and the legendary Collyer Brothers, and survived none of them.

To bring alive the old City News home office near Park Row, you would have to imagine a room not too much larger than your living room. Or, imagine your living room, remove the furniture and replace it with four typewriter desks equipped with headset telephones, a miniature horseshoe-shaped copy desk, a switchboard, a cashier's cage, a general manager's desk, and eight Teletype machines. Then people every visible chair with individuals named Mac.

On my first day at work one of the Macs asked me my age. I promptly said I was 31 (I was 21). He winced and snarled, "Thirty-one! Hell, you're just a baby." At any age into my late fifties I would have been a baby compared to that bunch downtown, but they kept me there only long enough to put me on the payroll. Then they shipped me off to perform the bedrock job of City News—covering police and courts in Manhattan and the Bronx for all New York City newspapers and the wire services.

Somewhere in this vast mélange of opportunities the big chance should have come—but, I don't know . . .

True, I was in on the ground floor of the Hauptmann case. The night he was arrested and lodged in the Bronx County Courthouse I was told to stay with him. What this could mean in an imaginative someone's memoirs is one thing; what it actually meant was that I sat alone in the pressroom all through the night and, to stay awake, read the Manhattan telephone book. When the stars, the take-charge reporters, appeared in the morning I had reached *D'Appolonia-D'Arrigo* (I'm not the world's fastest reader), and that was the end of my connection with the story.

These were stirring times, it will be remembered, on the labor front. What can be said of a typical involvement of mine in that area?

A strike was called at S. Klein's, the mammoth low-priced dress establishment on Union Square. A group of us reporters showed up, interviewed the pickets, then went indoors to get management's side of the dispute.

Management, represented by a worried-looking man with a gardenia in his lapel, said oh dear, but this seemed a matter for Mr. Klein himself to handle. Up to this point, it's doubtful that any of us had considered that there was such a person as S. Klein. I think we had all looked on the name as representing an institution like Yankee Stadium or Interborough Rapid Transit. But we were adjustable; we said okay, we'll speak to him.

Oh, not everyone, said management; what papers did we represent?

We reeled them off—*Sun, Journal, World-Telegram,* etc. When I said City News, he looked at me uncertainly. Did I mean I was the Associated Press, he asked. Well, we serve AP, I told him.

Then *you* speak to Mr. Klein, he said. I looked at the other men and they nodded agreement.

Without another word, management turned and I followed him through a labyrinth of offices, cages, workrooms and corridors until we came to a small door. He opened it, switched on a light and beckoned me in. Then he stepped out and closed the door behind me.

It was a pine-paneled room, subdued under indirect lighting. The only furniture was a small table in the center with a phone resting on its polished surface. There were no chairs.

I waited long moments until I realized no one was coming to join me in the room. Gingerly, I picked up the phone. A voice immediately came on, identifying itself as that of S. Klein.

Dazedly, I carried on my interview. My conversation with the voice of S. Klein lasted perhaps 10 minutes. I must have remembered enough of it to fill in the notes of the reporters who were waiting for me when I was led back, bewildered and almost babbling.

But my heart wasn't in the fruit of my interview. I was completely bemused by the thought that somewhere in this fabulous building, somewhere above the mass of ladies wandering in their slips through downstairs aisles, fighting with their fellow-women for the $6.95 specials, was this mysterious merchant—disembodied, a voice in an earphone in a pine-paneled chamber.

For all I know, there still may be no S. Klein. Goodness knows there are no more $6.95 specials.

Nor does New York cover its police news as it did a generation ago.

In my time, and perhaps for 200 years before, covering Police Headquarters on Center Street meant spending one's days and nights in an old-law tenement behind the sprawling Headquarters building, exchanging complaints with other reporters, intermittently trotting to the police ticker across the street to check on possible stories.

Being the City News man on a job had many drawbacks, both professional and physical. Because City News served all New York newspapers, we had to hit on a dead medium in style; and because the other reporters knew that City News would have to cover every story, no matter what was going on—foul weather, a heated poker game, a crushing hangover—they would generally tip me off to what was going on and then remain behind while I trudged to the scenes of accidents or crimes. They could relax in full confidence that the unwritten law called for me to return and read my notes to all of them. This accomplished, each of us would call our respective city desks and relay the same notes to re-write men.

It was on such a day—a hot August Sunday, when my colleagues were too dispirited to move—that I was in a Mott Street basement, in the heart of Chinatown. The street-level sign attested that this was the office of Wong Foo, Importer, Noodles.

Because I was alone, because it was hot and because, perhaps, of pure oversight, none of the police thronging the little shipping room objected to my presence. I mention this because it has been my experience that, television to the contrary, reporters just don't move in on the scene of a crime and start looking for clues. What they really do is sit on the stoop outside the house where the crime has been committed and look up wistfully each time the door opens in the hope that it might be a detective who will tell them what is going on inside.

But this day I was inside and everyone—detectives, policemen, inter-preter, Wong Foo's assistant, and I—looked vaguely around the room and back to the desk where Wong Foo had been sitting when someone had fired four shots into him.

During the long interval of silence I noticed what appeared to be bits of glass on the desk blotter. When no one else spoke up, I asked the detective in charge whether the murdered man had worn glasses. He con-sidered my question, then turned to the interpreter and, pointing at Wong Foo's uneasy assistant, said, "Ask him."

The interpreter spoke rapidly in Chinese, received his answer and turned back to the detective: "He says no."

For a moment, I thought I saw a flicker in the detective's eyes. I even sensed a quickening of interest in the uniformed men. If the murdered man hadn't worn glasses, then the killer must have. In that case, the science laboratories at Headquarters could check the broken pieces. It would be simple enough to obtain the prescription, the opticians in Chinatown could be combed and who knew but . . .?

I was mentally shaping the modesty with which I would accept the congratulations of the other reporters, the respect with which the police would regard me in the future. I was even returning the firm handshake and brushing off the hearty thanks of then Commissioner Valentine, when the detective said to the interpreter, "Ask him for a dust broom so I can sweep up the glass on the desk."

I watched the expressionless face of the interpreter as he put the request, noted the equally blank face on Wong Foo's assistant when he responded.

Then the interpreter said, "This is not glass, he says. This is cellophane covering for noodle boxes."

The detective looked at me. The policemen looked at me. One of them nodded over his shoulder. I shrugged, walked out and sat on the stoop.

For Howard Dietz, a member of the celebrated Class of '17, journalism was the first step up to a brilliant theatrical and motion-picture career. A vice president of Metro-Goldwyn-Mayer (which he joined as publicity director shortly after leaving Columbia), Mr. Dietz is the author of the lyrics and librettos for some twenty Broadway shows and two operas.

His musical comedies include "Dear Sir" (with Jerome Kern), "Merry-Go-Round" (with classmate Morrie Ryskind), "The Little Show" and the "Second Little Show," "Three's A Crowd," "Bandwagon" (with George S. Kaufman) and "Revenge With Music." He lives with his wife, Lucinda, in Sands Point, Long Island, New York.

HOWARD DIETZ:

Fragments of a Preface

The same thing happened to me that happened to many Class of 1917 students at the Columbia School of Journalism—they learned the jargon of journalism, they became facile through journalism, but when they left the School they didn't practice journalism. Some became advertising men, some became publishers, some became song writers or librettists, some became press agents, some even became bankers. But few became journalists.

If you call a copy boy a journalist, then I was a journalist before I entered the School. The city editor of *The New York American,* Justin McGrath, had a friendly feeling for me and thought my lack of knowledge could be corrected. Mr. McGrath urged me to try for the School of Journalism. When one considers that I had gone to Townsend Harris Hall for only two years, it was a tall order. But when the editor implied that the copy-boy-turned-student might also become the Columbia campus correspondent, the order became not quite so tall.

The gap between high school and college meant an austerity program incompatible with my cavalier disposition. But I had company, notably

133

my solid, solemn, brilliant block-mate, Merryle Stanley Rukeyser, who
was certain to pass. The future financial editor of all the Hearst papers
predicted, "When I'm graduated from the School of Journalism I intend
to become a great financial editor." I retailed this offensive prediction
to Herman J. Mankiewicz, the campus wit, who said "That's the difference between Ruk and me. Before I entered Journalism I *used* to be
a great financial editor."

The star in the faculty during my time at the School was the late
Charles Austin Beard. I decided that his was going to be a tedious course
—until the Professor got started. He leaned his back against a window,
his head on the venetian blinds, his eyes closed, and he said with the
cadence of a metronome, "Today we are going to take up the budget in
state government. Now I am sure that this will sound to you like a very
dull subject. But if you will tell me how much a government spends on
its army, its navy and its public works, I will tell you as much about the
people of that state as if you gave me the output of its philosophers and
poets." Beard was in.

He didn't make me a Rukeyser, though, or any other kind of journalist. I never gave the School of Journalism a chance. I left in the third
year, having listened to Opportunity knocking. In fact, at every stage
in my educational experience I listened to Opportunity—except at
public school where my configuration was somewhat altered, and where
I received a diploma that made me eligible to enter (and then leave)
high school. I wrote some verses around grade-school graduation time
that made a comment on the system:

> At public school I made no sense
> But learned the art of self-defense;
> From kindergarten to 6B
> I went to P.S. 103,
> And what with all the cons and pros
> I left there with a broken nose.
>
> Continuing the local war,
> I went to P.S. 24;
> My tongue as usual was glib
> I left there with a broken rib.
>
> I went to P.S. 165,
> The only ones who there survive
> Are those whom Darwin termed the "fittest"
> The students who the hardest hittest;
> I left there with a souvenir
> A slightly cauliflowered ear.

> I held my end up, if you please,
> With several Pyrrhic victories;
> It's give and take, the golden rule,
> At any New York public school.

The knock that ended my stay at the School of Journalism was the fabulous windfall of 1916, when I won an advertising contest and the $500 prize. Stout Cortez may have stood on a peak in Darien looking at some new planet swimming into his ken, but nothing can compare with my ken when it was swam into on an April morning by the Liggett and Myers Tobacco Company. My problems seemed all cleared, with something left over for an impersonation of a not-so-sober sailor. As I recall it (not total this recall), I took a great number of classmates, as guests of my windfall, to Lorber's or Gertner's or some such restaurant where you got all you could eat for a dollar and a quarter. As I remember, Bennett Cerf was one of my guests.

Everyone thought the advertisement I had submitted was preposterous, and so did I. It showed two gentlemen on a roof garden with palm trees. One chap was disconsolate over the prospect of spending a dull evening in these stilted surroundings. "Isn't this a stupid affair?" he said to his more enthusiastic companion. Whereupon the enthusiastic companion offered him a cigarette. "Do you think so?" he said. "Then have a Fatima."

Good or bad, what cared I? But to my surprise I received offers of jobs from various advertising agencies. I thought I'd better accept one of the offers, since later I might be a drug on the market. Besides, there was a war on the horizon and I wanted to enlist in the Navy so that I could write saltwater ballads. If I took a job now, it might be kept open for me when the war was over. I accepted the Philip Goodman Company offer because Goodman had a literary turn which appealed aesthetically. He particularly knew a lot about Boswell and Dr. Johnson. He owned a first edition of *Rasselas,* and used to eat as though he were in some Mermaid Tavern washing the food down with ale. Such things can affect a young man.

Later on Goodman became a theatrical producer. He produced Don Marquis' "The Old Soak" as well as my first musical, "Dear Sir," in which Jerome Kern took a chance on my lyrics. He also became a publisher, publishing George Jean Nathan, H. L. Mencken, Benjamin de Casseres and Arthur Hopkins, the producer and director.

I had a faint influence on Goodman's enterprise. The first assignment I received was to create a trademark for the newly-formed Goldwyn Pictures Corporation. In other words—Sam Goldwyn. Having just come

from Columbia and having been on the staff of *Jester,* I felt partial to
the lion. Goodman called in a commercial artist to make a lion's head
and I supplied some words from a Latin insignia. "ARS GRATIA ARTIS"
sounded right, but I've never been sure. I was willing, however, to apply
the capsule philosophy learned extra-curricularly from the late Frank
Tinney, the comedian.

The Old Grad will remember Tinney's performance with Vernon
Castle in Irving Berlin's "Watch Your Step." He had a special method
(there is a "method" in musical comedy, too) of telling a joke. It was
to explain the joke with full significance before he actually told it, and it
was not too far from Professor Walter B. Pitkin explaining the shadow
world of Plato—except that Tinney commanded more attention. He
said to Castle: "Vernon, I feel a joke coming on and you'll just have to
be used. I'll see how good a dancer acts." "Very well, Frank, if you
think I have Thespian traits." "I don't know about your traits, but in this
joke you go off-stage and come on again saying 'Good Morning, Frank,'
and then I tell the joke." "What joke?" asked Vernon. "Never you mind,"
said Frank, "just go off and come on like I told you." So Castle went off
and came on saying "Good Morning, Frank. How are you feeling today?" *"Don't improve it!"* said the seemingly exasperated Tinney.

*Matthew Gordon "lived" the U. N. in his post
as head of press services for the United Nations
Secretariat for fifteen and a half years. The Saturday Review said that "the operation which Mr.
Gordon organized and directed is unique in the
annals of journalism," and expressed doubt that
the U. N. would ever again have "so powerful a
press figure." The late Secretary General of the
U. N., Dag Hammarskjöld, wrote Mr. Gordon
that ". . . your talent, professional experience
and skill have contributed in an important way
to the successful conduct of the work of the organization."*

*Matthew Gordon left the United Nations in
1955, and has since become director of information of Communications Satellite Coporation. He
is a member of Columbia Journalism's class of
'32.*

MATTHEW GORDON:

Vertical Town on the River

Events of high drama and melodrama have been routine in the history
of the United Nations, but the "heads of state" assembly—the Fifteenth
Session of the General Assembly, held in the fall of 1960—was excep-
tional by any standards.

The vertical town on the East River was jammed with more newsmen
than had ever before covered a U.N. meeting, drawn there by an un-
precedented concentration of headline-makers—Tito, Nehru, Nasser,
Gomulka and Castro, for example, and Nkrumah, Sukarno, Macmillan,
Eisenhower and Khrushchev.

Some will remember the meeting because of the antics of the Soviet
premier—the two-fisted table thumping, the bitter banging of a shoe.
Others will also recall the sudden mass descent of the Cuban delegation
on the U.N. after their surprise exodus from a midtown hotel; Castro
and his followers threatened to camp out on the U.N. grounds before
deciding finally to move on to a Harlem hotel.

After all the self-conscious tumult and shouting had died, however, and after the heads of state and the dictators had departed, the effects of this session traveled on: Khrushchev had mounted a head-on attack against the person of Dag Hammarskjöld and the office of the Secretary-General, and for the U.N. a period of strain and trial had begun. Powerful forces battered into the inner structure of the organization, setting fundamental and irreversible changes in motion. Among them, for instance, was the bringing to the fore of national and political distinctions as criteria for the international secretariat, replacing the hitherto paramount charter requirement for efficiency and integrity.

Fourteen newly-emergent African nations were scheduled to take their seats at this session, with Nigeria to follow shortly thereafter. This audience of new voters presented Khrushchev with perhaps his chief impetus for making the journey to New York. And when he decided to come, so decided those in his orbit, and thereupon other heads of state were inspired to participate in the international act scheduled to take place on the spotlighted U.N. stage.

When the members of the cast became known, applications and importunity funneled into the U.N. press offices from news organizations all over the world. Everyone from every county and country wanted, as a matter of course, to have maximum access to the news and the newsmakers, plus maximum facilities for disseminating the resulting reports, photographs and films. And everyone, naturally, was more equal than everyone else.

Since I was in charge of press services of the Secretariat, it was my job and the aim of my international staff to meet as many of these requests as possible—to admit all the journalists unstretchable space would accommodate, to enable them to gain access to the delegates, to help newcomers learn the ground rules, and somehow to do all this within a framework of rigid security and amidst the crowding which security abhors.

At that time the hard core of journalists providing daily U.N. coverage was perhaps fifty. For this session we were to accredit 1,600 media representatives to the building. Each of them had to be identified, photographed and cleared in accordance with security regulations imposed by both the U.N. and by suspicious security men accompanying the various heads of state. A prime difficulty in accomplishing this stemmed from the natural reluctance of journalists to stand in line or to conform with regulations or to follow any "standard" procedures.

Since not even the delegates had enough room (the second-floor North Lounge was always packed, with a television monitor placed there for the convenience of delegates who couldn't make it to the Assembly Hall), logistics were our chief problem. The familiar third-floor press area—known as the "bull pen" or the "corrida de los toros" —was extended as far as we could go down the corridor outside the third-floor entrances to the Security Council, Trusteeship Council and Economic and Social Council. And since we couldn't wedge even a substantial fraction of those accredited into the Assembly Hall for the really major convocations, closed-circuit television receivers had to be set up in supplemental press areas. We also extended our public address system, over which we made continual, multi-lingual announcements of press conferences, names of speakers at the rostrum, availability of press releases, translations, and so on. The best way to cover the Assembly, it seemed to me, was not to be present in the Hall.

Reporters had to be given access to the delegates. We went through various stages in this effort. First we issued a number of non-transferable special-access cards for accredited correspondents; that proved insufficient. Then we worked out a system of shared allocation within nationality groups, but competition strained the cooperative spirit among the shareholders. Finally we evolved a system of transferable passes that probably unnerved the security people but aided (and sometimes amused) us. I recall giving Marquis Childs a lounge-access card that attested to the fact that he was a member of the Turkish press. Allen Drury, then covering for *Reader's Digest,* became a pro-tem Danish correspondent. In any event, the systems worked: The lead article in the October 1 *Editor and Publisher* was gratifyingly headlined: UN PRESS OFFICE MEETS CHALLENGE WITH INGENUITY: *Amid Necessary Restrictions, System Gives A Break To All.*

One continually baffling problem was the traffic and crush that developed when Khrushchev or Castro or one of the other headliners moved out of the prescribed area. Khrushchev moved in nondescript ensemble. If he went one way, a tide moved in that direction. If he stepped off in another, the tide shifted. If he stopped to chat with someone, the crowd swelled. Newsmakers were followed down halls, up escalators, and into men's rooms.

Castro and his men were a particular worry. Some were, as they put it, "in disguise"—clean-shaven. They were aggressive, sensitive—and armed. And if they did not like a line of questioning or the manner of the correspondent who was doing the questioning, things could get exceedingly tense. There was one specific instance in which U. N. security forces had to intervene to rescue a visiting *Chicago Tribune* correspondent.

With the heads-of-state part of the assembly finally over, the news pressure was reduced, but Soviet pressure on the Secretary-General continued with boycott, needle and harassment. The Soviet demanded key spots in the Secretariat and got some of them at least. The pressure on the international Secretariat and the merit system mounted. The pressure on Dag Hammarskjöld occupied his mind and time in continuous contest until his death by plane crash in Africa just before the Sixteenth Session of the Assembly.

I joined the U. N. in March of 1946 as a consultant, asked to help set up and organize a Department of Information. I agreed with one proviso: that it be understood that I would stay for only a few months, since I had other plans. The next time I looked up from my work it was September, 1961.

During this time there must have been some quiet periods, but these fade from memory. What I recall now are such times of intensity as the parallel Suez-Hungary crises. Then there were no hours, and we all went on in perpetual motion. Dag Hammarskjöld worked all the time, and night was better than day, and we followed his example because we had to. A favorite running gag then—it was the fall of 1956—was that we had regular hours at last, nine to five. Nine A.M. to five A.M.

Before the U.N. settled on the East River site, it had its temporary headquarters at Lake Success and Flushing Meadow. During Assembly periods these were used simultaneously, with much shuttling back and forth between twin press set-ups. Flushing was for plenary sessions; Lake Success, home base, was used for meetings of committees and the Security Council.

We did not have any interior public address system of the sort incorporated into the Manhattan headquarters for simultaneous notification to various press offices in the building. So we got an old ship's bell, hung it next to our press documents counter, and rang it whenever we wanted to inform the press that a new press release was to be had or a press briefing was to be held. I think we tapped it lightly for a minor press release and really hit the gong when there was urgent need to summon everyone for a press briefing.

We inaugurated a system of "running" news coverage of such meetings as the Security Council or the First (or Political) Committee of the Assembly. Our staff was trained to report the story in "takes," issuing stories in progressive stages as the news developed, thus providing increasingly complete accounts as the meetings progressed.

Not all correspondents who came to the U.N. were conversant with news terminology. We know of at least one occasion when a seeker of information came to our press documents counter and followed directions literally. Where it said "Take one," he took one copy; for "Take two," he took two; and so on up to and including "Take fifteen." Our press distribution was uneven that day.

The methods which the U.N. press services used at Lake Success and Flushing, and later in New York—and at the two assemblies in Paris as well—were really decided upon at the outset of the U. N.'s appearance in the United States. It may come as a surprise to most people, but the U.N. actually began its operations in the Spring of 1946 in New York City at 610 Fifth Avenue, Rockefeller Center. Here Secretary-General Trygve Lie had his office, and here we organized the set-up and arrangements for press coverage in the converted gymnasium at Hunter College in the Bronx, where the first meeting of the Security Council in the United States were held. A day or so after Andrei A. Gromyko walked out during the Iranian case, a private meeting of the Council was held at 610 Fifth to consider the situation. There was a prevalent Council thought that Gromyko might show up at this private meeting. He did get into his chauffeur-driven car and he actually drove down Fifth Avenue, trailed by some reporters. But finally he rode by, went along the Avenue a piece, and then drove back on the other side.

The first international meetings on control of atomic energy began at Hunter College on June 14, 1946, with Bernard Baruch's statement that "We are here to make a choice between the quick and the dead." There was very heavy press attendance and strong news interest. But there was a lack of understanding between the U.S. and the U.S.S.R. even then, and these efforts at atomic energy control were in early deadlock.

I remember one instance when Dr. J. Robert Oppenheimer directed his remarks to the Soviet scientist, Dmitri V. Skobeltsyn, declaring:

"We have a law in the state of Iowa that says that when two trains come from opposite directions on the same track, one train must stand aside at the crossing to let the other train pass. Do you understand that?"

After it was translated for him, Professor Skobeltsyn asked:

"Why is it necessary to have such a law?"

The news handling of these scientific meetings, held in the shadow of the first mushroom clouds, was a matter of sensitivity for the U.S. representatives, who were enjoined from giving away any secret information. We were then sole proprietors of The Bomb. The meetings began in lecture style, with Oppenheimer drawing a flow chart of the atomic energy project on the blackboard. At one point in that diagram, an X was put in. For nuclear fission there was U-235, enriched uranium, plutonium—and X. All the scientists in the room (and they included Australians and British who had worked on the bomb project in the U.S.) knew what X was. Finally, the U.S. scientists got the official go-ahead and announced that they were now authorized to disclose that X was U-233—thorium. No scientist present had been enlightened. At the end of the meeting I went to the blackboard and drew tic-tac-toe lines around the "X." Someone put in an "O," and we were off. The Australian scientist drew an Australian game, and then the Nationalist Chinese added their contribution. The Soviet scientist, who was getting ready to leave, saw the group around the blackboard and instead of going out rushed forward and peered at the new equations on the board.

He finally decided that, though it was puzzling, it was certainly no major contribution to the state of Soviet atomic knowledge.

Although no one, Frank Scully remarks, is giving him a birthday party, he has led a full literary life in the 50 years since he first entered the newly-opened doors of the Columbia School of Journalism, from which he was graduated in 1917.

Mr. Scully, Hollywood correspondent for Va-riety, has written many magazine articles and some twenty books, including Cross My Heart, This Gay Knight *and* In Armour Bright. *Mr. Scully is himself a Knight of the Order of St. Elizabeth (founded by Isabella of Spain for Elizabeth of Hungary) as well as a Knight of the Order of St. Gregory the Great. Mr. Scully, who is married and has five children, lives in Palm Springs, California.*

FRANK SCULLY:

A Story for the Occasion

On April 28, 1963, I was 71—a full 21 years older than the Columbia School of Journalism. In honor of its attainment, the school is being feted in this book—and, presumably, will also receive endowments, scholarships and new blackboard erasers.

But what about Scully? For years I have been impressed with how other persons reaching such milestones as the biblical age of seventy have been made the warm and nostalgic vehicle of some big charity event, or joshed by the Friars, the Lambs or the Elks, and awarded Georgie Jessel as Roastmaster General. Although I read the chatter columns faithfully throughout 1962, I saw no hint that any such thing was going to happen to me. And it didn't. In 1962 I performed my habitual writing stints for *Variety* and other magazines, and I wrote a book of 140,000 words, but no books were written about me and there were no televised banquets.

I am grateful to Columbia. It has given me a place to tell a joke. It gave me a great many other things too, useful in my profession—but this is a joke that cost me $3,000, and you never heard it before, so don't stop me.

143

About five years ago a covey of doctors found that I had an aneurysm of the aorta, a bulging of the heart's main artery which might blow out at any minute. Some were sure surgery could help. Others advised a long layoff, maybe for the rest of my life. All agreed, however, that if I could get to a certain Dr. Michael De Bakey (a Lebanese who looks much like Danny Thomas but operates better) he might save me. But how, you ask, could a bum like me get to a man like De Bakey?

How? I'll tell you how. I wrote him a letter at the Methodist Hospital in Houston. (I'm a Catholic but no bigot, and in the physical world I play the field.) I wrote the letter and air-mailed it from Palm Springs on Friday. My guardian angel must have marked it "Special Delivery" because the next day, Saturday morning, Dr. De Bakey, in person, called me from Texas.

If I came down a week from the following Tuesday he would fix me up. "The main thing is to repair that aorta. If you can pay the hospital bill, that's your only immediate worry." And that's all there was to it.

When I got to Houston I didn't know a soul there. The last time I had been in the town was in 1925, when its population was 75,000. Now it was 1,200,000, not counting me and milady Alice. But unlike *Variety,* those newspapers down there have morgues. They found that I had been a patient in 39 hospitals in seven countries and was now honoring Houston with a 40th opening. The interviews were front-paged with run-overs.

One editor said he left my room in tears. "The poor guy," he told a doctor. "He has a typewriter under his bed. He won't be able to cough even a comma for six months, if he lives."

In a way he was right. I couldn't write a line for six months, but that was because the De Bakey team spent three hours cruising around my wide-open gizzards snipping off everything except dangling participles. Then they inserted about nine inches of Dacron porous tubing in place of the bulging aorta. Finally they sewed me up and waited for nature to accept the Dacron as a friend of the family.

Dacron, of course, is a duPont product. It's the only duPont stock I own, but it is sewed in and regardless of what happens in Wall Street I can't lose it.

That's how I got my joke.

I was swimming not long ago. A doctor saw me and shouted, "What are you doing in that pool, you crazy guy?"

I came up for air and said, "I'm *watering* my stock."

Now if someone had honored my seventieth or seventy-first birthday, I'd have found a place for a gag like that, wouldn't I?

Herbert Brucker, editor of The Hartford Courant, *was elected president of the American Society of Newspaper Editors in 1963. He is the author of three books about the newspaper business: "The Changing American Newspaper," "Freedom of Information" and "Journalist: Eyewitness to History.*

A recipient of a Pulitzer Traveling Scholarship upon his graduation from the School in 1924, Mr. Brucker returned to Columbia Journalism to serve with the faculty for 12 years. In 1959 he received the John Peter Zenger award of the University of Arizona, and in 1961 the Yankee Quill award from the New England Society of Newspaper Editors. Mr. Brucker lives with his wife in Avon, Connecticut.

HERBERT BRUCKER:

The World

Looking back through the fog of almost four decades to my days as a beginning reporter, in New York, I can still see a light: *The World.* And THE *World* it was—not *The Morning World,* as some had it. There were, to be sure, an *Evening World,* a *Sunday World* and a syndicate. But they existed only to make money. What counted was the heart and soul of the operation at 63 Park Row, and that was *The World.*

As a student in Columbia's School of Journalism I had learned to look upon *The World* with awe. Here was the monument erected by the man who had founded our school. Here was the model of all that was exciting and all that was noblest in journalism. The paper's reporting was a model of Joseph Pulitzer's command of terseness, and of his three rules for reporters: accuracy, accuracy, and accuracy! On the editorial page and on the Page Opposite, that unique invention of *The World,* there was wit, comment, and insight into the day's affairs—and in a concentration that has not since been matched.

No wonder any student of journalism, or any other young newspaper

145

hopeful, dreamed that one day he too might be one of this happy company. Thanks to William Beazell, assistant managing editor who did some part-time teaching in journalism at Columbia, I was hired as a reporter. So at 1 P.M. on the day appointed I entered that hallowed city room on the 12th floor—or was it on the 11th? I was assigned to a desk next to a young fellow named Frank Sullivan, whose ability to turn a routine birth at the zoo or a politician's picnic into hilarity had already given him bylines on local stories (and such bylines were hard to come by in those days). On the other side sat the elderly J. Otis Swift, organizer of the Yosians, a group devoted to exploring the beauties of nature in and about Manhattan. Beyond him was C. B. Allen, himself a pilot, assigned to cover aviation when there was any of it to cover in those days before Lindbergh.

The time was 1925. Already the great *World* building was growing dingy. Its golden dome was tarnished, its walls were covered with lower Manhattan soot. But nobody minded that. The desks were of familiar yellowed oak. The décor was old hat. But then, those were primitive days. Not long before I had sat in the hot emptiness of the news room of *The Morning Union* in Springfield, on an August Sunday afternoon, listening to the clack-clack of the old Morse instruments that brought in the news in those days. Suddenly the operator who could read those sounds shouted through the stillness, "Harding is dead!"

In those days, too, crowds used to stand in the street outside newspaper offices as telegraphed bulletins from distant places were shouted through a megaphone. And one of my early assignments on *The World* was to cover the crowd that stood outside 63 Park Row, on the afternoon the World Series began, to watch the game replayed in skeleton form on a miniature mechanical diamond on the building's facade, as the play-by-play account was flashed in from the game itself.

We didn't know then that such newspaper mechanics would soon be old-fashioned. All we saw was the incandescent light that seemed to glow in the staff, giving the daily printed product a vitality and spirit that had to be felt in its own time to be understood. Joseph Pulitzer had been dead for a decade and a half, yet his paper lived on as he had taught it—never letting the counting room influence the news room to the slightest degree. *The World* still was what he had said it should be:

"An institution that should always fight for progress and reform, never tolerate injustice or corruption, always fight demagogues of all parties, never belong to any party, always oppose privileged classes and public plunderers, never lack sympathy with the poor, always remain devoted to the public welfare, never be satisfied with merely printing news, always be drastically independent, never be afraid to attack wrong, whether by predatory plutocracy or predatory poverty."

So it was that our boss told every newcomer, "We have no sacred cows." The boss, as far as we were concerned, was, of course, that race-track devotee Herbert Bayard Swope—erect, ruddy, a big-chested bundle of energy who, as a reporter, had won for *The World* the very first Pulitzer Prize in reporting.

Gradually one got to know who was who; gradually one realized that the journalistic greats with whom one was rubbing elbows were human beings. One day I went to the little window that memory tells me guarded what would now be the library but was then the morgue. There, waiting for the desired dusty envelope of clips, was an unimpressive fellow in shirt sleeves, a cigar stump in his mouth. This, I learned, was F.P.A., the Franklin P. Adams who made his "Conning Tower" column a daily must for intellectual New York. And that great mountain of a fellow in rumpled clothes in the nearby cubbyhole was Heywood Broun. Now and again duty led me up into the sacred dome itself, and there one might see a clean-cut, youthful Ivy League type who presided as editor over the cleanest, punchiest, most literate and most reliable editorial page of the day—Walter Lippmann.

In the corridors and in the news room one would run into the whole galaxy that lit up the Page Opposite: not only Heywood Broun or F.P.A. or William Bolitho, but also Laurence Stallings, Alexander Woollcott, Samuel Chotzinoff, Allison Smith, Wells Root. And so in the news room, where an awed newcomer realized that in one sense he was now the equal of the top reporters of that day: Oliver H. P. Garrett, Ernest K. Lindley, Dudley Nichols, Henry Pringle, and all the rest.

In a corner of the room on a raised platform was the city desk and the attendant assistants' desks, presided over by the owlish Jim Barrett, who after the death of *The World* (which he vainly tried to save with employees' dollars and enthusiasm) ran that extraordinary phenomenon of the battle between newspapers and the upstart radio, the Press-Radio Bureau. There too sat the kindly Alex Schlosser, who kept things going and took an interest in new reporters.

I had heard tales of the barking type of city editor. They didn't have that kind on *The World*. Alex used to inquire of a recruit, as the weeks went by, what kind of assignment he would like best. So when the chance came I could tag along with the top political reporters, and watch in fascination as a campaigning Al Smith impatiently thrust aside the unaccustomed microphone on the table before him. This gesture spoiled the broadcast, but it let the old pro talk directly to the crowd, as was the custom in that day before speeches were prepared for delivery by ghost writers. Or I could see Jimmy Walker, the well-dressed mayor who introduced tomato juice for breakfast after the Prohibition night before. All through the campaign, at rally after rally, he would have to stand and listen as some beery tenor or hard-faced soprano rendered his own "Will you love me in December as you did in May?"

At night there was the helping hand of Joe Canavan, another bluff-outside, soft-hearted-inside type who saw to it that a young fellow wasn't frightened but was helped along.

No doubt in those days the mighty *World* was already on its way to the rendezvous with death that came just six years later. But we didn't know it, did not even dream it might ever be. The paper seemed lustier, livelier, more scintillating and more inspiring than ever.

By the time *The World* was sold I had left it. But like everyone else who had worked there or still worked there at the end, I felt that it had been betrayed, murdered for profit. Now, looking back upon those times, one can see that an earlier society had bequeathed to the New York of the Depression too many newspapers. *The World,* for all its integrity and all its spirit, had neither that combination of skill and raffishness that was to give *The New York Daily News* the biggest circulation in the country, nor that relentless devotion to getting and publishing *all* the news that has made *The New York Times* unique among the world's newspapers. Something had to give, and included in what gave was *The World.*

With it went a kind of journalistic life's blood that this country and its newspapers could well use today. This was the net distillation that comes out of telling the news as one can best find it out, exactly as it is, with no punches pulled no matter whether the great or the rich or the powerful like it. As Walter Lippmann put it at the end of his valedictory editorial:

"Farewell! Let the last words of the *World* be those of Mr. Valiant-for-Truth in *The Pilgrim's Progress:*

" 'Though with great difficulty I am got thither, yet now I do not repent me of all the trouble I had been at to arrive where I am. My sword I give to him that shall succeed me in my pilgrimage, and my courage and skill to him that can get it.' "

Today, when a newspaper is bought, the buyer cares nothing and pays nothing for good will. All that counts is tangible assets—real estate, mechanical equipment, and such other things as one can see or touch or turn in for ready cash. Yet a newspaper should be something more than that. And *The World's* light still shines across the years to tell us how incomparably much more it can do.

*Allan Keller has been praised elsewhere in these
pages for his contributions as an adjunct professor
at the School of Journalism. A winner of many
awards, he has traveled widely as a reporter; but
it is for his day-to-day feature coverage of New
York in* The New York World-Telegram and Sun
that he is best known.

Mr. Keller is the author of Thunder at Harper's
Ferry, Morgan's Raid *and* Grandma's Cooking,
and co-author with Anne Putnam of Madami. *He
is married to the former Ima Elberfeld, and is the
father of two married daughters. Mr. Keller graduated from the School of Journalism in 1926, and
served with the U.S. Navy during World War II
as a commander.*

ALLAN KELLER:
Having Wonderful Time . . .

A man can have a wonderful time as a newspaper writer. We ought
to noise this fact around, proclaiming it proudly, if we want to attract
talented young people to journalism.

I can sum up the case for a career as a news man with one question:
Will someone tell me how many other life pursuits there are that pay
a man to travel the world, to look at new things and places, to go to
sea, to fly in tomorrow's planes, to inspect industrial complexes, to talk
to men and women with great minds, to watch history being made,
close-up?

I go back a long way. Back to a time when the Lindberghs, Alcocks,
Byrds, Chamberlains and Acostas were making their perilous flights
across the Atlantic in planes resembling orange crates with Model-T
engines. If a wife phoned around in search of her husband, some other
reporter might flippantly—or quite correctly—reply: "He was last seen
flying low over Halifax, Nova Scotia." And before I'm through, that
answer might just possibly be: "He was last seen leaving the launching-
pad at Canaveral."

There are times when newspaper life is dull, of course; when the

149

death watch on a prominent figure keeps you waiting in the bitter cold, when an investigation drags on in court or when a stint on the desk makes you almost envy insurance adjustors, bank cashiers and manufacturers. When I began, the nights seemed uniformly long. Waiting at police stations, standing in the snow at fires, watching the drab processional of the night courts, viewing the mutilated victims of wrecks and gangfights in the emergency ward at Bellevue. Or eating wet turkey a la king and soggy vegetables at dinners where men who should have known better talked for hours and said nothing; wolfing hamburgers on the run at Thanksgiving; touring the night spots on New Year's Eve, but staying sober, to earn the right to spend the next day at home with one's family. And wondering again and again why the best stories so often happened on the wind-swept docks or in the Jersey meadows or at Sheepshead Bay, miles from the nearest telephone.

But all things change—with experience—and the long climb out of anonymity brings the moment when the reporter suddenly senses that half a million people are reading today what he wrote yesterday. And above his words is—his name. Perhaps there's a touch of hemlock in the realization that his grocer won't accept a front-page story with a 14-point byline in exchange for a yeast cake, but time erases that trauma.

For me time brought the ugly fascination of the Lindbergh case and the trial of Bruno Hauptmann with its tension, color and excitement. Here were Damon Runyon, Kathleen Norris, Adela Rogers St. John, Stanley Walker, Courtney Riley Cooper—the trained seals—floundering about where less famous men, veterans in the field, walked with sure step.

I watched Hauptmann die in the electric chair. It wasn't a pretty thing to see, but a reporter goes where he is sent. Harry Ferguson and I wrote our stories with the help of a pint of applejack apiece, and when the dawn came and the stories were marked "end" it was as if we had drunk well water.

In the years that followed there were floods in New England, where reporting had to wait while we helped people out of second-floor windows, where Coast Guard cutters nosed ten-story-tanks of gasoline out of the rampaging Connecticut onto the flats below Hartford. There were hurricanes, when a man drove almost blind to get the story of New London in flames or of Winsted with its heart ripped out by a stream justly called the Mad River.

Better communities are the result when newspapermen help fight greed and oppression. Compensation for this never runs high. Sometimes there are awards and prizes, but the best remuneration is the feeling that comes when a reporter walks into a city hall or a courthouse or any place where opportunistic politicians, land sharks, racketeers and venal officials congregate, and senses that these evil men fear him and the big black ribbons of type in his paper more than they fear the police or courts.

Cincinnati and Milwaukee have possibly the best police forces in the country, and so I traveled from New York to the Midwest to see how my city could improve its department. When the war in Europe cast its shadows here, I toured the Army camps to see merchants and teachers and soda jerks and farmers being trained in the art of battle. Organized vice flourished at the gates of many of these camps, and I helped, with investigations and articles, to clean it out. There was tyranny and oppression in the potato patches and truck farms of New York; and there was danger in those fields, too, where greedy men ruled little empires with shotguns. But the work of the journalist was done, and new statutes were put on the books. And there were other crusades—to end fraud in crooked charity drives, to keep thieves out of the public till, to stop the sale and purchase of justice in the courts, to stanch graft in highway and construction, in housing and public bidding.

Or if it's fun you want . . . There was the morning spent with Katharine Hepburn talking of the stage and Siamese cats; an afternoon when Mary Astor entertained me with her piano playing just to convince me that she, not a double, had been at the keyboard in a movie. There was the day when Marilyn Monroe broke her bra strap at a press conference. There were interviews with strip-tease artists and opera singers, with clowns and comics, nights at the horse show and previews of the circus, birthdays with Bernard Baruch and talks with Winston Churchill. There were flights to South America and voyages to Europe, trips on tankers and in freighters and even in a railroad caboose.

There was a film director who wanted to grouse about how temperamental Bette Davis was, and a press agent who tried to prevent it by keeping my highball glass filled. How could he know I was pouring the Scotch into the tub that held a rubber plant? But I'll wager the hotel people knew a few days later.

Who but a reporter gets to travel with a tent carnival for a week, and gets paid for it? Who else watches skating stars train on the ice rink at Atlantic City, or is the first passenger on a piggy-back train, or accompanies lighthouse tenders as they make their rounds, or inspects bourbon distilleries in Kentucky, or can dive in submarines? Only a newspaperman.

In the trade papers and at solemn academic meetings I learn that
there is an urgent need to recruit more young men and women for
careers in journalism. I suspect that the fault is ours. Perhaps we
haven't told them what we know to be true: Men in other professions
may make more money. But which of them can look back over the
years and find the stars so bright and the sun so warm?

A co-founder of Simon and Schuster in 1924, M. Lincoln Schuster is now president, editor-in-chief and chairman of the editorial board of the publishing firm. He was a member of the Columbia Journalism Class of 1917.

Mr. Schuster began his career as a copy boy on The New York Evening World *but, as he points out here, was drawn from the very beginning to "creative publishing." (In 1961 he received the Carey-Thomas Award for Creative Publishing, along with the Journalism Alumni Award.) Fittingly, for a man who started out on a Pulitzer newspaper and in a Pulitzer-founded journalism school, Mr. Schuster has lived for the past twenty-five years in the building that was once Joseph Pulitzer's New York City home—a Stanford White palazzo now cooperatively owned.*

M. LINCOLN SCHUSTER:

Fifty Years—A Personal View

The Class of 1917 had the good fortune to reach Columbia University at one of the great turning points in modern history. An old world—the century from Waterloo to the First World War—was ending. The lights were going out in Europe; a new world was about to be born.

When we arrived as freshmen at Morningside Heights in September, 1913, to begin the first full four-year course at the School of Journalism, there were giants on the University faculty—John Dewey, James Harvey Robinson and Charles A. Beard, to name just three. A brilliant group of top-flight newspapermen like Robert E. MacAlarney and Franklin Matthews formed the first Journalism faculty. The greatest city in the world and a world in upheaval served as our classroom. And as students in that classroom, we were not only learning a craft, but were also building our training on the firm foundation of the humanities and the liberal arts, taught and interpreted by towering men.

The School of Journalism was a bold new concept, a radical and

153

untested experiment, and, by a process of natural selection, most of us were therefore dissenters, nonconformists, volunteers for this experiment, adventurers on the road opened by Joseph Pulitzer's dream—*to make journalism a learned profession and to keep it a free one.* The class was so small—about thirty of us in the first year—that we were able to learn almost as much from one another as we did from our teachers and our books. Professor Walter B. Pitkin's courses in philosophy and psychology uncovered new windows on the world, stirring us so deeply that we asked him to conduct a supplementary series of lectures and Socratic dialogues after academic hours. One of our classmates, Irwin Edman, continued to lead these extracurricular sessions while he was writing his first book, "Human Traits," and qualifying for his Ph.D.—steps in a career later to be climaxed by his appointment as chairman of the Philosophy Department at Columbia University.

This led to a turning point in my own career, because, while still a freshman, I suggested to both Professor Pitkin and Irwin Edman that they write a basic book on the lives and the wisdom of the great philosophers, from Plato and Socrates to John Dewey and Bertrand Russell. The elation and inspiration I derived from *sensing this need* and from urging two scholars *to fill it*—the sheer, exquisite excitement of *taking the editorial initiative* and *discovering needs yet to be met by books yet unwritten*—was an unforgettable experience. This, I felt, was the career for me, and I vowed to aim my journalistic training toward book publishing, and to do my home work and to save my money with that goal in mind. Ten years later, Simon and Schuster was launched, and two years after that we published "The Story of Philosophy" by Will Durant. And ten years and one million copies later, we published "A History of Western Philosophy" by Bertrand Russell.

Let me go back to the first of the fifty years we are celebrating. On June 30, 1913, the morning I was graduated from high school (note the word "was," a grammatical nicety I learned in my first course in news reporting and copy-reading), I took the subway to 63 Park Row, and applied for a job as copy boy on *The World.* Joseph Pulitzer was already my hero and guiding star, and The Pulitzer Building was for me the most exciting place on earth. Herbert Bayard Swope, executive editor of *The World,* was considered the greatest of all newspaper men, the reporter's ideal reporter. (Some years later, he was elected an honorary member of the Journalism Class of 1917—and four decades after that, S & S signed a contract with E. J. Kahn, Jr., of *The New Yorker* to write a biography of "Swope of *The World.*")

Without any such nonsense as letters of introduction or resumes or references, I went directly to the toughest and most celebrated city editor in the newspaper business, Charles E. Chapin, already a legend on Park Row (he spent his last years in Sing Sing, serving a life sentence for murder). I told him of my ambition for a newspaper career and my hero-worship of Joseph Pulitzer, and the next morning I began work as a copy boy at $5.00 a week. Six months later, I was enrolled in the Pulitzer School of Journalism.

Coming as I did, fresh from a Swope-filled room at 63 Park Row, I promptly became Columbia University campus correspondent for *The Boston Evening Transcript*. At space rates of $5.00 a column, I was working my way through college. I was in good company. Frank Scully was covering Columbia for *The Sun,* Howard Deitz for *The New York American,* Clarence ("Ike") Lovejoy for *The New York Times,* Merryle Stanley Rukeyser for *The Far Rockaway News* and *The Morning Telegraph.*

These Columbia University campus correspondents were not content to wait for news to happen, or to accept passively news releases and handouts. We *made* news by participating in it, and sometimes even by instigating student revolts and uprisings, and other newsworthy situations. One such was Morrie Ryskind's battle with President Nicholas Murray Butler over an editorial article Morrie had written for *Jester,* in which he called Butler "Czar Nicholas." Another was a furor arising out of the "fixing" of a student board election during a period of intense rivalry between the students of Columbia College and those enrolled in the School of Journalism. The issue made the front pages under headlines that spoke of "Jews, Jesuits, and Journalists." Morrie gave me a clean scoop on this explosive story. The battle was carried on with charges and countercharges, usually in heated prose but occasionally in verse—poetic parodies, for example, of the Odes of Horace. A few were even in Latin, which of course made the story of particular interest to so sophisticated and high-brow a newspaper as *The Boston Evening Transcript,* a legendary paper immortalized in poetry by T. S. Eliot and in prose by John Marquand. (Incidentally, Morrie was expelled and didn't get his degree with the rest of us in 1917, but a few years later, when he received a Pulitzer Prize for "Of Thee I Sing," he was officially reinstated in our class.)

The day after I received my B. Litt. in 1917, I joined the Washington staff of United Press, then headed by Roy Howard. I covered Treasury, Commerce, I. C. C., and the Federal Trade Commission. My opposite number on The Associated Press was Willard Kiplinger, who later became an S & S author.

My first years as a book publisher were strongly affected by my four years in the School of Journalism. Our first S & S list, in 1924, included "Joseph Pulitzer—His Life and Letters," by Don C. Seitz; two books by classmates—one on investments by Merryle Rukeyser, and the other a book of poetry by Irwin Edman. In rapid succession came books by other classmates—Silas F. Seadler, Sir Francis Joseph Xavier Scully, "Ike" Lovejoy—and Walter B. Pitkin's masterpiece, "A Short Introduction to the History of Human Stupidity" (a mammoth volume!). Some years later we published a number of other books that reflected the professional training offered at the School of Journalism. One of them was "A Treasury of Great Reporting" by Louis L. Snyder and Richard M. Morris; another was "The Story of The New York Times —1851-1951," by Meyer Berger.

Before I drop the subject, I hope I may be forgiven if I drop a few names:

The roster of S & S authors became for me a post-graduate faculty in literature as well as journalism—continuing and enhancing the courses we took at Columbia. Thus I had the high privilege of publishing three Nobel Prize winners, and several Pulitzer prize-winning books. Between 1924 and 1962 we published books by Bernard Berenson, Bertrand Russell, Charles de Gaulle, Winston Churchill, Will Durant, Wendell Willkie, James Thurber, Franklin P. Adams, Clifton Fadiman, Walter Kerr, Bennett Cerf, Bob Hope, Groucho Marx, Bruce Catton, Quincy Howe, Walt Kelly, Cole Porter, Rodgers and Hammerstein, Alan Lerner and Frederick Loewe, S. J. Perelman, Mortimer Adler, William Laurence, George Gershwin, Robert M. Hutchins, Ogden Nash, Joseph Alsop and Robert Kintner, Edward R. Murrow, Max Eastman, Averell Harriman, Max Lerner, J. David Stern, P. G. Wodehouse, Peter Arno, Eric Hodgins, Max Beerbohm, Ephraim London, Leonard Bernstein, William Bolitho, J. Robert Oppenheimer, Christopher Isherwood and Albert Einstein.

Our S & S "Treasury of the Theatre" and our Inner Sanctum Editions of classics like "War and Peace," "Rabelais," "Leaves of Grass," "Pickwick Papers" and "The Canterbury Tales" were simply an extension of the courses in European and American Literature we took with Professor (and Dean) John W. Cunliffe at the School of Journalism.

At the School during the early stages of the First World War, I was obsessed with the idea of a new kind of foreign correspondent—the reporter-as-historian. This inspired us to publish such books as "I Write As I Please" by Walter Duranty, the celebrated *New York Times* correspondent in Moscow; "We Saw It Happen," a symposium by a group of *Times* correspondents who had covered history in the making the world over; and, just recently, one of the most spectacular best-sellers of modern times, William Shirer's "The Rise and Fall of the Third Reich."

Some three years before Simon and Schuster was founded, I covered the Dempsey-Carpentier heavyweight championship fight in Jersey City as a special correspondent for *The New Bedford Standard,* on assignment from its famous managing editor, George A. Hough, father of two of the most illustrious graduates of the School of Journalism—George A. Hough, Jr., and Henry Beetle Hough. (George was a classmate—in fact, the president of our class—and is now co-owner and co-editor with another School of Journalism graduate, Clara Sharpe Hough, of *The Falmouth Enterprise.* Henry came to the School a year later, and is now, with *his* wife and school-mate, Betty Bowie, co-owner and co-editor of *The Vineyard Gazette* ("The Thunderer")—one of the most famous country weeklies in the United States.)

In years to come, I had more than one occasion to recall that exciting Battle of the Century which I covered for *The New Bedford Standard.* Henry was at ringside with me in Boyle's Thirty Acres. In my junior year at the School, I had been greatly inspired by his passionate interest in the life and works of Henry David Thoreau. I told him then that he ought to write a biography of Thoreau. Thirty years later, he did so and we published it with great joy. And, in the next decade, there was another reason to be glad that I had seen the fourth round of that famous fight with the "Million Dollar Gate"—we published Jack Dempsey's autobiography.

Over the years, we at S & S have had our share of hits and misses, and plenty of *successes de fiasco* and *flops d'estime.* But there also have been many pioneering breakthroughs, too—the paperback revolution, the new world of Golden Books for children, the development of mass markets and the democratization of the whole book publishing process. We were unalterably committed to a policy of better and better books for more and more people at lower and lower prices. Much of this series of publishing revolutions and cultural explosions I saw, some of it I was. Since 1924, S & S has published more than three thousand books; about one thousand are still in print; over 360 have been best-sellers. Perhaps the deepest joy of all is the fulfillment of the hopes I cherished and the instruction I received at the School of Journalism between 1913 and 1917.

*On one of the early S & S lists just described by
M. Lincoln Schuster, there was a crossword
puzzle book that sent an entire nation on an un-
ending search for rare three-letter words. That
first book in the field was printed by Maxwell
Geffen; and for him it was also one of a number
of firsts in a many-faceted career. He has developed specialized book clubs, unique publications
for business and the professions, and he heads
organizations active in every form of publishing.*

*A member of the Class of 1916, Mr. Geffen is
chairman of the boards of The Blue List Publishing Company, Arrow Press, and Book Club
Guild, and is publisher of* Medical World News.

MAXWELL M. GEFFEN:

Never Far from the Presses

On May 31, 1916, the German High Seas Fleet clashed off the coast of
Denmark with the British Grand Fleet. The Battle of Jutland, a turning-
point of the First World War, had begun.

That happened to be the day on which the graduating journalism
students of Columbia University's Class of 1916 received their diplomas.
With mine in hand I journeyed down to 238 William Street, where I
quickly found employment as a cub reporter on *The New York American.* I was to receive a salary of $15 (not an hour, not a day, but once
a week) if my work proved satisfactory.

When I reported for duty in the city room at about 9 o'clock on the
night of June 1, the first edition of the *American* was already out in the
streets, headlines bannering the fearful toll in the first great meeting of
the rival naval forces. As I remember it (this was almost a half century ago, so don't hold me to details), the night city editor tossed a copy
of the paper in front of me and said: "Look it over. You're a college
man [college men were rare in the newspaper business in those days].
Let me know if you see anything wrong."

Maybe he thought of me as a "college man," but he was talking to a scared kid who'd never held a man's job before. I gave him a confident "Yes, sir," and went off to a desk to study the front page. The news in itself was as dramatic then as the Battle of the Solomons was to be for a later generation. My memory is that some 9,000 men were killed— over 6,000 of them British. I recall that my eyes blurred as I realized that I was *working* on history, not just reading it.

When the fog lifted I walked out to the newspaper's library and picked up a copy of *Jane's Registry*. I checked our story and sidebars at the only level I could possibly verify them, and found that we'd made more than a modicum of errors in designation and tonnage. (There were also the usual typos that plague any first edition put out under unusual pressure.) When I brought these corrections to the night editor—a wonderful man with a wonderful name, Percy Edrop—he stopped the presses to replate for the next edition. A number of cruisers on both sides became light cruisers or destroyers (or vice versa), and tonnages and complements were more closely related to reality.

"Well done," said Percy Edrop—and with that my job at *The New York American* became secure.

The printed word is the product of many talents. The writer, the typographer, the financier, the administrator and the editor are among the many who contribute to its appearance. My career began with the reporting of routine fires, attempted or successful suicides, clubhouse political meetings and dreary night-court processionals, but soon it took me into far different areas. Printing salesman. Proprietor of a printing company. Publisher of specialized magazines. Book publisher. Yet no matter what my hat or where my offices, I was never far from the presses.

"Expect the field to change," we'd been told at the School. "There'll always be new ideas. Try to look ahead to tomorrow's needs. Try to be among the first to fill those needs."

Let me tell you of several such attempts. For twenty years I published *Omnibook,* the magazine of book abridgements, and watched its circulation climb from 10,000 to a million. Then it dropped back to 10,000, and we left where we came in.

The Blue List is a daily publication launched in 1935 by our company, Geffen, Dunn (long-distance telephone operators frequently asked for "Deaf and Dumb"). It has several distinctions: *The Blue List* was

one of those fortunate responses to a genuine need, one which clicked
at the very beginning and has grown ever since. Until it began publication, the municipal bond dealer had to rely on what must have been a
prodigious memory, plus hundreds of scribbled notes on desk spikes, in
order to know what bonds were available, at what price, bearing what
interest, etc. Now, practically every municipal bond dealer in the nation
has on his desk at 9:00 A.M., every morning, a compilation of state and
municipal bonds being offered for sale that day. For our part, we carry
on an operation of fact-gathering, setting type, rearranging pages, printing at night and rushing copies to airports and terminals, which is as
exciting and demanding as any newspaper business I know. Recently
we merged this specialized publication with one of the giants in the
financial field, Standard and Poor's.

We began two book clubs—Scientific Book Club, which may very
well have been a few years ahead of its time—and the first religious
book club in the United States, founded in association with S. Parkes
Cadman and Harry Emerson Fosdick. The Religious Book Club continues to grow under the editorial leadership of Dr. Samuel Cavert,
former executive secretary of the World Council of Churches.

Medical World News, a bi-weekly edited by Dr. Morris Fishbein, is
the publication that now keeps me closest to the presses. A magazine
that reaches every doctor in private practice, it covers the latest developments in medicine, research, personal news for physicians, and
legislative news. Started when I was sixty-three years old, it has turned
out to be one of the most successful ventures with which I've ever been
identified.

I hope and expect that at the School today they're telling students
that there will always be new ideas—that they can "expect the field to
change." It *will* change; it always has. Life in journalism will continue
to be a series of exciting gambles and guesses. Our best hope is to be at
the right place when the opportunity or crisis shapes up—to be able to
check a fact, spot a trend, develop a concept, or start the presses on another new venture.

When journalists talk among themselves, they trade
memories---of the big or unforgettable stories,
of the problems of their craft, of the teachers who
guided them, of lessons learned.

They reflect, tell anecdotes, sum up. In moments
of frustration, some dream of getting out of the
big city. Some others determine from the start
to choose a small town, to edit a country weekly
or to write.

*The good story, as Hal Borland delightfully ex-
plains, needn't be noisy, large or catastrophic; it
may be quietly growing in a sunny field.*

*Mr. Borland (Class of '23) worked for a dozen
newspapers and two press associations before joining* The New York Times. *He is now the outdoor
editorial essayist for the Sunday edition. A pro-
lific writer, he has published books of poems,
plays, fiction, non-fiction (including "How to
Write and Sell Non-Fiction") and novelettes. His
most recent works are "Beyond Your Doorstep,"
"The Youngest Shepherd" and "When the Leg-
ends Die," a novel. Mr. Borland received the
Columbia School of Journalism alumni award in
1962. He lives with his wife, Barbara, in Salisbury,
Connecticut.*

HAL BORLAND:

The Oldest Story on Earth

Almost twenty years ago I assigned myself to one of the oldest running
stories on earth. I had been nibbling at it most of my life, but had been
too busy at other matters—as a reporter, copy reader, news editor,
daily book reviewer, editorial writer, staff writer—to settle down to
this job until the end of World War II. Then I quit my daily job at
The New York Times Sunday Magazine, moved to the country for good,
and went to work on the story of a hill, a valley, a brook and a river-
bank, the natural environment of man. Ever since then I have been
interviewing trees and rocks, investigating swamps and woodlands, attending conventions of crows, gathering statistics on milkweed seeds,
goldenrod flowers and snowflakes, being on hand for sunrises, thunderstorms and harvest moons.

I still haven't really covered this story. Nobody ever will. But I have
set down progress reports in several books and in a long series of editorial essays and magazine articles. Along the way I have had a variety
of surprises and personal discoveries as well as my full share of false

leads and wrong guesses. Any reporter does, and I am essentially an interpretative reporter.

Take the instance of the bumblebee. Bumblebees have always fascinated me, in part because according to the theories and equations of flight the bumblebee was theoretically unable to fly. Eventually the engineers revised their theories and equations to include the big bumbler's improbable skill in the air, one of the few instances I know of in which an insect upset the dicta of the slide rule. But even the entomologists and most of the all-round naturalists are somewhat vague about the bumblebee, so one fall day I set out to see how well a bumblebee chosen at random follows the rules.

I found one of the big bees just getting out of bed in an orange zinnia flower in midmorning. It was still stiff from the night chill, being a cold-blooded creature, so it sat in the sun till its blood temperature rose and its joints loosened. I marked it for identification and watched it at intervals all day, since it never went more than fifty yards from the flower in which it had spent the night. Only a few late flowers were still in bloom, among them the petunias. For its first meal that day it chose petunia nectar. But instead of entering the trumpet-shaped blossom as it was supposed to, and extending its long tongue down to the nectar sac—a precarious performance for a bumblebee with the equivalent of a severe case of arthritis—it perched at the base of the blossom, where its stiff legs could get an easy foothold. There it slit a neat hole directly over the nectar sac, thrust in its tongue and got its first snack the easy way. Several other bumblebees, already warmed to a greater degree of agility, were busy at other petunias getting the nectar in the conventional way, but my bee kept on using its shortcut until it had a full breakfast. By then it was warmed up and made the rounds of the wild aster clumps like any other bumblebee.

That afternoon I took up the trail again and followed this bumblebee to a place where the gentians were in bloom. I knew that bumblebees feed at fringed gentians on occasion, but my bee went to a bottle gentian, a flower tightly closed at the top even when in full bloom. I had been assured by two naturalists that bottle gentians are self-pollinated, and that bumblebees are unable to enter them. Curious, I watched my bee climb over and around a bottle gentian as though looking for the entrance, and finally perch on top and thrust at the stiff, tightly closed petals with its front legs. It opened a crack, thrust its head in, pushed with the four hind legs and disappeared inside. The blossom bobbed for several seconds as the big bee moved around, undoubtedly rifling the nectar sac and incidentally pollinating the flower. Then the petals parted a crack, the bee's head emerged and it hauled itself out like a burly workman emerging from a manhole. It rested briefly, then flew to another bottle gentian and did the same thing, proving that bottle gentians are at least occasionally cross-pollinated by bumblebees, no matter what anyone may say to the contrary.

That bee taught me to take hearsay and even some of the things in books with a grain of salt.

Or take the instance of the fox and the railroad track.

The red fox is one of our most insistent wild animals. It succeeds in living not only in well-settled farm areas but also in suburbs and even in the fringes of cities. John Kieran has seen red foxes in New York's Van Cortlandt park and even in the Spuyten Duyvil area. Several families of foxes live on my mountainside and I see them from time to time. One dawn, sitting in a still-watch at the edge of the woods, I watched a vixen show two kits how to catch field mice in the grass not twenty yards away. One afternoon a big dog fox stood just across the pasture and barked an invitation to my old hound to chase him. The hound accepted, and they circled the mountainside for an hour, the hound belling wonderfully, before they called it enough and the dog came home.

Foxes are surprisingly clever and have a reputation for playing tricks on hounds as well as hunters, but I never knew how full of fun they can be until one winter morning. Four inches of snow had fallen overnight and I went out to take a census of my wild neighbors, to read the tracks they had left. I crossed the pasture to the spur line of the New Haven railroad that crosses my land. It is used by a freight train that runs from Canaan to Lakeville and back every other day, some fifteen miles. This was a no-train day and the snow, which had fallen without a whisper of a breeze, lay four inches deep on the rails, undisturbed.

I came to the railroad track and started to cross it, to the timbered mountainside beyond. Then I saw the trail of a fox. It had been trotting up the railroad tracks a few hours earlier. I followed the trail to see whether the fox had stalked a rabbit, a partridge, or what. But that fox hadn't been hunting. It was out enjoying the beautiful winter morning. Fifty yards from where I first started trailing it, the fox had paused and then stepped onto one of those snow-covered rails. It had walked the rail about twenty yards, then slipped off. It had gone a few yards further, and then up on the rail it had stepped again. That time it walked the rail successfully a good hundred yards before it fell off again. A third time it mounted the rail, just like a small boy fascinated by the challenge. By then it had mastered the feat. It walked that rail a good three hundred yards, then stepped off, satisfied with its achievement, and made its leisurely way up into the woods.

I have known foxes to walk stone walls and even rail fences to throw pursuing dogs or hunters off the track, but that is the only time I ever knew a fox to walk a railroad rail. And that fox did it for fun, apparently. There was no other reason I could imagine. I never saw the fox that day, but the whole story was written, clear as text, on the white page of the snow. I could almost see the fox grinning in triumph at his boylike achievement.

Those are two days I shall never forget. They are personal highlights in this assignment I have set myself, unimportant in the big story of this hill and valley and its inhabitants, perhaps, but significant to me as well as satisfying. I no longer take anything about this story for granted, and I am sure that I can spend the rest of my life working at it and still not cover it completely.

One more day I shall never forget.

It was the day I had an argument over how many seeds there are in a milkweed pod. I said five hundred. A botanist friend insisted it was nearer a thousand. So I went out and gathered a dozen ripe milkweed pods, brought them into the living room and started counting. Before I was half through the air was foggy with milkweed floss. My wife and I were chasing milkweed fluff through the house for two weeks. But I made the count. How many? Those pods averaged out to 256 seeds per pod. And if anyone doubts that, let him make such a count himself, in his own living room. And take the consequences.

*Among the specialized fields of news writing, labor
reporting grows increasingly important. Damon
Stetson is now chief labor reporter in New York
for* The New York Times. *This piece, however,
was written when he was still chief of that paper's
Detroit bureau. Mr. Stetson was graduated from
the Columbia School of Journalism in 1937; ten
years later, after having worked as a labor reporter
for* The Newark News *and serving in the air combat intelligence branch of the Navy, he was back
at the Journalism School as an instructor in labor
reporting.*

He joined The Times *in 1953, and two years
later became its Detroit correspondent. He is married and has two children, Nancy and Dave.*

DAMON STETSON:

Midwest Reporter

There is, I suspect, a consensus among those in the newspaper field, and
those aspiring to it, that for romance, high achievement and distinguished
status you must work in Washington, Paris or Moscow.

As a regional correspondent for *The New York Times* in the Midwest, I do not observe Senators or congressmen from Capitol press
galleries, nor do I mingle with them at cocktail parties at the embassies;
but I see them shaking hands at factory gates in Mishawaka, addressing
a Kiwanis Club in Lansing and a Negro group in Columbus. I do not
interview Acting United Nations Secretary U Thant at the United Nations, but I can observe the reaction of a Soviet delegation as it tours
the mighty Rouge Plant of the Ford Motor Company. I cannot look out
my office window and see the Eiffel Tower, but I can crane my neck
and look out at the gleaming expanse of one of America's lifelines, the
Detroit River, where giant ore boats pass in a steady line.

Perhaps the greatest news dramas are enacted in Washington, New
York, Paris and Moscow, but there are moments and incidents to remember as a regional correspondent in the Midwest:

167

There was that gray morning in Eau Claire, Wisconsin, when a Senator named John F. Kennedy, campaigning desperately in the 1960 primary, walked up to a farmer in a truck stopped at a red light. The youthful-looking Senator stuck his hand through the open window and started to introduce himself. But the farmer scornfully ignored the proffered handshake, clashed the gears and drove off huffily as the light changed. Probably he still doesn't know that he left the future President of the United States standing in the middle of the street, with hand extended and looking a little foolish and embarrassed.

*

At 2 A.M. one morning the telephone awoke me from a sound sleep and New York gave orders to fly to New Castle, Indiana, immediately to cover an outbreak of violence in a bitter strike at the Perfect Circle Company. And once in New Castle there were the morning excursions each day, with other newspapermen, down the short residential street leading to the plant. What was different, however, were the menacing barrels of machine guns behind sand-bag emplacements and on tanks manned by National Guardsmen trying to quell the violence. Was this a quiet and sleepy mid-America or an armed camp with emotions boiling over?

*

There was bitter journalistic irony on a night in June, 1955, when the General Motors Corporation and the United Automobile Workers reached agreement on an historic and precedent-setting contract providing for supplemental unemployment benefits for laid-off workers. While reporters (I among them) waited outside the negotiating room for the final word, a General Motors teletype message flashed news of the about-to-be-announced settlement to plant managers across the country.

A wire service reporter sitting in the office of a General Motors executive in Kansas City saw the message and immediately flashed word of the new agreement, thereby scooping by a few minutes the worn and weary regulars outside the conference room in Detroit who had been covering negotiations on a daily basis for three months.

*

For three years I listened to Democratic protestations that former Governor G. Mennen Williams never saw Walter P. Reuther, president of the United Automobile Workers—the man who, according to critical Republicans, dictated the Governor's every move. Then one day I was sitting in Mr. Reuther's book-lined office in Solidarity House, overlooking the Detroit River, and was trying to interview him. Actually, he was delivering a speech at me.

The telephone rang and Mr. Reuther answered and said, "Sure, send him right in."

The door opened and Governor Williams walked in, explaining that he was nearby and thought he'd drop in to congratulate Mr. Reuther on his recent reelection as president of the U. A. W.

*

Dateline: Ann Arbor, Mich., April 11, 1955.

"The vaccine works. It is safe, effective and potent."

With those words, written by a public relations man for the University of Michigan, the United States and all the world learned that the Salk Vaccine was to become another great boon to mankind in the battle against disease. The announcement of the Francis Report on the vaccine's successful testing was one of the great medical stories of the last decade.

The story broke shortly after 9:15 A.M. in the Rackham Building of the University, where Dr. Thomas Francis Jr., director of the group evaluating the vaccine, was scheduled to begin a formal report to 500 scientists and medical men at 10:20 A.M.

About an hour ahead of Dr. Francis' lecture and the formal release time, staff officials wheeled 300 copies of the now-famous report into the press room on dollies. A melee involving some 150 reporters ensued. The staff members finally began throwing copies of the meticulously-written document to those who couldn't get close enough to grab one.

Those reporters with an immediate deadline got on the phone and began dictating a story from the press release rather than from the long report that had taken a year to prepare. William L. Laurence, now science editor for *The Times,* and I were fortunate enough to have some time, so we read and assessed before we wrote.

*

There was the convention of 600 magicians in Colon, Michigan, known as the magic capital of the United States, to which I took my wife and son.

"Baker the Faker" mystified my 10-year-old with disappearing quarters while Duke Stern, a magician from Indianapolis, placed a cabinet over my wife's head and then thrust twelve arrows through the cabinet. My wife said that I should not have smiled, but it made a good picture for *The Times*—my wife in the cabinet, I mean.

For two days we lived in a world of magic, watching magicians fool magicians and then instruct each other on technique. I stood by, always amused and usually baffled but jotting notes as one magician after an-

other, at the drop of a rabbit or an ace, put on a private or public per-
formance—whether on the sidewalk of Main Street, in the M & M
Grill, in the vestry of a church, or in a demonstration tent of the Abbott
Magic Manufacturing Company, which has made Colon famous.

*

There was the long swing South in 1956—through Arkansas and
Texas—as part of a *Times* team effort to assess the impact in Southern
states of the United States Supreme Court's decision outlawing segre-
gated schools.

I traveled from the cotton country of Eastern Arkansas, where rickety
sharecropper shacks dotted the fields and Deep South attitudes prevailed, to Fayetteville, seat of the University of Arkansas, nestled in
the Boston Mountains in Northeast Arkansas. A young Negro, Silas
Hunt, was enrolled in the School of Law there six years before the
Supreme Court decision.

From Arkansas I traveled to Texas and the old antebellum city of
Marshall near the Louisiana line, where the scent of magnolias, with
their Southern symbolism, was still strong; and then on across the state
to El Paso at the far west, where school integration began easily.

In view of later events, however, my experience with Governor Orval
E. Faubus of Arkansas at Little Rock stands out in my recollection. I
had requested an interview on my arrival there and had made clear that
I wanted to discuss with him his attitude and policy toward implement-
ing the Supreme Court decision. He agreed to see me on a Monday
afternoon.

When I was ushered into his office, he rose, smiled, shook my hand
and said he was glad to see me. But he looked deadly serious and not
especially happy as I expressed a few amenities and explained my reason
for being there.

The Governor, who seemed a mild-mannered man, had formerly
been the editor of a weekly newspaper in a small town in Northwest
Arkansas. Throughout the early part of his administration he had carefully avoided any commitment on the segregation issue. White Citizens
Council members, in fact, were charging at the time that he was an
integrationist at heart.

"What is your policy going to be toward the court's decision?" I asked
the Governor.

Governor Faubus tilted back a little farther in his chair and clasped
his hands across his chest. He frowned as he pondered my question.
There was a long embarrassing pause. Then he replied tersely:

"I'm not going to answer."

I tried another tack, asking him to give me some insight into the thinking of Arkansans about the problem. He again declined. I asked several more questions and he refused to answer any of them. The interview was fast becoming an abortive farce, so I asked the Governor if he would answer some written questions if I submitted them.

"I might," he said.

My most frustrating interview was over. I thanked the Governor and hurried to the Capitol press room, typed out a dozen questions and left them with the Governor's secretary.

During the next few days, as I traveled to various sections of the state, I called the Governor's office periodically to inquire whether he had prepared any answers. Finally his secretary told me to drop around the next afternoon. I did, and cooled my heels for two hours before being invited in to see the Governor again. Several of his cabinet members and assistants were there.

Governor Faubus handed me a sheaf of papers on which answers to each of my questions were typed. He still was unwilling, however, to carry on any further discussion. As I started to leave he told me that he was releasing his answers to my questions to the wire services and to Arkansas newspapers.

I protested, particularly since I had initiated the questioning and had not planned to use the material until I had completed my swing through Arkansas and Texas. But he was adamant, so I rushed to my hotel and beat out a spot news story for *The Times* and filed it for the next day's paper.

In the light of future events in the Little Rock school crisis, his answers were revealing and doubly significant. He said, for example, that at his request a public opinion poll had been taken, and that it showed 85 per cent of the people of Arkansas to be opposed to school integration.

"I cannot be a party to any attempt to force acceptance of a change to which the people are so overwhelmingly opposed," the Governor said.

Subsequently, in his answers, he summed up prospects for integration in Arkansas as follows:

"The people of Arkansas are, as a whole, moderate, reasonable and honorable. If left alone, they will work out their own destiny—a destiny that will do no violence to any Christian principle.

"But they will not be bullied, abused or vilified without fighting back with all the means at their command. They do not approve extremists, dictation or demagoguery. They resent outsiders' attempting to enforce a code of behavior to which they are not accustomed."

These words were more prophetic than I knew.

*

And then there was a meeting of a group of neighbors in an attractive home on an all-white, middle-class Detroit street where the first house had gone on sale to Negroes. I listened as some of the group—tense, frightened, angry and obviously prejudiced—talked of methods by which Negroes could be kept out of the area. They didn't know a re porter was present.

"We've got to keep our property values from going down," one man said.

"Once a Negro moves into this block, others will flock here like locusts," another said.

A timid-looking, gray-haired woman said she would be afraid to walk on the streets if the area became heavily populated with Negroes.

Then another element took over. Irving J. Rubin, the courageous and pioneering president of the Bagley Council—a neighborhood group— took the floor. He emphasized that property values wouldn't be depressed unless people "panicked" and put up their houses for sale. He said that the Negro families who might move into the area would probably have an income level and educational background at least equivalent to the present white residents.

"We're not trying to encourage or discourage the settlement of Negro families in this neighborhood," he said. "But we do feel anyone ought to be able to buy a home where he pleases.

"What we're trying to do is to stabilize our community, improve the schools, get better library and better municipal services, and generally make our area a better place in which to live."

The discussion went on for about two hours. Some urged banding together and trying to buy the house that was up for sale.

"That just doesn't work," Mr. Rubin said. "Pretty soon someone else will have another house for sale, and then you'll have to buy that. You just can't keep doing that as people come and go."

Others who supported Mr. Rubin's point of view joined in urging tolerance and calmness instead of hysteria and panic.

As the gathering broke up, an elderly lady stopped to shake hands with Mr. Rubin.

"My husband and I like our neighbors, Mr. Rubin. We'll stay if they do."

In a simple, unostentatious way this episode had a symbolic significance in terms of one of America's major problems of the North —residential segregation. Perhaps it did not have the drama or violence or regional impact of a Little Rock or an Oxford. But it did represent a bold facing up to the problem of neighborhood integration and an attempt to resolve it morally and justly without wholesale turnover. It was a story for *The Times*.

The Bagley area has not, to date, given way to panic. There has been no "block busting." Other Detroit neighborhoods have studied the Bagley experience and are adopting the approach used by Mr. Rubin and his supporters. Both white and Negro leaders of Detroit have hailed the positive attitude of the Bagley Community toward a problem that is not local but national.

*

And so I would argue that some of the great journalistic opportunities today are in the wide expanses of America, where people do things —where they make cars rather than pass laws; where they grow corn and hogs, and go to high-school basketball games instead of Broadway plays; where attitudes both mean and meaningful emerge; where life has a distinctive, all-American flavor.

*When Charles Alexander left Washington to take
a job in a "middle-sized" city, none of his friends
or co-workers seemed to understand why. Here
Mr. Alexander, who is managing editor of* The
Wilmington *(Del.)* Morning News *and* Evening
Journal, *puts the case for the smaller daily.*

*Mr. Alexander, who was graduated from the
Columbia School of Journalism in 1956, started
his career on* The Washington Star, *where he
began as a copy reader and left as an assistant
city editor. He is married and has one daughter.*

CHARLES T. ALEXANDER, JR.:
Why Wilmington?

During my first 18 months in Delaware, the state distinguished itself by
reinstating capital punishment—by hanging—and by sentencing a
wrongdoer to 20 lashes, well laid on, at the whipping post. The friends
I had left behind when I quit as an assistant city editor at *The Washington* (D. C.) *Star* must have thought either that I was daft or that I
fancied myself an Albert Schweitzer of the journalistic frontier.

To most of them, a few cities—and but a few newspapers in those
cities—have caught the vision of journalistic excellence. New York,
Washington, Chicago, Los Angeles, Miami, Minneapolis, St. Louis—
these and cities like them are the pinnacles against which many newspapermen prop their ladders and begin to climb. After making the club
in such places, they plan only to stay there. My move was incompre-
hensible.

Yet after a number of years in Washington, preceded by stays in New
York and Boston, I had come to view big cities in ways perhaps best
expressed by Stanley Walker after his return to his native Texas. He referred to "the great mass of nuisances . . . the lung-defiling smog . . . the
dreadful noises, the eternal jangle of the telephone, rent paying, taxicab
fares, strike threats, conferences and committee meetings, movements to
save the world, the harsh chatter of pip-squeaks with definite opinions."
New York City, he said, is like some "jangle-nerved, gin-soaked old

174

lady friend [who] grows ever more raucous, high-pitched, garish, troublesome and generally messy."

A lot of people who don't like cities continue to live in them because they feel they can't afford to leave, financially or professionally.

How about the respective merits of large and middle-sized newspapers? That's a question I explored before I joined *The Wilmington Morning News,* a paper which then had a circulation of 34,000 (now, happily, pushing 36,000). My conclusion was that the philosophy and attitude of the individual organization, not its size, determine the effectiveness of the job the newspaper does. Some smaller newspapers do a superior job by any standards; some in larger cities squander their resources or pay them out in dividends. There can be no generalizations.

It is obvious that the more resources an organization has, the better it ought to fulfill its journalistic functions; but it is also true that in a smaller area with smaller circulation, the demands are less. Thus, it is possible in some areas to do a far better job with fewer dollars while still maintaining the quality of coverage and salaries and employe benefits on a level with those of larger newspapers.

The day of the provincial little sheet in the middle-sized city is passing. Readers in these areas are coming to realize that they are citizens on the international as well as the local level. Some may scorn entangling alliances, but all know that their fortunes are inextricably bound up with the destiny and aspirations of people the world around.

The intelligent and broad coverage of foreign news has become a must; the wire services now cover Cairo and Karachi with the same fervor as Washington and London. The readers are demanding ever more news and more of its significance.

While increasing its worldwide coverage, the middle-sized press is also called on to raise the breadth and quality of local coverage. Acting as the daily journal of local activities is the unique role of each newspaper in its community. No imported big-city daily or newsmagazine can fulfill it.

In the area of local news, middle-sized cities have relatively the same amount of crime, the same interest in schools, planning, taxes, economics, business, society, public administration, other people, the whole gamut of human activity, as larger cities. This is becoming the story not of the American city but of America.

The middle-sized area requires a vigorous press to foster good government. In Wilmington, the newspapers—both owned by one company—have brought about reforms in one public agency in recent months which extended to the forced resignation of the executive director; they have freed from prison 21 inmates who were given sentences by magistrates in excess of the maximum allowed by law (and the papers are currently seeking reform in the magistrate system); they brought to public attention the sale by the city of a prime business location to a syndicate represented by an attorney who was also the city chairman of the party in power (and the sale was subsequently nullified by the courts); they uncovered ethically questionable practices in the administration of the state insurance office, through which insurance agents who rendered no service to the state were receiving commissions. The result here was that the insurance commissioner, who had been nicknamed "Landslide" because of his previous election victories, was defeated in the 1962 elections. The papers are currently keeping the whipping-post issue before their readers.

As a member of the Columbia Journalism Class of 1956 I went with a group of classmates and the late Roscoe Ellard to a small city in upper New York State to take over publication of the local paper for one day. The fact that the paper was willing to let such a group assume control for a day was, I suppose, some commentary on its seriousness of purpose. There was no doubt that this 9,000-circulation daily wasn't doing the job.

A new organization came to that town, however, and locked horns with its entrenched rival. Now the newspaper readers in that city—and there are about 25,000 of them—receive a paper which is doing a signal job, the product of a consolidation between the newcomer and the old-timer. The paper has won awards both for its appearance and for its public service. This is typical of the vitality of the press in smaller metropolitan areas.

What of the journalist's professional status, his working conditions, his opportunities for advancement on a middle-sized paper? It seems to me obvious that success can come more quickly to the talented young journalist on a middle-sized paper. He gets the opportunity to tackle the big assignments sooner, to acquire more varied experience—and to gain real professional satisfaction at an earlier stage. (My own experience is a questionable example. I was originally supposed to begin with the *Morning News* as assistant city editor, moving up to city editor as soon as I became familiar with the area. By the time I reported for work on April 2, 1961, I had been named managing editor to succeed a man who had unexpectedly decided to retire to his seashore home.)

On a smaller paper, a good city editor can give his staff of from ten to 15 reporters individual supervision and training. Those reporters will generally have started at a pay scale commensurate with or even slightly above that of the larger dailies. They can become specialists—or, over the years, expert in many facets of their craft.

Why Wilmington? Why Richmond? Why Charlotte? Why Nashville? Why a lot of other medium-sized cities with metropolitan newspapers?

Because these are places that are demanding and getting better newspapers. But beyond that, because they're good places in which to live, and challenging and satisfying places in which to work.

*Some people sell newspapers; others buy them.
Since his cub days on* The New York Tribune, *F.
F. McNaughton has bought two dozen newspapers
and radio stations. Currently, he is an owner of
five daily papers, five radio stations and a number
of weeklies, all in Illinois, California and Arizona.*

*A member of the School of Journalism Class of
1915, Mr. McNaughton is editor of the* Pekin
(Ill.) Daily Times, *but prefers the title of "old
man" of what has become a family enterprise; two
sons and a son-in-law are active in its various operations. (A third son is general counsel to the
Defense Department.)*

F. F. McNAUGHTON:

Small-Town Journalism

On a Spring day in 1912, I was wandering idly on Columbia University's
South Field—then mostly an open expanse, now the crowded site of the
library, John Jay Hall, and many other buildings.

At the northwest corner of the field, a group of laborers had gathered.
I joined them.

"What are they building here?" I asked.

"A place to teach newspaper fellers."

"I'll be a charter member of that school," I answered.

Many things must have inspired my response—uncertainty about the
future, perhaps a touch of bravado, possibly a feeling that newspaper
fellers led exciting lives and were amply rewarded for their work. But
I said it and meant it, and while an illness in the family prevented me
from enrolling in the first class, I did enroll in 1914.

Robert E. MacAlarney, later the managing editor of *The New York
Tribune,* taught us two rules of journalism in his class. After almost fifty
years of experience, I still consider them vital if food for your family
depends on whether people read your paper or your competitor's. "Put
your best brains into your first paragraph," said Bob MacAlarney. "If
they read the first paragraph and like it, they'll go on into the story. But
if the first paragraph looks dull, they'll never even start the story."

178

Rule number two: Put a loving touch on every story.

I tried to apply these two rules to my pieces at the *Tribune,* where MacAlarney gave me my first newspaper job. Often the opposition did it better. Once each paper sent a reporter to watch a beauty cavorting, for some reason, atop a skyscraper. When I saw that the *Sun* had sent Frank O'Malley, my heart sank. My pitiful little story got about five inches inside. But O'Malley, after teasing the reader all through a front-page column, finally concluded: "Reader, do you really want to know what she wore? She didn't wear."

I had been working at the *Tribune* for about a year. Then something happened.

On my day off I went out to see the international polo matches. When I got there I noticed that the June grass was heading. To myself I said: "It's summer, and you didn't even see the spring go by."

I reflected that I had only one life to live. A farm boy likes to square himself by looking at the North star. He likes to hear the bleat of hour-old spring lambs. (As I type this there is the honking of a V of geese overhead. A letter today from a son says that he plans to take his family back to Brown County, Indiana, to see the "full glory of autumn.")

I decided that I belonged back home again . . .

In Indiana, at a tiny college near my home, I had received my undergraduate degree in liberal arts. I had been a high-school principal in Madill, Oklahoma. I had gone to Columbia to get my master's in education, and had then switched to economics. After I received that degree I went on to the School of Journalism. A mighty amount of time had thus been spent in classrooms.

But nothing I'd learned had prepared me for newspaper ownership. The Pulitzer School was intent on turning out writers, not publishers.

I bought a weekly—yet I didn't know a pica from pi. When I turned the weekly into a daily I was so ignorant of simple newspaper facts that I hedged by taking my foreman in as a partner, accepting his note for his half. In no time at all his note was paid off from profits. Then when he wanted to go it alone, he of course demanded a higher price, and I had to mortgage the plant to buy back something I had recently owned.

It seems to me that the fun of newspapering is ownership. True, ownership has taken some terrific jolts in the half century this book covers. I think back to my first daily; nearly *all* information then reached the people of our city through my paper. On a screen across the street we threw the inning-by-inning story of the World Series. "THE WAR IS OVER!" was pasted in our window, and all hell broke loose. A mine disaster killed 52. The wives did not hear of the tragedy by radio—

someone told them it was on the *Daily News* window, and our street was jammed as women and children watched the lengthening list of the dead.

I tried to acquire other small dailies. There'd been a high-school co-ed in Madill whose picture I had carried in my mental photo file over the years; during my time with the *Tribune* I'd saved enough to buy an engagement ring fit to send to Cecille McMillan. And now, married and searching for good schools for our "five in seven years" youngsters— Cecille and I took the big risk of buying a daily that was practically a giveaway.

It had first been owned by whisky interests. Then when prohibition came, the Ku Klux Klan took it over. From this you can sense how little standing the paper enjoyed, especially among church people. I recall with dismay my first trip to a local barber shop after I'd bought the paper. I saw a copy of our paper on the floor, still unopened, right where it had been thrown by a newsboy the afternoon before. Meanwhile the barber's customers were reading sections of a paper published in a nearby town; what's more, they were discussing its contents enthusiastically.

That night I was to cover my first important story in this new location. One of the city's old Lutheran churches was holding its final service in an old building, and this occasion was also terminating the 50-year ministry of a beloved pastor.

All through that evening the voice of Bob MacAlarney kept telling me: "If *ever* you put a loving touch on a story, put a caress on this one. If *ever* you put your heart into a first paragraph, do it now. It may mean success and happiness for your family, or it may mean defeat and a stumbling life."

I finally found my loving touch in the last long farewell glance old Pastor Witte gave that sanctuary as he was stepping out the door. Somehow I must have said it right. After our paper came out the next afternoon, people began dropping in to buy copies at the counter. One person bought six papers! And that evening we began receiving phone calls. The most meaningful compliment come from the wife of the man who had just peddled the paper to me. She said: "If you write more stories like that one today about Pastor Witte, you will make a success of this paper."

It was not really a good story. I am not a good writer. But just as a woman will forgive much clumsiness in a man for one right word or gesture, so people will forgive—oh, maybe even misspelling and bad grammar in exchange for a loving touch that convinces the reader that the writer had his heart in the story.

If he is willing to hurl himself into it, the owner-editor of a small-town newspaper can do a world of good for his community and for himself. He'll frequently hear dirges, however, sung for his role in journalism. When radio came, people warned us to quit the newspaper business. When TV came, my closest adviser declared insistently: "Get out of the newspaper business." We safeguarded ourselves by sprouting a few radio towers, but we hung right on with newspapers. Next came free sheets, and now it is trading stamps that may bankrupt us. But still ownership is fun, and I'm sure our sons agree. Recenly our youngest son started a new daily in California; a half million dollars wouldn't pry it loose from him.

We've evolved some rules for buying that we try to apply as regularly as MacAlarney's rules for writing. They're simple: County seat of over 10,000; not overshadowed; only publication in town. And we follow three simple rules in operation: Dig, *Dig,* DIG for local news; see that your advertisers get results; and keep your payroll under 41% of gross. Observe those rules and a hard worker can hardly miss.

Newspapering has been good to Cecille and me, and to all our children; and we foresee that it will be good to their children and to their children's children. And it may all be because I once told a laborer that when they finished the Columbia University School of Journalism building, I'd be one of the "fellers" to go there to be taught newspapering.

James R. Gallagher, co-publisher and editor of
The Belmond *(Iowa)* Independent, *was graduated
from the School in 1936. He has worked on
the copy desk of* The Des Moines Tribune, *as
news editor of* The Antioch *(Ill.)* News, *as advertising manager of* The Madison *(N.J.)* Eagle *and
as the news editor for two Iowa papers,* The Oska-
loosa Tribune *and* The Grinnell Herald-Register.
*Mr. Gallagher is married and has four children.
During World War II he served as a lieutenant
with the U.S. Navy.*

J. R. GALLAGHER:

Fitting Targets Anywhere

"Break a lance!"

Anyone so fortunate as to have had the late Dr. Douglas Southall
Freeman as a professor at the Columbia University School of Journalism
heard that advice on repeated occasions.

It was delivered in the "Go! Go! Go!" spirit of a coach at half time;
and I've often thought that if Columbia Journalism were ever to adopt
a motto, the choice might most appropriately be the famed Pulitzer prize-
winner's admonition.

As a laborer in the journalistic vineyard, my plot has been a 750-
square-mile area of Iowa corn country that would seem to lend itself
very poorly to cultivation by lance. Editing and co-publishing a country
weekly like *The Belmond Independent* provides no opportunity to conduct world-shaking crusades. But the lance is nevertheless a very suitable
tool when reminding perpetrators of provincial corruption that the press
is looking over their shoulder. And as a prod to supplant inertia with
action, it's hard to beat.

When we came to this community in American agriculture's heart-
land in 1949, the population was about 350 fewer than today's 2,500-
plus. The *Independent* then claimed a circulation of less than 1,500
compared to the present more-than-2,000 (plus a "shopper" covering
an additional 2,000 homes).

182

There was much about the town that was pleasing, but, as the phrase has it, Belmond was sitting on its hunkers. There were few new homes. Main Street's business district was blighted with frame store buildings that sagged wearily and were beyond being spruced up. No streets had been paved in 30 years.

It was by no means a "dead" town, but it was certainly in the doldrums. More distressing than its lethargy was the prevailing attitude toward its shortcomings: "Too bad, but nothing can be done about it."

It was taken for granted that such municipal needs as a new sewage disposal plant, a systematic program of street paving, a zoning and planning commission, a swimming pool were out of the question. "They" would never stand for any such innovations.

Endowed years earlier with a fine library by a well-to-do citizen, the community had permitted the institution's usefulness to shrivel as a result of the indifference of a self-perpetuating board of trustees and the influence of an elderly librarian retained simply because she needed her meager salary.

Pride was taken in the fact that the city wasn't "in debt for a cent"— although businessmen and homeowners (neighboring farmers, too) found it possible to live by desired standards only through utilizing credit.

On the other hand there was a progressive element in Belmond that saw those shortcomings only too well. It was encouraging that one of the first public gatherings we covered had to do with the formulation of plans for a new hospital to replace the rambling, converted residence that was serving the purpose at that time.

Inquiry made it apparent that the stultifying element known as "they" was in a decided minority. Here was a community that needed mainly to think in terms of "we"—and then things might begin to happen. With a lance dipped in printer's ink, *The Belmond Independent* set about to transmogrify a pronoun.

Iowa has been abustle with school reorganization since the early fifties; the "little red schoolhouse" and its dubious blessings have given way to educational progress. In many communities much bitterness has arisen as confused citizens have voted down reorganization proposals or have denied the new buildings needed to implement them. Belmond has gone through two successful reorganizations with controversy virtually absent, and has approved bonds for more than a million dollars' worth of new buildings. In the words of the local superintendent, the *Independent* "helped immeasurably" in bringing these accomplishments about.

About that hospital? The *Independent* campaigned strenuously for the project, and Belmond was fortunate in having an exceptionally fine staff of doctors to help inspire hearty support for it. The hospital was completed in 1951. It was the first hospital in the nation in a town so small to be fully accredited by the Joint Commission on Accreditation.

Another editorial campaign emphasized how poorly the city was utilizing a valuable asset under the prevailing administration of the library. It was privately pointed out that the librarian could retire under the Social Security system with little loss in income. A change in trustees ensued as miffed board members resigned. A newspaper-sponsored fund drive made possible the purchase of $1,800 worth of new books. By 1961 the library, as one outstanding in the rural field, received a $5,000 federal grant to conduct an experiment in expanding the use of its facilities by attracting more rural patrons.

For years "everybody" had been saying Belmond should have a Community Chest. Through editorial endeavor (not to mention considerable personal effort) a Community Chest was established. It has reached or surpassed its goals with remarkable consistency.

A dedicated but weary group of septuagenarians had served for years as the Cemetery Association, and wished desperately to have the city relieve them of their responsibility. The city fathers were not disposed to do so. An editorial campaign pointing out the advantages of so doing brought a change of heart. The city accepted deed to the property, and has since expanded it so that the cemetery will serve its purpose properly and well for many generations to come.

New sewage disposal plant? We've got one. Zoning and planning commission? That, too. Also a swimming pool. In 1962, 50 blocks of new paving were laid. Moreover, plans call for another paving project just as soon as the level of municipal debt will permit. As a side effect, those warped and tired frame fronts have all but disappeared from Main Street in the sweep of progress.

We save some of our lances for county government, too.

As recently as 1955 there was not a mile of secondary road in the county that had been paved with county funds. Road money was eaten up by purchases of new equipment, by the cost of "repairing" the constantly replaced machinery and by grossly inefficient maintenance of the graveled roads.

But when private inquiry by the *Independent* raised the spectre of a grand jury investigation, the county board hurriedly came forth with a ten-year paving program. Close to 75 miles of road have been paved in the past six years, and another 20 will be surfaced next year.

There was the time that the *Independent* brought to the taxpayers' attention a proposed 35 per cent increase in the county tax levy in a sin-

gle year. The resulting hubbub achieved a quarter-million dollar cut in
the levy, with not the slightest perceptible sacrifice in services performed
during the year affected.

For years the county had been buying its road machinery fuels "across
the counter." That was editorially cured in 1952, with savings of more
than $50,000 since purchases have been contracted on bids.

On our office wall hang three plaques representing years in which the
Independent was judged to have performed the most outstanding community service of any weekly newspaper in Iowa. Three other citations
denote lower placings or honorable mentions.

A framed award names *The Belmond Independent* as winner in 1959
of the Iowa Press Association's contest in Editorial Excellence. There's
another for being one of three weeklies honored in this category in 1961.

We honestly take no undue pride in these achievements. They have
been no more than by-products of an effort to do a proper job. Neither
do we wish to imply that in the hands of a country editor, a lance becomes a magic wand—nor to pretend that *we* never get the shaft.

But it's our suspicion that our city brethren sometimes discount the
opportunity for effective journalism that exists in the weekly field.

There are vegetating weeklies, just as there are namby-pamby dailies.
But as Dr. Freeman suggested, you can find fitting targets for lances almost anywhere—if you keep your eye peeled and your hand artillery
sharp.

*With his wife, Elizabeth, Henry Beetle Hough is
editor and publisher of* The Vineyard Gazette, *the
country weekly serving Martha's Vineyard, Massachusetts. A 1918 Journalism School graduate,
Mr. Hough won one of the first Pulitzer Prizes for
a special report on the American press.*

*He is the author of 16 books of fiction and non-
fiction, including "Country Editor," "The New
England Story," "Great Days of Whaling" and a
new novel, "The Port." He has written for many
magazines and, in 1942, was awarded the Columbia University Medal for Excellence. Above all,
the Houghs and their* Gazette *epitomize "The
Vineyard" for everyone who visits or lives on that
lovely Massachusetts island.*

HENRY BEETLE HOUGH:

Country Editor's Recollections

After a certain number of years, or of decades, things no longer stand
out; on the contrary, they retreat, and one comes to believe with David
Copperfield that trifles make the sum of life. If you are reminded of
something in years past, it becomes memorable, but soon it is lost below
the surface again—a trifle.

In a scribbled note from long ago I find that a hostess to the Want
to Know Club served a collation of segments of tangerine oranges and
ice water. For a moment or two this brings back the lavender hue and
fragrance of the aunts and mothers and grandmothers who met to read
or listen to papers about foreign scenery, remote wild life, and curious
customs of the world abroad.

Mrs. Flo Pease, a neighbor of ours, kept a journal of the refresh-
ments served at meetings of different clubs; she knew what the rewards
of attendance were likely to be in the case of different hostesses, and
governed herself accordingly. Another neighbor owned a husband and
an automobile, and she would not trust the one to drive the other unless
she was along. Accordingly, when he drove her to a club meeting he

would have to leave the car, walk back home, and then walk back to resume the wheel after the meeting had adjourned and his wife was ready to take her seat beside him.

One of our subscribers, a Gay Head Indian, occupied the somewhat contradictory positions of deacon of the Baptist Church and medicine man of his tribe, but in our day both titles had become largely honorary. A church woman and mystic of our town went to consult Judge Draper as to whether it was all right for her to inform people that she saw visions. The judge said that anyone fortunate enough to be able to penetrate the unseen should certainly be allowed to say so. It was Judge Draper who wrote to members of the S.A.R. to say that if each one would send him twenty-five cents it would "more than make up the cost of the recent entertainment." Some members mumbled that they would like to know how much more, but they sent their quarters.

Over the years we had the usual country newspaper troubles over things that appeared in the paper, but one Main Street businessman of advanced years didn't much care what was in the paper. What he did care about was who had put it in.

One time a city man went to see the chairman of the board of assessors because he had found that his father-in-law's estate was being taxed for two buildings that had burned down and a windmill that no longer existed. The chairman of the assessors advised him to do nothing about it, because if the assessors were to look over the property and bring the valuation up to date, they were likely to double the taxes. So the estate continued to pay the taxes on vanished property.

I don't know how general the custom may be, but our branch of the W.C.T.U. has a Natural Fruit Juices Director.

We used to see much of an old-time school teacher who had taught the first two grades to at least two generations in our town. When balked in some attempt at recollection she would say, "I can't think of it if I suffer!" She called *The Gazette* office to order a copy of the paper sent to a relative in the West, and gave the address distinctly: "Seattle, Washington Territory."

She experienced a good deal of difficulty with one knee that would stiffen when allowed to remain in one position. When she learned that a gold watch was to be presented to her at commencement, she arranged with the superintendent of schools to have "America, the Beautiful" sung immediately before the presentation, so that the entire audience, herself included, would rise. Thus she would be limber for the honor and for her response.

It was a different old lady who confused the Red Cross with the

W.P.A. And it was at a different ceremony that Albertus Poole Wither-ell, a retired gentleman of dignity, threw out his shoulders and his trousers fell off.

At one time when a stranger would have said nothing at all was going on in town, Walter M. Thorpe was busiest at research tending to prove that Sir Walter Raleigh wrote a number of the Shakespeare plays. His death finally terminated the research prematurely.

An income tax investigator came to town to look into the circum-stances of Lonnie Summerton. He found Lonnie, friendly and unper-turbed, living in an old fur coat in an abandoned privy. Much shaken, the investigator reported that the amount due the government was uncol-lectible.

Mr. Middlebrook used to put in the window of his Main Street restau-rant a large show card announcing the daily specials and prices. Then he and Mrs. Middlebrook would keep a sharp lookout, and as soon as their competitor from up the street had walked by, Mr. Middlebrook would revise the schedule by adding five or ten cents to most of the items. The uncle of this competitor used to occupy a stool at the Middle-brook lunch counter and sit there, a morose brooding figure, for long intervals. He was taken for a spy and treated accordingly, until one day he hanged himself. He hadn't been a spy but an exile.

Trifles now, in long retrospect, trifles that make up the sum of life; but none to be remembered unless for some oddity or irony or charac-teristic reflection of our own lives, as distinct from others. To me it is significant that most of my memories go back to the first twenty years or so of the more than forty Betty and I have exercised our editorship. The tradition of self-will and individualism was strong then, and we watched the passing of the generations that were the last to be brought up in it.

Though we reject the label of "mass communication media" as apply-ing to newspapers of any size, the conforming influence of mass com-munications is everywhere to be seen. A woman whose neighbor sawed off a limb of her sycamore maple tree would no longer insist that the limb be nailed back on again. Civilization cares more and more about images of itself, and there are fewer and fewer styles in the way of images that are sufficiently sophisticated for the new age.

We suspect that, despite the present ascendancy of mass communica-tions, all this is not final but, quite to the contrary, another phase to be lived through. Meantime, though, how shall we advise an inquirer who desires to launch himself in the career of small-town editor? How should we know what it is like to start a newspaper in this the day of offset printing, photo composition, teletypesetting, photo-electric engraving, and of a baffling multiplicity of government reports and remittances— we who, in innocence, founded our editorial lives upon a hand press, some cases of worn-out type, and a single typewriter, long before the Presidency of Calvin Coolidge?

The evidence of growth that impresses me most is that our office now possesses seven typewriters, and on occasion all may be in use at once. Verily, we have seen the accomplishment of wonders!

There is, of course, one piece of advice or instruction we may safely offer any beginner, and it cannot be better put than in the words of a former editor of our paper when he looked around from the summit just short of a hundred years ago:

"The editor of a country newspaper occupies a place that is not in every respect enviable, although many seem to be impressed with that idea. There are lots of people who know how the labors of the station ought to be performed, and if they only had the helm they would show the local world wonderful things. . . . The labors of the position are arduous, the duties are multifarious, the thanks are few, the curses, often-times, heavy."

When journalists talk among themselves, they trade
memories---of the big or unforgettable stories,
of the problems of their craft, of the teachers who
guided them, of lessons learned.

They reflect, tell anecdotes, sum up. In moments
of frustration, some dream of getting out of the
big city. Some others determine from the start
to choose a small town, to edit a country weekly
or to write.

All speak of <u>people they have met.</u>

Milton Bracker has been with The New York Times, *both in this country and overseas, since his graduation from the School of Journalism in 1931. He is the recipient of three major journalism awards: The Maria Moors Cabot Prize from Columbia, the George Polk Award for foreign reporting (with his wife, Virginia Lee Warren) from Long Island University, and the Page One Award of the New York Newspaper Guild.*

A versatile writer, Mr. Bracker has contributed fiction to The New Yorker, *poetry to "The Conning Tower,"* Saturday Review *and* This Week, *and articles to* Saturday Evening Post, Look, *and* The Reporter. *Late in 1963 he became chief of the Rome bureau of* The New York Times.

MILTON BRACKER:
"Bless You, Mr. Frost"

The most impressive man I ever met was, by all odds, Robert Frost. I saw him only four times, twice as a reporter on public occasions and twice as an individual interviewer. The last time was on the eve of his eighty-eighth birthday, at his gray clapboard house on Brewster Street in Cambridge, Massachusetts. The interview made a gratifying piece in the daily, but it was interlined with foreboding. In the less than four years since I had seen Mr. Frost for *The New York Times* Magazine, he had obviously failed. As the room darkened, somehow (I was impelled to report) "it seemed filled with the ticking not of one clock but of many."

Ten months later, Robert Frost was dead. He died during the printers' strike, the most desolate period in the history of journalism in New York. It limited the access of New Yorkers to obituaries and appreciations of the poet, which was certainly more their loss than his. For Robert Frost's fame and meaning could not be encompassed in any particular amount of space in any particular newspapers on any particular day. Indeed, on the midwinter morning following his death in Boston, it suddenly struck me that here was one encounter in thirty-two years of reporting that wholly transcended a professional relationship.

I never saw Robert Frost socially or "personally." Yet the two interviews were personal in the extreme. At the close of our first meeting, in the Westbury Hotel on Madison Avenue, he wrote in a collection of his poems, which I had been both selfish and careful enough to bring along, "To Milton Bracker, from his friend for many reasons—Robert Frost." In March, 1962, with the light fading and the clocks ticking in the house in Cambridge, he wrote in his brand new (and much thinner) volume, "In renewed friendship, after real talk one afternoon . . ." And in the act, he filled my heart with shame for having produced the book, because he now had such difficulty in managing a pen. In fact, a measure of the attrition of time is explicit in the comparative strength and weakness of those autographs, separated by three years and four months.

But a more significant measure—of the man himself—is suggested by the fact that later the same year, 1962, he was to travel all the way to Moscow, where he found Khrushchev "not a coward" and "no fathead." At a time of the Berlin crisis, he read "Mending Wall" at a Soviet literary evening. In American circles, this occasioned more quotation of the opening line—"Something there is that doesn't love a wall"—than of the subsequent " 'Good fences make good neighbors.' " Well aware that this would be the case, Robert Frost let his poem speak for itself.

He was a giant whose talent and personality fused into an absolutely infrangible whole. The man and the poetry could not be separated. He spoke himself of his "ruthless" dedication; and perhaps his

> supreme merit
> Lay in risking spirit

to prove it. With avowed "recklessness," he charged past the "unnecessary commitment" he made when he wrote the first line in the second stanza of a poem called "Stopping by Woods on a Snowy Evening." The line was

> My little horse must think it queer

and indeed, a lesser poet (and man) might have backtracked and sought to extricate himself—to go around the problem instead of solving it. But as Robert Frost later recalled, "I was riding too high to care what trouble I incurred. And it was all right so long as I didn't suffer deflection." The poem, of course, became perhaps his most celebrated single lyric.

Robert Frost was pure courage, not only in a line but in his life. He went unrecognized for very nearly half of it; and although he was flesh of the flesh and bone of the bone of America, that recognition came first in Britain. He survived personal tragedy as well as professional frustration. When he wrote in "Tree at My Window,"

> You have seen me when I was taken and swept
> And all but lost

he was hinting at the kind of turmoil he had undergone and survived. His courage had the granitic quality of the New England with which he was invariably associated (although he was born in San Francisco). He said to me in 1958 that "I have done many of the things that it looked as if it was impossible to do—like going on the platform. I did it because I didn't have to face bullets." And he also said that he wondered what it must be like to stand before a firing squad. I told him I had seen a German general face one in Italy in December, 1945.

"Did he do it bravely?" Robert Frost asked.

In his own case, intelligence and wit added a flashing shield to his innermost courage. Aware of the tragic joke that life plays on man, he was capable of playing jokes right back.

Perhaps the most celebrated incident occurred at the inauguration of John F. Kennedy on January 20, 1961. The young President-elect had invited Robert Frost, nearly twice his age, to "say" a poem at the ceremony. (Frost insisted he never "read" poems; he always "said" them.)

When the time came, the old man advanced to the lectern, the sheets bearing his new poem, called "The Preface," in his hands. But a skittish January wind and a glaring sun combined to thwart him. For a moment, he hesitated. (This was the moment that was caught for all time in a photograph of Dwight Eisenhower and Jacqueline Kennedy, the former frowning with almost disciplinary resentment at the inimical elements, the latter verging on tears.) Only Robert Frost himself knew how to handle it. Unable to read, he shifted quickly to a poem he knew by heart. It was "The Gift Outright," beginning—most appropriately for an intimately national occasion—"The land was ours before we were the land's." The triumph was complete; and fourteen months later, Robert Frost had the additional satisfaction of taking to Washington an original draft of a revised and expanded version of "The Preface." He had retitled it "For John F. Kennedy His Inauguration" (without punctuation), and he gave it to the President personally.

The qualities that came across in talks with Robert Frost included concentration, patience, constant sympathetic awareness of his guest's objective, and a sense of humor that could be turned against himself. In his last book, "In the Clearing," which became a best-seller and had sold 94,000 copies by the time of his death, there is a short piece called "Version." Robert Frost acknowledged that a close friend and Cambridge neighbor, the poet and anthologist David McCord, had "asked what it meant."

"What modern editor would ask that a poem should mean anything, anyway?" the author commented, blandly. "I left it that way in order to be in fashion."

Actually, being "in fashion" to Robert Frost meant only one thing: being himself. Some of his poems seemed simple. But his own simplicity was deceptive; or perhaps it simply went deep. "There's nothing in me to be afraid of," he assured an interviewer familiar with his work and approaching him with some awe. "I'm too offhand; I'm an offhander." But a twinkle of warning followed the very assurance. "I bear watching," he added. "I'm not confused; I'm only well-mixed." And he might have added of himself, as he frequently remarked of some of his most quoted and picked-apart poems, that he was "loaded with ulteriority." He always said what he meant but he did not always mean what he seemed to be saying.

"You have to look out for everybody's metaphors," he went on. And of course he was himself the biggest metaphor of all. As he aged, he *looked* more and more like a symbol. His white hair was really silky; a mass of it tended to sift down to the left side of his forehead, like snow to one corner of a window. His eyes were pale blue, occasionally tinged with green. They were cragged by heavy brows wintered by white curls.

One of the most moving things I heard him say came during the interview at Cambridge. "A real poem," he put it, "is sort of an idea caught in dawning—you catch it just as it comes. Think it out beforehand and you won't write it." Knowing a rare and lovely utterance when they see one, the editors of *The Times* chose that for the next morning's "Quotation of the Day."

It struck me early in our first conversation that Robert Frost had the curious inability to speak a cliché or to arrange English words in a commonplace fashion. In the present context, perhaps an even more relevant remark was "I don't like to write anything I don't see." Unfortunately, this is not a rule that journalists can always obey, but it is no less a valid and admirable guideline. And in the case of Robert Frost, it explained what a superb reporter he was, notably of the details of the country life around him. He disavowed any specialized knowledge of natural history; he knew, like countless poets before him, that there are sermons in stones. But he also knew, unlike too many poets and reporters, that there is an *exact* way to describe something seen with one's own eyes. There are lots of approximate ways, but there is only one *exact* way. Viewing Robert Frost perhaps narrowly, this was to me the one almighty thing about him.

Take "Blue-Butterfly Day." When he wrote of the wheels that "freshly sliced the April mire," he chose the absolutely correct verb, the one so uniquely evocative as to renew and fix for many readers for all time the experience of observing such a wheel in such mud. Or the other exactnesses: The swimming buck pushing the *crumpled* water, the ice crystals from the birch branch *avalanching* on the snow crust. And, in the final collection, in "Pod of the Milkweed," he saw the "intemperate" butterflies cluster so avidly on the honeyed blossoms that

> They knock the dyestuff off each other's wings. . . .

It was when we were discussing the butterflies—he had seen them just outside his "voting" home in Ripton, Vermont, in his mid-eighties—that I noticed that the room was darkening and the clocks were ticking louder. It was time to go.

Robert Frost rose, a heavy, slightly stooped figure in a gray suit. The lower right edge of his jacket was frayed, almost as if it had been burned. His white shirt was tieless, open at the throat. He led the way to the door.

Not far from his stoop were sites identified with Henry Wadsworth Longfellow and James Russell Lowell. Just outside the house, a bare tree was somewhat less bare because a bird's nest in it stood out like a black clot against the twilight.

Across the street, a brown and white cat limped along over the vestiges of snow. The cat's right hind foot shunned the ground, like a creature in space trapped in a low and painful orbit. From up the block, a child's voice tinkled. It had the clarity of a bell; timed if not tuned like Gray's tolling curfew.

At the head of the seven steps leading to the brick wall and into Brewster Street, the visitor turned and said:

"Bless you, Mr. Frost."

The poet, who was to leave for Washington the next day, snapped it up approvingly.

"Bless is a good word—that's what I'm going to tell the President," he said. " 'Bless your Irish heart.' "

Then he went back inside. I never saw him again. On the morning of Tuesday, January 29, 1963, my wife heard the news on the radio and told me. I experienced that welling of tears, not so much *to* the eyes as *behind* them, that told me that a friend "for many reasons," indeed, was gone.

Joseph Jones worked as a copy boy for a small Missouri newspaper before attending Drury College in Springfield, Missouri. Then, even before his graduation from Columbia Journalism in 1922, he joined the staff of the United Press (now United Press International). He's been with that news service ever since.

Mr. Jones has been a vice president of United Press since 1942. Before he became general foreign manager in 1937, he was assigned to London, Lima, Santiago, Buenos Aires and Caracas—the last of which he writes about in this piece. Mr. Jones lives in Pelham, New York.

JOSEPH JONES:

The General

Before the air age began, Venezuela was off the main travel routes. Few reporters visited the country, and that was quite all right with the government. If a correspondent somehow did make his way in, he faced cable censorship, insecure mail channels and clammed-up sources. One official even told me that the constitution was out of print and unobtainable.

Not only did news fail to get out of Venezuela—it also failed to get in. Until early 1929, the newspapers of Caracas obtained their world news from a hand-out prepared by the French Cable Company; for this each paper paid thirty cents a day, the cost of making a mimeograph copy in the cable office. And for what they got, the price was high.

I was in Venezuela for the United Press in 1929, waiting for a new cable connection to tie that country in with the already-established (and otherwise complete) UP network in South America. In the meantime a remarkable election was taking place, and I was able to witness it.

Venezuela's congress was meeting in joint session to elect a president of the republic. Voting was by ballot; the 124 senators and deputies turned furtively from each other as they wrote their choices on blank

198

sheets of white paper. One member used his straw hat to conceal his selection.

The honorable senators and deputies seemed troubled as they then put their ballots in two white enameled boxes in the front of the chamber. There two deputies and two senators dumped the folded slips onto a table, and began to call out the votes.

"General Gomez . . . J. V. Gomez . . . El Benemerito General Gomez . . . Gomez . . . General Juan Vicente Gomez, el Gran Rehabilitador. . . ."

An ancient clerk, with glasses far down on his nose, held his pencil poised in air, ready if another name were called. There were 124 votes —but all were cast, by name or title, for Gomez.

The vote was announced; the assembly stood and sang the national hymn. After sending a telegram to the town of Maracay, 75 miles away over the Andean foothills, notifying the general that he was in again, the congress adjourned.

Yet the congressmen had every right to be worried. They didn't know whether the man for whom they had voted would serve. There had been no electoral campaign, nor was there an opposition party.

For more than 20 years, General Juan Vincente Gomez had been the undisputed master of Venezuela. All power flowed from Gomez. All official favors were in his hands. He ran the country as if it were a rich hacienda—and it was a magnificent property, bigger than all France.

But now it was 1929, and Gomez was 72, and he had given signs of wanting a change—disturbing signs, because without him who could be sure of office or of a government job or of any place in the Establishment?

Then back from Maracay came the word that many had feared: El Benemerito wired that he declined to accept. Congress hurriedly sent a commission to persuade the general, but without success. Now the whole legislature, senate and chamber, rushed in a body to Maracay.

Gomez reiterated his refusal of the presidency, but said that his services were at the command of the country in any circumstances.

Congress "accepted the services so nobly offered, putting under his expert hand the supreme command of the army. And thus," their announcement ended, "national peace was assured."

The general named his choice as president; and congress rapidly set about reforming the constitution, appropriately dividing the powers of the president. Within a month the amendment had passed three readings in both houses of congress and had been ratified by all state legislatures. Justice Perez was elected president—and General Gomez continued to run the country. Some eighteen months later there were rumors of revolt, and Perez resigned. Gomez succeeded him, put down two minor uprisings, and the constitution was re-amended to put the presidency together again.

In sum, the governmental structure through which Gomez ruled Venezuela, certain niceties aside, worked like this: The president was elected by the congress . . . which was elected by the state legislatures . . . which were chosen by the municipal deputies . . . who were named by the state governors . . . who were appointed by the president. A conveniently closed circle, with all the formalities of a representative system.

Back of the constitutional formalities was a national 12,000-man conscript army. It belonged to Gomez; he had led it, in skirmish and battle, as far back as 1901. There was another small army of informers. Police posts spread chains across the highways and took down the names and movements of all travelers. Dark stories of tortures and 70-pound leg-irons seeped out of the prisons. Landowners who refused to sell out to the general's favorites found themselves jailed, freed, then jailed again until the offered prices seemed acceptable. The Ins prospered with governments jobs, farms, concessions.

When congress made the pilgrimage to Maracay, it traveled a well-worn path. The Old One lived there, far from Caracas and its city ways. He rarely went to the capital, rarely saw Miraflores Palace, the presidential residence. Cabinet members journeyed to Maracay for weekend meetings; diplomats presented their credentials there, and a steady stream of less consequential visitors followed.

Set in the fertile Aragua valley, the town had 10,000 civilian inhabitants and 2,000 troops were quartered in it. One of the barracks stood across the plaza from General Gomez' residence, a rambling old one-story building with a graceful patio. The tiny air force trained a few blocks away, and the only long-distance radio station in Venezuela was nearby. A first-class concrete highway led to the capital and its port.

The general rarely received in his home. The hundreds who arrived weekly to shake his hand had to go to Las Delicias, three miles from Maracay.

Las Delicias was one of many Gomez ranches, but a favorite, where he built an open-air restaurant and the largest zoo in that part of the world. In the restaurant, or seated under one of the big trees in front of it, Venezuela's president attended to the social and some of the more weighty duties of his office.

Usually this power center became active in late afternoon. At five o'clock on a typical day, half a dozen persons were sitting at the tables, waiting. Just before six, a caravan of automobiles whirled up bringing the general, his aides, members of his family, friends and petitioners. The president walked to a line of chairs against a wall and sat down. The people, by then 50 or 60 in all, stood.

They saw a middle-sized, straight figure which had lost the fat of middle age; a plain khaki field uniform with a wide turned-up Panama hat; dark gloves which, like Clemenceau, Gomez wore in public; a grizzled mustache, and a pair of sharp eyes that did not miss a single pretty face, including my wife's.

Men and women, they approached, some of them politicians, candidates, or concession hunters who had come halfway across Venezuela to make their bow or, failing that, simply to stand where the general might see them. Sometimes they went to Las Delicias for several days in succession, but without apparent result.

Gomez' day began at 4:30 A.M. After coffee, he set to work with a secretary answering official mail. After breakfast at 7:30, he would go for a drive in the country. At one of his ranches, officials would report on government matters, probably while sitting under a tree. The more important the problem, the more likely it was to be settled out of town.

Lunch was at one, siesta till 3:30. Then an hour to receive reports on private affairs—cattle sold, condition of the coffee crop, factory output—before the trip to Las Delicias. Dinner came at seven. At eight the Chief Executive, surrounded by aides and followed by a little crowd, walked over to the little movie theatre. He was an inveterate movie-goer, a fan of westerns or military stories. He usually saw movies five nights a week. He was always in bed before ten.

On Sunday mornings he liked to see the cock-fights, held in a little roofed arena at the back of a garage. I saw him sit there from 8:45 A.M. until 12:20, flanked by seven cabinet members, watching a dozen bouts. Around him eddied the impassioned cries of bettors, who made so much noise they had to use sign language.

With a crony, the general bet on about half the fights, $100 or $150 on each, with varying luck. The bookies, scuttling around the ring, took off their hats before approaching his wicker-bottomed rocker —carried in for the occasion—to take his wagers.

Gomez was one of the world's rich men, thought to be rivaled in South America only by Simon Patino, the Bolivian tin king. His fortune was estimated by a close associate at one hundred million dollars, but with the reservation that no confirmation was possible. His personal pay-roll was given as $52,000 a week, with 12,000 persons depending on his enterprises for a livelihood.

The country was his barony. His friends and relations held their lands in fief, and his frown was banishment.

Gomez' family life was as off-beat as that of a Mongolian khan. Never married, he was said by close friends to be the father of eighty natural children by numerous mothers.

Gomez, who had put down a dozen armed revolts, died in bed in 1935. Official mourning was proclaimed. When the victims of his dic-tatorship were sure that the report of his death was no trick, emo-tions exploded. They burned his newspaper, seized and sacked his properties, looted the homes of his favorites and tore some mansions down brick by brick. The Gomez family and friends fled secretly to Curacao on a gunboat furnished by the government. The jails were emptied of political inmates.

But by the time Gomez died, Venezuela was no longer in the dark ages of news dissemination. About the time the congressmen went to Maracay, Caracas papers, notably *El Universal,* began to receive a thousand words of cabled news daily from UP. Before long, this daily file would become 50,000 words of radio-teleprinter copy in Spanish. In the subsequent years, fast air transport, instantaneous radio trans-mission of news, telephoto service, scholarships, the sturdy Inter-American Press Association—even dictatorial outrages against the press like the *La Prensa* case—drew newsmen of the western world together in a way unimaginable when the incidents related here took place.

Sooner or later, such free dissemination of the news must make the personal power of a Gomez impossible.

John Hohenberg was graduated from the School of Journalism in 1927 and returned to it in 1950 as a member of the faculty. In the intervening years he worked as a newspaperman in New York, Washington and overseas for The New York World, United Press, *the* Journal-American *and* The New York Post, *for which he served as United Nations correspondent.*

Professor Hohenberg is the author of two books, "The Pulitzer Prize Story" and "The Professional Journalist," a comprehensive volume in wide use as a text. Since 1954, he has been secretary to the advisory board on the Pulitzer Prizes. He lives with his wife, Dorothy, in New York City.

JOHN HOHENBERG:

Paris, Fate and Mr. Dulles

On a dour November afternoon in Paris, General George Catlett Marshall interrupted an extraordinary proceeding at the Palais de Chaillot. He did not mean to do it, of course, being soft-spoken, courteous and considerate in all things. But he happened at the moment to be the Secretary of State of the United States, and the mere fact of his entrance at the Palais was enough to attract the attention of any thoughtful foreign potentate. There were a few hundred around. The United Nations General Assembly was in session.

At another door of the Palais, flashbulbs were winking, singly and in mass effect, like star shells over some half-forgotten cinema battlefield. A horde of shouting photographers had gathered around an almost totally obscured figure, another personage who was making a grander entrance. From the contorted mass came a babel of commands in a half-dozen languages, accompanied by multilingual imprecations. They added up to:

"Look this way, Mr. Secretary . . ."

"Okay, Mr. Secretary. Let's have a big smile, now . . ."

General Marshall murmured a polite inquiry to a member of the

203

United States Mission. Who was this particular Mr. Secretary? Why so
much interest in him? There was an air of quiet desperation about the
little group that surrounded General Marshall, and he perceived that
his question had produced a certain amount of embarrassment. Just
then it was answered for him. The ranks of the photographers parted
and a big, balding gentleman in brown, his tie awry and his eyeglasses
slightly askew, strode out beaming. It was John Foster Dulles, who
was in the pleasant process that day of being publicly anointed as the
next Secretary of State of the United States.

The photographers, of course, instinctively realized that they now
had a much better picture, and they rushed to get both General Marshall
and Mr. Dulles together. Had it not been for the quiet good humor of
the French foreign minister, the wise and friendly Robert Schumann,
the scene might have been painful. But M. Schumann, closing in ahead
of the photographers, slipped between Mr. Dulles and General Marshall,
linked arms with them and announced with the serenity of an experienced diplomat, "Let me pose with both Secretaries of State."

There was, of course, only one small detail that everyone had overlooked. That dour November day in 1948 was Election Day in the
United States, and not a vote had yet been counted. The elegant British
and the realistic French had, for the most part, already concluded that
Thomas E. Dewey was bound to defeat the hapless Harry S. Truman
for the Presidency of the United States, and few Americans were brave
enough to challenge them. That being the case, there was no need to
consult either the diplomatic experts or *The New York Times.* Everybody who was anybody at the United Nations knew that John Foster
Dulles would be the next Secretary of State. Hadn't General Carlos P.
Romulo of the Philippines already arranged a party in his honor?

Under these circumstances, the correspondents descended on Mr.
Dulles in a body for interviews (on a hold-for-release basis, of course)
to be published after Election Day.

What policies would he recommend to President-elect Dewey? The
next Secretary of State was graciousness itself. He pointed out that it
would be best to have the formality of the election out of the way
before he made any pronouncements; on the morrow, therefore, he
would see us one at a time at his hotel. As luck would have it, I was
able to obtain an appointment with Mr. Dulles for 7 A.M. the next day
at his hotel, the first newspaper correspondent on his list.

I was a little ahead of time at the hotel for my interview. Although I
had read the Paris edition of *The New York Herald Tribune* and the
French papers (which carried the early returns, merely confirming what

everybody had forecast), I phoned the AP for the latest word. The best they had at that hour was a summary put out shortly after midnight, New York time, which showed Dewey still in the lead. I settled down to wait. Seven o'clock came, but no Dulles. Five minutes passed. Then another five. I was about to telephone to his room when I saw him walk slowly across the lobby toward me, his face solemn, his head slightly bent. When we shook hands in the mechanical way in which diplomats and correspondents greet each other, I noticed that he was wearing a black tie.

"I'm afraid I'm not giving any interviews right now," Mr. Dulles said soberly.

"Why not? Dewey's ahead, isn't he?"

"I'd rather not comment."

"I can understand why you might not want to be quoted directly," I said, feeling a little uneasy, "but what's wrong with talking for background?"

He shook his head. "I've just talked with New York."

"What do they say?"

"That's the trouble. They don't say."

"Well, is it or isn't it true that Dewey's ahead?"

Mr. Dulles, shrewd lawyer that he was, never let himself be drawn into a fast question-and-answer exchange. He would always pull back ever so slightly, deliberately hesitate before answering, and stare a correspondent down. That was what he did now and he seemed quite grim and weary, as if he hadn't had much sleep.

"I've had a little experience with Presidential elections," he said, finally. "I remember one particular election in 1916. I was at Wilson's headquarters that night and I'll never forget it."

"Oh," I said.

He adjusted his black tie and blinked. "So you see, I'd better not give any interviews."

"Shall I call you later?" I asked.

He shook his head sadly. "I guess not."

He walked across the lobby and returned to his quarters. As other correspondents came in or phoned, he was unavailable. That was why *The New York Post* never carried a post-election interview with John Foster Dulles, and why nobody, to my knowledge, ever published the gay picture of M. Schumann with his two American Secretaries of State. As for General Romulo's party, he gave it anyway in Mr. Dulles's honor. It was, as he soberly explained, for the ex-Secretary of State.

*Richard Schaap attended the Columbia School of
Journalism on a Grantland Rice Fellowship; he
was graduated in 1956 and is presently a senior
editor of* Newsweek.

*A former president of the Magazine Sports
Writers Association, his stories have appeared in*
Saturday Evening Post, True, Sport *and other
magazines, and have been represented in three
annual editions of "Best Sport Stories." He is the
author of biographies of Mickey Mantle and Paul
Hornung, and of a new sports history, "An Illus-
trated History of the Olympics." He received his
B. A. in Industrial and Labor Relations at Cornell
University in 1955.*

RICHARD SCHAAP:

In Defense of Sports Writers

Sports writers are popularly portrayed as frustrated athletes, sycophants,
freeloaders, hacks, clichémongers and alcoholics. This is a gross libel.
Some of them do not drink.

I have overstated, of course, the mass indictment of the sports writer;
yet there are those who would insist I have been too kind. Even many
of the sports writer's journalistic contemporaries, who should know
better, seem to consider him an inferior breed—a type to be tolerated
most of the time, to be cultivated at World Series ticket time, but
never to be accorded equal status. The sports writer is the James
Meredith of journalism. He is in only under protest.

He does not present the great issues the way the political reporters
do. He does not clarify the great issues the way the political analysts do.
He does not judge the great issues the way the political pundits do. He
makes his living by writing about grown men playing the games of
children.

My modest proposal is that there is nothing wrong with writing
about the games of children—provided that the writing itself is not
childish. Any decent sports writer, as many decent sports writers have

206

said, knows that he is working in the toy department of his newspaper or magazine. He realizes that no matter how important a World Series or a heavyweight championship fight or a Grand Prix auto race may seem at the moment, its cosmic significance is, at best, infinitesimal. A sporting event is no more enduring than today's rape or yesterday's ax murder.

In defending sports writers, I admit I'm in a fairly vulnerable position. For five years, from the time I left the Columbia Graduate School of Journalism in 1956 until the fall of 1961, I was a fulltime sports writer. Now, as a senior editor of *Newsweek* concerned with seven so-called "back-of-the-book" departments, I devote perhaps 10 per cent or less of my fulltime job to sports. Still, as a freelance magazine contributor, I devote perhaps 60 per cent or more of my spare time job to sports. I am, you might say, a half-ex-sportswriter.

To me, what makes sports writing worthwhile is surely not the events —it is the people who participate in those events. The sportsmen, not the sport. This is the whole lure of writing about sports; it affords one the opportunity to write about ordinary people thrust into extraordinary circumstances. The way these people react—emotionally as well as physically—can provide drama and pathos and humor, basic ingredients of fine journalism. If a sports writer can capture the essence of one man —his "grace under pressure," in Hemingway's classic definition of courage, or his "choking up," in the athlete's classic definition of cowardice—then he may have matched in value anything the political reporter or pundit can produce.

My most memorable experiences in sports writing therefore, concern people, not events. I cannot single out one individual, but I will limit myself to three—three men whose company I shared on critical days in their careers. Under extreme pressure, each reacted differently. My intention is to give you merely an impression of three different, yet appealing men.

On the day Floyd Patterson fought his savage third bout with Ingemar Johansson, a small group gathered in his temporary Miami Beach home to spend the waiting hours with the man who was then heavyweight champion of the world.

Patterson has his flaws. He is introverted to a fault; he is overly suspicious of people; he is at times so determinedly humble that he borders on mawkishness. Yet all his flaws are understandable. He grew up in ugly poverty, spent his adolescent years in a school for disturbed children and then, although his instincts are gentle, earned fame and

wealth by pounding people with his fists. He is truly modest, truly compassionate. He is, as trite as it sounds, a good man.

Now, on the day he was going to risk his title, he scanned wonderingly
a batch of mail he had received from Sweden, strangely proud that so
many Swedes wanted him to defeat their countryman. He made certain
that his guests were comfortable. And he played cards—quietly, almost
lethargically. He played a game called Tonk, a five-card version of gin
rummy. I won $5 from the heavyweight champion of the world; he
paid in cash.

Before and after lunch, he took long walks, strolling the streets of
Miami Beach, smiling and waving at the people who recognized him,
embarrassed yet pleased by the recognition, and condoning the little
girl who rushed up and said, "You'd better win tonight. My father has
a lot of money bet on you." And now the first sign of nervousness appeared. Patterson yawned. When he gets nervous, he gets drowsy; he
was once so afraid to make a speech at a banquet that he almost fell
asleep at the dais. Patterson slept the afternoon of the fight and he slept
in the dressing room before the opening bell.

Then came the fight and when Johansson struck suddenly with his
right hand, Patterson fell to the canvas, his pride hurt more than his
body. He came up and went down again. I was supposed to be an im-
partial observer, but knowing both men and liking only one, I felt
pained, too. When Patterson came back and floored Johansson in the
first round and destroyed him in the sixth, I shared his elation. Then
Patterson hugged his opponent and complimented him, and the nervousness was gone and Patterson was wide awake. Later, when Jimmy
Durante, entertaining at the victory party, singled out Patterson for attention, the champion was embarrassed once more. It seemed an appropriate touch.

If tension serves as a sedative for Floyd Patterson, it serves as a
stimulant for Stirling Crauford Moss, the Englishman who is, for sheer
virtuosity, as fine a race driver as ever lived—and almost died. On the
morning of the first Grand Prix de Cuba in 1956, Stirling and his future
wife, Katie, and I ate a fast, light breakfast, and he bubbled over with
small talk and energy.

"Grand Prix racing is a simple art," I once wrote in an article for *True*
magazine. "You drive a low car at a high speed and if you do it better
than anyone else, you win. That's all there is to it. Except there isn't
much room for error. You depend upon a complicated machine to
storm down straightaways at 170, 180 miles an hour and you depend
upon complicated skills to drift through curves at 80, 90 miles an hour,

and if your machine fails or your skill fails, you pay in blood. The name of the game is survival.

"Nobody plays the game harder than a short, wiry, balding, bold, superstitious, shilling-pinching, teetotaling extrovert with a name that looks riddled by typographical errors. Stirling Crauford Moss is British and brash and 33 years old, and if you want to bet he never makes it to 34, you've got a case. He almost didn't make it to 33."

Typically, on the day of the Cuban Grand Prix, Moss drove to the course in somewhat unusual fashion. He had ten people in a Hillman Minx, a neat trick with three in the front seat, four in the back and three in the trunk (featuring a blonde stretched across the legs of two young men). He chattered constantly as he slipped into his racing outfit, gave Katie a quick kiss and then, with a cheerful wave, began the race. For several laps, he held first place. Then he dropped back into second as he passed the pit area. Then the first place car came around and Moss didn't. Twice more the field circled the course and Moss never came into sight. Katie, standing beside me in the paddock, gripped the fence in front of her so hard her hands shone white. Finally, after what seemed an interminable time, Moss appeared far down the road, unscarred, running, walking and swearing, cursing the machinery that had failed him. He and Katie and I returned to their hotel and, within an hour, he was showered, shaved, dressed and laughing, the mishap that might have been fatal apparently forgotten completely. If another car had been available, he would have been eager to risk his life again.

Boxing is brutal and auto racing lethal, but baseball is rather a pleasant game, and Jim Brosnan, the pitcher-author, is a pleasant man. Even on the morning of the opening game of the 1961 World Series, when after a decade of journeyman pitching Brosnan was anticipating his first World Series appearance, he was in a pleasant mood.

Brosnan is a unique athlete. He writes books about his sport, and, doubly shocking, he writes them himself and he writes them honestly. He takes pitching and martinis with equal seriousness, and he takes managers and sports writers with equal grains of salt. He is a delightful person.

The morning his Cincinnati Reds were to begin their Series with the New York Yankees, Brosnan, his wife and I ate a leisurely, heavy breakfast at a New York hotel. As we prepared to order, Brosnan turned to me with mock seriousness and asked, "Tell me, what does a relief pitcher eat for breakfast the day of the opening World Series game?" He ate a ham steak.

Brosnan can kid about the pressures of baseball; he has no inflated notion of the importance of his game. But he is also a dedicated professional, and as long as he is playing, he wants to win. I watched the World Series and watched the Yankees smother him with base hits, and for me it was the same as seeing Patterson pounded or waiting for Moss to reappear. Brosnan suffered deeply, but when I saw him again a few months later all the pain had disappeared. It is amazing what a winter of well-mixed martinis can do for an athlete—or a sports writer.

Floyd Patterson. Stirling Moss. Jim Brosnan. I could add a string of names—the happy hams, Paul Hornung and Cassius Clay; the geniuses of their arts, Pancho Gonzalez and Wilt Chamberlain; the men embittered by discrimination, Bill White and Oscar Robertson. They are all fascinating individuals. They are the men who make sports writing worthwhile.

John H. Crider, who was graduated from the School of Journalism in 1928, won two major awards in 1949 for editorial writing: The Pulitzer Prize and the Sigma Delta Chi Prize. A Nieman Fellow at Harvard in 1954, Mr. Crider is now assistant information director of the Committee for Economic Development.

His previous experience runs the gamut of the profession—reporter, The New York Times; *Washington correspondent,* Time; *editor-in-chief,* The Boston Herald; *news analyst, CBS; assistant editorial page editor,* Life; *Washington correspondent,* Barron's Weekly, *and diplomatic correspondent, INS. He lives with his wife, Maxine, and three children in White Plains, New York.*

JOHN CRIDER:

The Fellowship of the Press

It is said that writing is a solitary and lonely profession. Journalism is not; rarely is a reporter entirely sufficient unto himself.

I remember back to a relaxed, triumphant Sunday in New York. I'd been out late the night before; I'd slept late; now I had the Sunday *Times* to keep me company for the remainder of a restful day. And on the following morning—I would go out to White Plains to become Westchester County correspondent for *The New York Times.*

Then the telephone rang. It was the *Times* city desk.

"Crider," a voice said calmly, "there's been a torch murder up in Westchester. We can't find our stringer up there, but we'd like to have a staff man cover this anyway. It might be quite a yarn."

The desk couldn't give me much more information. Everything it had I could find in the late edition of one of the tabloids.

I dressed, reached into my pocket and discovered that my Saturday night celebration had stripped me of cash. I had fifteen cents. White Plains was twenty-five miles away from Manhattan. The brand new

Model-A Ford I'd ordered couldn't be picked up for a week or two. Railroad fare would be far more than I had.

There were two alternatives. I could go down to *The Times* and borrow some money. But for a cub reporter on his first big assignment, this would be humiliating.

Or I could walk a mile to an elevated train that wound its way across lower Harlem and then connected with the line running out to White Plains Road in the Bronx. There I could walk down a hill to the Bronx end of the new Bronx River Parkway and try to hitch a ride for the remaining 12 miles to the Westchester County seat. This seemed risky, slow—and necessary.

So I walked to the "L" station and bought the tabloid (first nickel). Then I boarded a rattling old train (second nickel) and settled down to get informed. But there was practically nothing new there—just a few paragraphs saying that the charred, nude body of what seemed to be a young girl had been found along a roadside in the town of Greenburgh, somewhere between Ardsley and Scarsdale. A final line added that a suspect might soon be picked up in North White Plains.

No matter what, the sensational press of New York would blow the story sky-high. *Torch murder!*—it was a natural for them. Ordinarily this would not be much of a story for the august *Times,* but we had to be covered and—who knew?—the body might turn out to be that of a Rockefeller.

My train stopped at every station. It was already getting on past mid-afternoon. The girl's body had been found some twelve hours earlier. Other New York correspondents would already be on the scene. The whole case might be washed up by the time I got there.

I waited for ten minutes on the parkway before a kind-hearted driver stopped to give me a lift. Luckily he was just out for a Sunday afternoon spin and didn't care where he went; he delivered me to the center of White Plains. From there I took a bus (last nickel) to North White Plains. Somehow, that seemed the only sensible thing to do.

The bus driver had heard about the murder; what's more, he knew that a little side-street house had now become the center of activity in the case. He let me off at the right corner, and sure enough, down the street I could see a knot of people—photographers, policemen, curious bystanders.

The first thing I heard when I approached was a cordial, "Hi, John —what are you doing here?"

I looked into the handsome Irish face of my old Mount Vernon neighbor and schoolmate, Bill O'Donovan—now on the news staff of *The*

White Plains Daily Reporter. No sight was ever more welcome. Bill had been on the story ever since it broke. He not only filled me in on all the developments, but also lent me some money. I called my office, and then we drove around together in his car until the story was wrapped up.

During my only assignment as a war correspondent, thirty years later, I received instructions to proceed immediately from Cairo to Port Said to replace Howard Handleman, a fellow INS correspondent who was covering the British occupation forces. To reach my destination in ordinary times would have been simple—the distance was only some 100 miles. But there had been fighting between the Israelis and Egyptians, with the British and the French supporting the Israelis. The truce of the moment was by no means secure.

If I had not been ordered to proceed "immediately," the trip could have been easily made. A stretch of "no man's land" at El Cap—patrolled by contingents of the United Nations Emergency Force—separated the Egyptians and the British and French. Had I been able to wait a day or so, I could have crossed the buffer zone in a white UN jeep under the protection of the little pale blue flag that was becoming so meaningful internationally. But I couldn't wait.

So I cabled Howard Handleman, by way of New York, saying that between three and four the next afternoon there would be a character in slacks and sports jacket crossing "no man's land," carrying a portable typewriter in one hand and a beat-up brown canvas bag in the other, and would he please ask his British and French friends not to shoot!

I made the trip in five stages. A remarkable colleague, a Greek named Angelopoulos, sped me the 50 miles from Cairo to Abu Suweir Air Base. "Angel" had, incredibly enough, a brand new Oldsmobile "88," and nothing gave him more pleasure than to drive it at about 90 miles an hour along the canal, terrifying any Arabs, camels, donkeys or other live stock unfortunate enough to be on the road.

At the air base, an Egyptian officer—Brigadier Amin Helmi, a dapper little man who looked and acted more British than the British themselves—arranged for Stage Two. He turned me over to a Yugoslav colonel who was about to drive to an advance UN base only a few miles from "no man's land." As the third man in a two-seater jeep, sometimes squatting and sometimes semi-supine, I completed the next 35 miles of the trip.

Stage Three was brief. At the Yugoslav camp, a Norwegian officer —the chief-of-staff to General E.L.M. Burns, commander-in-chief of the UNEF—took over. He had me driven a mile down the road to an Indian camp.

At the headquarters of this paratroop battalion from northern India, I was invited by the commanding officer to join him and his staff at dinner. (The curry we ate was so bitingly hot that I had a burning mouth for a week.) Stage Four was completed after we dined; in a caravan of brand new British Land Rovers, not yet painted a protective white, we crossed to the Egyptian side of the buffer area. Then, after a short delay while the colonel completed a necessary inspection, he drove me across "no man's land" to the British side.

Howard Handleman was waiting there with a jeep and driver. I suspect that he was even gladder to see me than I to see him; Howard was now free to move on to Paris.

. . . In White Plains, it had been *one* friend, come upon fortuitously. In Egypt it was a multitude of friends and strangers from numerous countries. Journalism is not a lonely profession—and not a profession for the lone wolf. You have to use your wits; but above all else, you need friends and friendly assistance.

*A. D. Rothman has been a newspaperman since
1917, when he was graduated from the School of
Journalism. Only the first of his many years in
journalism was spent covering developments in the
domestic field; the others have been devoted to
foreign correspondence. Mr. Rothman began as a
reporter with International News Service, and then
went on to serve as representative abroad for a
number of American and foreign (chiefly Australian) newspapers.*

*Mr. Rothman has covered such historic person-
alities as Wilson, Churchill, Roosevelt, Mac-
Arthur, Nehru and Khrushchev. He now makes his
home in Rhinebeck, New York.*

A. D. ROTHMAN:

The Power of a Question

During World War I, one of the leaders in the fight against Great
Britain in the "Irish troubles" was Archbishop Mannix. A dedicated
and tireless man, the Irish-born prelate not only dominated his diocese
in Victoria and the whole hierarchy of Australia as well, but also so
stirred the spirits of men that his name had become a household word
even among Americans of Irish extraction. Ireland was already a thorn
in the side of Britain; Archbishop Mannix worked implacably to make
the thorn grow into a lance.

The "troubles" in Ireland reached new heights in 1916. After a week
of bloody fighting, the great Easter Rebellion had been suppressed. Sir
Roger Casement, landed on the Irish coast by a German submarine
in this abortive effort to make Ireland a German base, had been captured. Now, as was due his rank, he was to be hanged with a silken
rope.

At the height of the disturbances, the Archbishop decided to visit
Ireland, pausing en route in the United States to strengthen opposition
to American entry into the war on the side of Britain. He was met at
the boat in New York by a mob of newspapermen. I was among them.

215

From the Columbia School of Journalism I had gone to Hearst's International News Service, where my work had ranged from running copy for Damon Runyon to organizing a tri-state (Kentucky, West Virginia and Ohio) news bureau. Then, after a period on the INS cable desk, I joined the newly-formed Australian Press Association, representing the group in America and (later) abroad.

For the newspapers of Australia, this visit by Archbishop Mannix was serious news. The brief statement he made to the crowd of reporters upon his arrival was scarcely sufficient for readers at home. I arranged to meet him privately that evening in the rectory on Madison Avenue behind St. Patrick's Cathedral.

Although I arrived late at the rectory, the company was still at dinner. Archbishop Mannix nevertheless came at once to the reception room and permitted me an extensive interview. His replies to my persistent questions were so startling that I finally said, "Does Your Grace realize that you are in effect asking for a declaration of war by the United States against Great Britain because of her failure to give Ireland Home Rule?"

"That's precisely what I have in mind," the Archbishop replied grimly.

"That being so," I said, "I should like to write the dispatch and have you approve it before I send it."

Mannix pointed to a writing desk in one corner of the room. I went to work while he rejoined the company. In about an hour he returned, just as I was finishing the last sentence. He read the news report, his face extraordinarily immobile.

"That will do," he said. "You are reporting faithfully what I said to you."

I filed my dispatch at "urgent full rate," which in those days was $1.95 per word. It proved a bombshell in Australia. Fiery Billy Hughes, then prime minister of the Commonwealth—the man who later was to give Woodrow Wilson so much trouble at the Versailles Peace Conference on questions of race equality and the German colonies—reacted promptly. He sent a preemptory signal to Prime Minister Lloyd George of Great Britain to have Archbishop Mannix removed from his ship, which by then was on its way to Ireland. Some days later a British warship carried out the order as the vessel was approaching Cobh. Eight-column, front-page streamer headlines in American newspapers blazoned the news. Further fuel was thus added to anti-British sentiment that smoldered in the United States—that divided the country, as a matter of fact, until early 1917, when unrestricted submarine warfare and the Zimmerman Note led to the American declaration of war against Germany.

I recall this incident from among a multitude in a 50-year career as a journalist—a period that has permitted me to meet with and cover the monumental activities of Woodrow Wilson and Franklin Roosevelt, Nikita Khrushchev and Sir Winston Churchill, General Douglas MacArthur and Prime Minister Nehru. I recall it as an example of the fact that with his questions the journalist can *make* news.

After half a century, the responsibility still seems to me to be exciting —and awesome.

Dorothy Ducas started her journalistic career as a reporter. She has worked for The New York Herald Tribune, The New York Evening Post, The London Sunday Express, *and* INS. *Miss Ducas also served as an editor at* McCall's, *Woman's* Day *and* House Beautiful, *and, from 1942 to 1944, was chief of the Magazine Bureau in the Office of War Information.*

Formerly public relations director of the National Foundation-March of Dimes, Miss Ducas is now a special consultant to the Surgeon General, U.S. Public Health Service, and public service consultant to Lobsenz and Company, public relations. When she was graduated from Columbia Journalism in 1926, Miss Ducas was at that time the youngest girl to win a Pulitzer Traveling Scholarship. She is married to James B. Herzog and has two sons and three grandsons.

DOROTHY DUCAS:

In Touch with Greatness

Newspaper reporters meet so many interesting people that the phrase long ago became a cliché. Meeting *great* people, however, is as rare as finding a pearl in an oyster.

Like most reporters, I have met my share of famous men and women, some of whom have merited the adjective "great"—Franklin D. Roosevelt, Sinclair Lewis, Dr. Jonas Salk. I can't say I knew them in an intimate sense. The stories I wrote about them by and large said all I knew; my readers had as much information as I.

But one truly great person encountered in my career as a reporter became a personal friend, and the circumstances under which this happened are the high spot of my professional life.

It was an assignment in 1934 to Puerto Rico and the Virgin Islands that gave me the opportunity really to know Mrs. Franklin D. Roosevelt.

The trip was scarcely the biggest story of that time, although it was

218

the first overseas inspection journey made by a First Lady acting as
eyes and ears for her husband, a role which became frequent for Mrs.
Roosevelt thereafter. And it was not my first close association with
Eleanor Roosevelt, for I had been a member of her press conference in
Washington from the beginning of that precedent-breaking activity;
also, during both the 1928 and the 1932 presidential campaigns I had
covered her public appearances. But until I became one of her Puerto
Rican party, our relationship was entirely that of interviewer and in-
terviewee.

I met Mrs. Roosevelt in 1928 in the Democratic State Committee
offices at the Biltmore Hotel. She sat very straight at her desk, wearing
a long-sleeved white shirtwaist and dark skirt, with a gold lapel watch
pinned over her breast in defiance of fashion. She spoke in a highpitched
voice, rather slowly and with a touch of shyness. I had no glimmering
of her remarkable character.

I began to see it, I think, the day after she moved into the White
House. I called about 9 A.M. and asked for Malvina Thompson, her
efficient and friendly secretary.

"Miss Thompson isn't here," said a voice from the White House.
"May I help?"

"Who is this?" I asked incredulously, suspecting the answer.

"Mrs. Roosevelt," she said.

"I didn't mean to trouble you," I apologized. "I just wanted to ask
Tommy what your schedule is for today."

"That's all right, I'll tell you," said the First Lady.

And she did. On her initial day as chatelaine of the White House,
she was taking her secretary's calls without thinking twice about it.

So I knew, before we left for Puerto Rico, that here was a woman
totally lacking in self-importance, an energetic, warm-hearted person
who cared deeply about people, even reporters. Indeed, she had created
the women's White House press conferences because she wanted to in-
sure jobs for women reporters in those depression days.

What I was not prepared for was the full measure of her humanity.
We were a small group: Bess Furman of the AP, the late Ruby Black
of UP, Emma Bugbee of the *Herald Tribune,* and I, representing International News Service. Lorena Hickok, then working for the WPA,
went along to observe and report to Harry Hopkins. And the lone male
was Sammy Schulman, one of FDR's favorite photographers, assigned
to cover the trip for a photo pool. Mrs. Roosevelt took us all to her heart.

We left Washington by train at midnight on March 4. Mrs. Roosevelt
arrived at Union Station after a Cabinet party and after a long session

with Tommy, spent signing mail and balancing her five checkbooks. She kept one checkbook for the Washington house, others for the New York house, Washington personal and New York personal, with the fifth for what she earned and gave away. She used a different signature for each—i.e., Anna Eleanor Roosevelt, Eleanor Roosevelt, A. E. Roosevelt, etc.

As one who has never managed to balance a single checkbook, I assumed that she would be tired and would sleep late the next day. But no, when we reached Fayetteville, North Carolina, early in the morning we were invited to step off the train with her to view an old slave market near the depot. It was the first of many side trips. Mrs. Roosevelt would not pass up an interesting sight, even during a brief train stop.

At Miami we boarded our Pan American Clipper and Mrs. R. (as we soon were allowed to call her) held her first ocean-flying press conference. She told us why she was making the trip—in quotable form. She wanted to see the condition of the people after three generations of depression, to let them know that the President was interested in their welfare. She hoped that out of her report might come some improvements.

During these press conferences I always managed to place myself on Mrs. R.'s left side, for I hear better with my right ear than my left.

"You are so thoughtful, Dorothy," said the First Lady, who was somewhat deaf in her right ear.

I confessed my real reason for the maneuver, aware at the same time that only a person finely tuned to the individual actions of others would even have noticed.

After a brief stop in Neuvitas, Cuba, where the Mayor of Havana told Mrs. R. of difficulties caused by a current railroad strike (everybody told his troubles to Mrs. R.) we called at Port au Prince, Haiti. There we were met by an escort of nine planes. The press was impressed. The First Lady just kept watching to make sure that the planes landed safely.

At San Pedro, Santo Domingo's president and his wife were on hand to greet Mrs. Roosevelt inside a wired-off enclosure, through which men, women and children peered for a glimpse of "La Presidenta." Between sentences, as she chatted with her host and hostess, Mrs. Roosevelt waved and smiled to them.

I think it was Emma who spied the big black limousine parked near the enclosure. It bore a large brass plate on its hood, reading "Primera Donna de la Republica"—the private car of Santo Domingo's First

Lady. We laughed at this ostentation, but Mrs. Roosevelt merely smiled politely. She wasn't good at laughing at people, only with them.

Back in the plane Mrs. Roosevelt fretted over what to do with a huge bouquet of some five dozen red roses presented to her.

"We must find a hospital in San Juan for these," she said.

In San Juan Mrs. Roosevelt stayed at La Fortelesa, the Governor's pink palace overlooking the bay, while we put up at a tourist hotel with a swimming pool. We thought ourselves very lucky. That was long before Puerto Rico became a top tourist site, but it is interesting to note that Mrs. R. predicted then that these hills and beaches would become a highly regarded and accessible vacation spot.

We were a little worried about keeping in touch with our story, being several miles away from her, but at 8 A.M. the next day I looked up from the blue waters of the pool, and there she was. She had come down to have coffee with us and tell us the day's plans.

We saw some evil slums in Puerto Rico—houses made of wood and pieces of tin, with two floors, each housing a separate family, the lower floors only a covered-over patch of earth. There were no windows; the light came only from doorways. Mrs. R. wondered how the women could produce their meager meals on the little stoves that stood in front of the houses.

Animals ran about everywhere. I caused some laughs when I stumbled over a pig, and then made it worse when I tried to convert the incident into cablese, writing: "Ducas onstepped pig running street eliciting squeal pigward and Eleanor remark quote poor thing unquote." Barry Faris, my editor, wanted to know later whether Mrs. Roosevelt was sorry for me or the pig.

Everywhere we went crowds gathered, shouting "La Presidenta! La Presidenta!" Mrs. R. never seemed to hurry. She had time to talk to people, mostly women, as she peered into their houses. She always spoke earnestly, without a tinge of condescension. We visited the countryside, meeting women who embroidered handkerchiefs in their homes for piecework wages of 60 cents a dozen. Little girls in rural schools often spent their lunch hours embroidering in order to add to the family income. That Mrs. R. was distressed we knew, but she never showed it. Despite her warm heart and ready sympathy, she maintained an Anglo-Saxon reticence that was part of her unique personality.

We called at a labor college, picnicking in a field from a luncheon hamper Mrs. R. had ordered for all of us. She liked picnics, as the world later realized when she entertained the King and Queen of England at Hyde Park.

In St. Thomas there was a reception at Government House given by Governor Paul Pearson, father of the columnist, Drew Pearson. It was, we learned, the first integrated party ever held there. Negro guests were invited at Mrs. Roosevelt's insistence. She stood in line for hours, shaking hands.

Next morning Bess Furman and I, who shared a room, were awakened at 6:30 by a familiar voice. We opened our eyes to see Mrs. R.'s head over the top of the shuttered half-door.

"Get up, lazybones—there's a lovely beach here," she said.

We swam and skipped rope up and down the deserted beach, Mrs. R. being the most agile. And she was, at this time, close to 50 years old. All six women dressed together in the ladies' cabana. We offered to wait outside while she changed, but she brushed the suggestion aside, saying: "We haven't enough time."

A quick trip to St. Croix ended with Mrs. Roosevelt's carrying a bottle of rare old rum in a large straw bag that never seemed to leave her hands for the rest of the trip. She meant to bring it safely to Franklin, who would appreciate it, as she would not.

Back to San Juan for a reception by Governor Blanton Winship and a typical Eleanor Roosevelt incident. We reporters learned that a Puerto Rican newspaper artist had just been fired because of a caricature he had drawn of the First Lady, showing mostly a set of protruding teeth. We told her about it.

"But it was a caricature," she protested. "And I *do* have the Roosevelt teeth!"

So, of course, the young artist was summoned to tea before the reception, to show her good will. And because of this, he got his job back.

We took off at dawn for home and flew into fog over Haiti. It was not a serious situation, but we were all new to flying and the journalistic part of the party was nervous. Mrs. R., peering over Bess' shoulder to read her lost-in-fog lead, said: "Why do you keep on writing? You know you can't file that story till we land—and anyway, it would only make people worry." She was not at all upset as we circled the Haitian mountains seeking a hole through which to land.

I never saw Mrs. Roosevelt afraid. When her husband was barely missed by the bullet that killed Mayor Cermak of Chicago during a campaign speech in Florida, she was asked: "Doesn't this make you worry about his future speeches?" I have remembered her reply every time I have given way to fear. "One can't go through life afraid," she said.

On the train from Miami to Washington we had our last press conference of the trip. The next day was her twenty-ninth wedding anniversary, so we prodded her for reminiscences of her wedding. Her uncle, President Theodore Roosevelt, had given her away. So great was the crowd and so carefully did the police guard him that some of the wedding guests never saw the ceremony. And afterward, most of the guests crowded around the President, leaving the bride and groom a bit forlorn.

"We were always careful, after Franklin became President, not to take the center of the stage at any wedding," she remarked. "The bride and groom should have the limelight."

The President was at Union Station to greet his wife, and she was still carrying her gift bottle for him. As they entered the limousine she waved to us, as if to say: "Till the next time!"

It was never my good fortune to make a prolonged trip with Eleanor Roosevelt again, though we kept in close touch over the years. But the Puerto Rican trip had brought me the most precious reward of my journalistic career: the privilege of having a great woman for my friend.

Why was she great? I think we reporters in 1934 were aware of her stature because we sensed that the nature of her greatness was *goodness*.

That word, goodness, is pallid in its usual sense, connoting morality, charity, piety. With Mrs. R. it was much more. Her overriding love for humanity, her desire to serve people, her daily efforts to be helpful to everyone around her, all sprang from an inner quality that also dictated her public actions and words. I can only describe it as—goodness.

She had her faults, of course. She trusted people too much. She was often gullible. She was not always a good judge of individuals, some of whom exploited her. But her values were true. She not only said and did the right things but *felt* them and *lived* them as well. That is why her enemies were never able to hurt her. That is why, when she died, she was almost without enemies.

When journalists talk among themselves, they trade
memories---of the big or unforgettable stories,
of the problems of their craft, of the teachers who
guided them, of lessons learned.

They reflect, tell anecdotes, sum up. In moments
of frustration, some dream of getting out of the
big city. Some others determine from the start
to choose a small town, to edit a country weekly
or to write.

All speak of people they have met. They recall
new ventures, first jobs and turning points.

*Immediately after his graduation from the Colum-
bia School of Journalism in 1925, Theodore M.
Bernstein joined the staff of* The New York Times
*as a copy editor. During World War II he headed
the foreign news desk, in direct charge of all war
news; and in 1952 he was appointed to his present position, assistant managing editor.*

His Watch Your Language *and "Junior," otherwise known as* More Language That Needs
Watching, *are both best sellers, and are in use as
texts in many schools and departments of journalism. Mr. Bernstein was a member of the faculty
of Columbia's Graduate School of Journalism for
twenty-five years, holding the rank of associate
professor when he retired in 1950. His major
work on usage,* The Careful Writer, *is scheduled
for publication in 1964.*

THEODORE M. BERNSTEIN:

Bonjour, TTS

The plans seemed clear, complete and foolproof when in 1960 *The New
York Times* decided to commit its prestige and a not inconsiderable
pile of cash to establishing an International Edition. Yet there were occasions during the nightmarish weeks just before publication when the
venture seemed to be slipping over the brink in spite of carefully drawn
graphs, flow charts and directives.

In late August I was sent to France to set up the new edition.
Our program called for the publication of a stripped-down version of
The Times, to be printed in Paris at about the hour the parent edition
went to press in New York. Edited stories in New York were to be
punched into Teletypesetter (TTS) tape. This tape would then be used
to transmit electronic impulses by cable to Paris. There they would au-
tomatically produce a duplicate tape that would feed into specially-
equipped linotype machines. Thus in Paris the type would be set "no
hands."

A precise timetable had been prepared to govern the printing and distribution of the paper. Trucks would rush copies to local outlets, to the railroads and to Le Bourget airport for delivery to London, Frankfurt, Milan, Rome—to all European countries west of the Iron Curtain, and to North Africa, the Middle East and India.

The Teletypesetter process had been successfully performed between cities, but it had never been attempted between continents. All that was necessary, however, was to substitute an oceanic cable for a land wire. It was a simple matter of a cable. A simple matter . . .

I had not been in Paris for three days when this simple cable matter suddenly became complex. My wife and I were giving a cocktail party for *Times* people in Paris. One of the guests, the man in charge of physical arrangements for the International Edition (henceforth to be known as the I.E.), remarked to me in a subdued and frightened voice, "Did you know we haven't got a cable?"

I took a quick look to see what he was drinking, and said I assumed he meant that the contract was not actually signed on the dotted line. He shook his head and spoke emphatically. Not only was nothing signed, there wasn't even a dotted line. There had been some misunderstanding between *The Times* and the French cable authorities. Arrangements were not, so to speak, "solidified."

From that moment on for more than two weeks, instead of merely setting up housekeeping for the new news operation, as I had planned, I was constantly preoccupied with negotiating with hard-headed Frenchmen, and seeking aid or sympathy from almost a dozen officials, right across the board to the United States Ambassador. It wouldn't have helped much even if I had been an expert in trans-Atlantic communications, but matters were probably made a little worse by the fact that I was a bambin in the bois. If you can visualize a kindergarten kid trying to negotiate disarmament, you will have a pretty good picture of my efforts.

Finally, in response to yelps for help, assistance arrived from the business office in New York. This move was successful in that it got the problem off my back, but it was not completely successful in solving the question of communications. What we wanted were six cable channels for six hours a day; what we had to settle for were three cable channels and three radio channels that would be reliable only when meteorological conditions were right. With much uncertainty and large doses of aspirin, this system has worked.

Meanwhile, back in the newspaper business, I had visited the future home of the I.E. on Rue La Fayette. It was a section of the private printing plant engaged to put out the paper, and it was all right if your taste runs to antiquated fire traps. The area designated as our news room was fairly large, windowless and unpainted. It was enclosed by four walls, a floor and a skylight that admitted stifling air on hot days and cold air or rain (or both) on wintry days. Little had been done to make it usable as a newspaper office, but after all this was early September and in Paris everything grinds to a halt for the August *grandes vacances*. Painters were now at work, painfully and interminably trying to spruce up the place. There were no telephones. For weeks there were no desks (they were on the way from Germany, presumably being pushed along the highways by little boys) and no chairs (at first we sat on packing cases, but at that our staff of five could not all sit at once). When the telephones were finally installed it took another week before a hireling of the PTT Ministry came around to approve them for operation.

Our staff began to assemble in Paris. It had been carefully selected for versatility, the vital ingredient for a small paper. There was Marty Gansberg, who had been assistant make-up editor in New York, had once run a printing shop, and was to be groomed to take charge of the operation when I left. There was Hank Kamm, a copy editor with experience in the sports department and in making up the editorial page. There was Ted Shabad, a copy editor on the foreign desk who had previously been a cartographer and geographer (useful for drawing maps, get it?); he was to spend a year in Paris before going on to Moscow as a correspondent. There was Sy Lutto, a copy editor in New York who had offered his services as a part-time copy boy while he took some courses at the Sorbonne, but who was impressed into full-time service when it became evident that a fourth editor would be necessary. There was Milt Bracker, our sole reporter, able to cover anything from an art show to a diplomatic conference. Finally, there was Henry Giniger, borrowed from *The Times's* Paris bureau temporarily because he knew everything about Paris and the French and could not only help organize the new office but also serve as a day editor. My secretary, who assisted with such editorial chores as compiling the shipping table, was Jeannine Duflou, a chic, bilingual Parisian who did extra duty as coffee maker and den mother.

As for me, in addition to such accustomed tasks as editing copy, writing headlines and laying out pages, I took on such unaccustomed duties as tinkering with maps and selecting, cropping and retouching pictures. My major triumph of retouching, when we finally got into publication, was an inadvertent one performed on a photograph of Times Square in a snowstorm. Because of faulty transmission it lacked contrast and did not show much snow. I went to work with the white paint, intending merely to touch it up here and there. But one thing led to another and soon I had Times Square buried in about a foot of snow. Fortunately, the storm lasted for several hours, so that by the time our paper appeared Times Square did look, so I was told, just about the way I had blunderingly depicted it.

In mid-September things began to move. We didn't realize how happy we had been before they did. First came transmission tests from New York. Since arrangements for the cable had not yet been completed, transmission was entirely by radio. Now radio is a great thing for selling corn flakes or summoning serum to Nome, but for an operation that requires a steady and uninterrupted signal, Marconi can have it. For the first three hours each evening it would perform with fair efficiency, but around midnight, Paris time, the signal would begin to fade and the Teletypesetter tape would begin to garble. Then we were dead ducks for the night, with perhaps half our news report received. Add to this the fact that the perforator operators in New York were not yet completely trained and that the linotype machines in Paris were not for some time properly tuned up and you have the completed picture of discouragement.

About this time we began producing dry-run editions. There were nights when we had radio transmission but no cable, nights when we had cable but no radio, and a couple of nights when we had neither. But in each instance we were able to assemble a paper, relying on Associated Press copy and manual composition. The successful meeting of various emergencies was invaluable in giving the staff the feeling that nothing could stop us. And this confidence paid off later on, when similar emergencies arose during actual operations.

Nevertheless the early dry-run editions were not papers that could have been offered to the public. The rehearsal operations went badly. In addition to the transmission difficulties, there was the unfamiliarity of the French printers with the English language, with American newspaper practice and with the new-fangled gadgets and tape that surrounded them in the composing room. They saw no usable results of the hard work and long hours they were devoting to this project. They were a baffled and frustrated lot.

I got wind of their muttering and decided to do something before their morale distintegrated completely. After we had finished operations one night I assembled the entire *équipe* in the news room and, with Giniger as interpreter, explained what we were trying to do, what the tape was all about, what the causes of our troubles were and how we confidently expected to surmount them. It was not so much what was said as the fact that someone had taken the trouble to explain things to the printers and show interest in them. They asked questions, there was animated discussion, and they left with their spirits obviously lifted. They performed magnificently from then on.

Naturally, in the interest of international understanding, we Americans had to make some accommodations, too. For instance, we learned to write the figure 1 with a lovely eyelash and the figure 7 with a little crossbar; we sized cuts not in columns or inches but in centimeters; and on a leaf of my desk I pasted a list of French equivalents to remind me, among other things, that a headline was a *titre,* that a bracket was a *crochet,* that a caption was a *légende,* and that indent was *découvert.*

On September 28 a moment of truth arrived. Back in the halcyon days of flow charts, October 3 had been set as the target date for beginning publication. For at least a week, however, it had been obvious to me—and I had convinced some others—that we had not sufficiently mastered the mechancial troubles to hold to this date. The department heads assembled, and each was asked how soon he would be ready to start. Advertising and circulation were, of course, prepared to go at once. The mechanical chief was asked when new machines would arrive and when certain controls would be installed on the linotypes. He said they were expected "next week." (This reminded me of little signs we had lettered and stuck on the wall in the news room as bitter gags. They reflected the kind of replies we encountered whenever we asked about equipment. One of them read, "We're getting that in next week." The others read, "This won't happen very often," "That can be adjusted," and "This is only a test anyway.")

We finally settled on October 20—somewhat earlier than I preferred, yet a date that made a cherished project possible. The last Kennedy-Nixon debate—the one on foreign policy—was scheduled for Friday, October 21. If our Saturday paper could carry a complete account of the debate, it would be a prestigious coup. *The Times* would be on the newsstands of western Europe over the weekend with a full report of a story that our opposition, the Paris *Herald Tribune,* would not have at all because of its earlier press time.

That's exactly the way it worked. In New York, five reporters operating in relays wrote a running account of the TV debate. It was punched into tape, transmitted to Paris and put through the linotypes a paragraph at a time. The I.E. went to press with a three-column story just 38 minutes after the candidates stopped talking. The four-column headline on the front page said: "Nixon Charges Kennedy Is

Inciting Cuban Civil War and Soviet Entry; Senator Defends Stand in Debate." A three-column head in the opposition paper's weekend edition said: "Nixon, Kennedy Square Away for Fourth Television Debate."

Right up to the first night of publication the shortcomings of the radio and the TTS were producing garbles in our type, but by this time we had a fine group of bilingual proofreaders, able to eliminate most of them. Reporters, magazine writers, photographers and radio and TV men now began descending on us to get the story of the I.E. We accommodated them all, but made a firm rule that on opening night itself the news room would be barred to everybody except the editors. We wanted no confusion to add to the expected normal stage fright.

There was no stage fright. We went through the operation as smoothly as if we had been doing it for years—and, indeed, by that time we felt as if we had been. The first issue closed exactly on time. We looked over the page proofs rapidly. In an emergency a quick correction could be made, but normally there was no opportunity for a second thought. The London plane, whose departure time had to be met, was a tyrant that forbade a second edition. But this first issue looked fine. With smiles and sighs of relief we—editors and printers alike—went out into the spacious lobby of the building, where snacks and champagne were waiting. We toasted the printers, the printers toasted the editors, everybody toasted *The Times* and from time to time the printers broke into part-singing of union songs. Greetings were even exchanged across the Atlantic, from a celebration at Sardi's on 44th Street to the news room on Rue La Fayette.

From that night on the production of the I.E. gradually subsided from Operation Panic to Operation Frenzy, and in that status it remains and probably will remain. There were emergencies, of course, and there were incidents large and small, grim and amusing. One incident deserves retelling because it has become part of the lore of *The Times*. One night we were all irked by a series of messages from New York criticizing minor points in the paper of the day before. At 3 A.M., when I was in the composing room struggling to put together that night's paper, a copy boy came in with the routine inquiry from New York: Were we in good shape and could New York have good night? I scribbled on a sheet of paper, "Good night from Paris," and, half to Giniger beside me and half to the boy, I muttered with a grin, "And tell them not to send any more stupid messages."

A half hour later, when the paper was safely locked up, I returned to the news room and went to the teleprinter to collect the night's file of messages sent and received. I stared at the machine in disbelief and horror. There, plain as anything, it said, "Bernstein says not to send any more stupid messages. Good night from Paris." I knew that at the other end of that wire had been Bob Garst, a long-time friend and colleague, who had performed a magnificent job of organizing the New York phase of the I.E.

In desperation I typed a postscript on the machine: "I deny all. I never said it. And if I did say it, I was kidding. And anyhow the boy doesn't understand English. Not only that, but there was an uproar in the composing room. And anyhow I was talking about 'more lucid messages' and he misunderstood. Not only that, but I never said it. Night now." This message was never received in New York; it had been tapped into a closed wire. But Garst, understandably miffed and puzzled at first, eventually saw the humor of my embarrassment. All is well now. Just as all is well with the I.E.

As a sociological reporter and interpreter, Vance Packard has found in American business and industry the material for dozens of magazine articles and four best-selling books, "The Hidden Persuaders," "The Status Seekers," "The Waste Makers" and "The Pyramid Climbers."

Mr. Packard, who received the 1961 Penn State Distinguished Alumni Award (he obtained his B. A. at Pennsylvania State University in 1936) was graduated from the School of Journalism a year later. He has taught at both Columbia and New York University. Mr. Packard lives with his wife and three children in New Canaan, Connecticut.

VANCE PACKARD:

My First Week Out

In thinking back over the quarter of a century of experiences I have had in various phases of writing, the period that remains most vivid in my mind is the month or so immediately after I left the Columbia Graduate School of Journalism.

My ambition in college was to become, ultimately, an expert on international affairs. I took special courses in international economics, in monetary problems, in social psychology, in the manners and mores of many cultures. At Columbia one of the major writing projects I undertook, for credit, was the assembling of a comprehensive report on the current status of all international treaties signed since World War I. It was a dismal picture of broken commitments and was published, as I recall, in *Current History*.

All this might suggest that I was not cut out to achieve first fame working for a Hearst tabloid, but in those depression days you considered any job an opportunity.

During my final weeks at Columbia the school recommended me for a job with the Hearst empire; someone had persuaded the Old Man at San Simeon that it might help check the declining fortunes of his news-

234

paper if he hired a few promising college graduates, and an interviewer had been dispatched to a number of schools and departments of journalism. I was one of eight trainees chosen, and I was instructed to report to work for *The New York American.* The day before I was to report the newspaper announced that it was suspending publication.

I went to the Hearst executive at the Eighth Avenue headquarters who had assigned me to the *American.* I suspect that he had already forgotten me, but he looked through some charts and said that I could take my choice of working in Pittsburgh, Rochester or Boston. I chose *The Boston Record,* a tabloid, for no better reason than that I had never been to Boston before, while I had been to Pittsburgh and Rochester on visits.

So I took the night boat to Boston (because I had never been on an ocean-going boat). I arrived on a Sunday and spent part of the day getting a room near the Harvard campus, an area I thought would be congenial, and then wandered about trying to get my bearings in this picturesque but confusing city.

The next morning I reported for work in the dingy third-floor city room of the *Record* on Winthrop Square.

During my first week I was ignored by all members of the staff except the man who had to deal with me—Eddie Holland, the city editor. He was a lean, bespectacled, solemn but kindly man with nervous ulcers who has remained one of my heroes of daily journalism. His dedication to his work was intense.

It bothered me to be shunned by the others, and I finally concluded that in their view I had three strikes against me: I was a collitch guy . . . I was an outsider, a non-New Englander . . . I was a non-Catholic. Another way in which I differed from many of them was that I had never been through the wringer of alcoholism.

One man did shuffle up and speak kindly to me. After a moment of chatting he asked if I could spare him a sawbuck. He had to explain that a sawbuck was a ten dollar bill. I had $16 till payday and being eager to become accepted socially I slipped him the sawbuck. (After a month I began asking him when the loan would be repaid. He kept saying "soon." Finally, after two months, to get rid of me, he used his power of the press to get me two complimentary tickets on a steamship to Provincetown. They were worth, in total, about $7. I accepted them as payment in full.)

As a cub, my first assignment was to go out with a photographer to Cambridge and stand amid high weeds, looking at a historic tombstone. This was to demonstrate to readers that weeds in important cemeteries

were a crying shame. I was sent on my second assignment to look in
on a fire in Dorchester, but I couldn't interest the editors in even a
paragraph on it.

It was my third assignment during this first week on the *Record* that
converted me overnight from a cub to a full-blown byline reporter. I
never did understand why Bostonians thought the story deserved attention, but they had many queer notions I didn't understand. At any rate
I was sent as a three-day-old cub to watch a girl's house.

Several days earlier the city had been entranced by the drama of
this girl's having been left at the altar. The groom, a soldier, disappeared
moments before the ceremony. His cruel leave-taking was the kind of
heartbreak drama the Boston papers loved to offer their readers. Virtually every newspaper had given the story banner treatment.

Would he return, as the newspapers pleaded, and do the right thing?
The newspapers assigned men to watch the girl's home for signs of reunion. As the days passed, however, the chances of reunion seemed to
die. My editor decided he could no longer spare a good man to stand
watch, and sent me. Most of the reporters from the other papers were
standing watch from bars in the neighborhood.

I found the house, a nondescript one, in South Boston, and knocked
on the door. When the girl's mother appeared I politely explained—in
my best school of journalism manner—my earnest interest in her daughter's future plans. I had taken off my hat. The mother seemed puzzled,
then pleased, invited me in and called her daughter, a gaudily ravishing
creature, from behind a curtain. She wasn't particularly articulate, but
I gathered there were no new developments.

The mother told me that if they heard from the soldier she would call
me—*and only me*—at the office. And the following morning I received
at the city room a whispered call from the mother urging me to hurry
right out.

The fiance had returned.

Why had she chosen me instead of the other reporters—all more
experienced—to get this exclusive story? I had not waved century notes
at her, as some of the other reporters subsequently did. I am convinced
she gave me the story because I had treated her and her daughter as
ladies. I gather that the other reporters, all hard-boiled types, had
affronted the mother by treating her daughter as something distinctly
less than a lady (which she may well have been).

When I told Eddie Holland about the soldier's return, he sternly
advised me that I had a scoop of major proportions on my hands and
not to flub it. We agreed that I would keep the soldier out of sight until

arrangements could be made to get the couple to a real hideaway. I raced out to the house; within an hour a car came to take the soldier, the daughter and myself to a two-bedroom-plus-couch cottage on Nantasket Beach.

Our strategy was to keep the couple in hiding while the *Record* told the world the glorious news—that a reunion had occurred, and that the wedding might still take place. For two days the *Record* front-paged my bulletins about the tempestuous efforts to effect a reconciliation that would culminate in marriage. The other papers could only copy and resort to conjecture.

A new wedding ceremony was arranged at the same church. It was to occur just in time for the *Record*'s first edition. But a complication, a real one, now developed. Suddenly the girl wasn't sure she wanted to go through with the wedding. I recall sitting on her bed, while she fussed with her hair before a mirror, urging her not to miss this opportunity for happiness for herself (and a scoop for me). She finally agreed. We slipped into the same church where she had been jilted. I served as best man, and saw them off on their honeymoon.

The veterans at the *Record* now began to wave to me and even stopped at my desk to chat. Soon I had a new specialty. With July approaching it was time for the Hearst papers to discover that a wave of sex crimes was sweeping the country. In those days the Hearst papers discovered the wave every July, and would crusade to stamp out the fiends molesting our nation's children.

My editors decided that I was the perfect man to document the molestations, since I had a proven ability to get along with mothers. And so I went on to new, if more modest, triumphs. Within three months after joining the paper I was assigned to write a daily feature column on the editorial page about interesting personalities in New England.

I was still doing this column when, the following spring, an economy wave hit the Hearst chain. My column was to be replaced by a canned beauty-advice feature that could be purchased, as I recall, for $6 a week, a considerable saving from the $30 being paid to me as a columnist. My editor, with tears in his eyes, told me that since I was the last hired I would have to be among the first fired. I tried to cheer him up by assuring him that I had a tentative offer of a job in New York that would pay more money, $40 a week. Dean Carl Ackerman at Columbia had proposed me for an opening at the AP Feature Service.

This AP job did materialize, and it brought me closer to what in school I had conceived of as worthwhile journalism. But I still regard the Boston interlude as one of the most eye-opening phases of my life.

Wayne W. Parrish, founder and editor of American Aviation Publications, was a member of Columbia Journalism's Class of 1929, and was the recipient a year later of a Pulitzer Traveling Scholarship. He's been traveling ever since, as his brief article indicates.

Before he launched American Aviation *Magazine in 1937, Mr. Parrish worked as a reporter for* The New York Herald Tribune, Christian Science Monitor, Literary Digest, The Decatur *(Ill.)* Herald, *and as editor of the magazine of the National Aeronautic Association.*

Mr. Parrish is married to Frances G. Knight, director of the passport division of the State Department. In late 1963 he received a Doctor of Letters from Missouri Valley College and his wife was given a Doctor of Humanities.

WAYNE W. PARRISH:

Flight Pattern

In the early summer of 1934, Transcontinental & Western Air—now Trans World Airlines—inaugurated a new service. It was an overnight, coast-to-coast flight on the mightiest plane then made—the DC-2, predecessor of the famous DC-3. Fourteen passengers could be carried, seven on each side of the narrow aisle. The flight was scheduled to leave New York in the mid-afternoon and arrive in Los Angeles at about eight o'clock the next morning—a great advance in travel time.

I was then a staff writer on the late, unlamented *Literary Digest*. And having had a yen for travel as far back as I can remember, I never missed an opportunity to find an excuse, or to create one, for going someplace new. And—I'd never been to the West Coast.

In those days there were no federal prohibitions against passes. If, then, I could develop an idea that would intrigue both my editor and TWA, it would mean a free round-trip journey.

I dreamed up the idea of swimming in the Atlantic just before departure and in the Pacific immediately after landing the next day. I would be the first person to perform such a feat in the U.S., and it might make a good yarn. (With today's jet flights this seems a little silly, but in those days it was an achievement.)

Everything worked out splendidly. I took the Long Island Rail Road to Jones Beach on Long Island, enjoyed a dip in the Atlantic, went to Newark Airport, boarded the flight and had an absolutely fascinating night trip across the country, a real thrill. I took meticulous notes.

Because of local fog we were late getting into Los Angeles proper. And the Pacific, I discovered, was some twenty miles from downtown. But thanks to the late Manchester Boddy, publisher of the old *Los Angeles Daily News,* I made it. He provided a reporter and a chauffeured car to drive me to the ocean, somewhere around Manhattan Beach, I believe, where I took my dip.

It was a good feature for *Literary Digest,* and TWA liked it so much that it reprinted tens of thousands of copies after securing our permission to eliminate one paragraph that described with reportorial enthusiasm the thunderstorms and displays of lightning I had seen while crossing the Great Plains.

One story can sometimes change a career. That trip was not my first airplane hop, but it cast a spell that has not waned since. I decided to specialize in aviation. My log says I've now flown 1,400,000 miles, covering much of the world and most of the countries on the globe. It's a good start.

*Elliott M. Sanger, who describes here the birth
and development of a unique radio station, is
executive vice president and general manager of
WQXR, radio station of* The New York Times.
*Graduated from the School of Journalism in 1917,
he received the annual award of its alumni association in 1952.*

*Mr. Sanger has written a good deal of broad-
cast material for WQXR, and is a frequent contributor to publications in the fields of broadcasting and advertising. Mr. Sanger and Eleanor, his
wife, are the parents of two sons, and make their
home in New York City.*

ELLIOTT M. SANGER:

The Birth of an Idea

This is a brief story of the origins of WQXR, the radio station of *The
New York Times.*

It is difficult to write about the growth of an influential idea without
appearing to take too much personal credit for its success. So if I describe
the way in which a concept became a pioneering trend in radio broadcasting, please give credit to the rightness of the timing and the fertility of
the soil in which the seed was planted.

WQXR was born because, one evening toward the end of 1935, I had
dinner with a well-known radio engineer, the late John V. L. Hogan.
Mr. Hogan owned a small experimental radio station in Long Island
City, New York, and maintained it as a sort of hobby, a place where he
could experiment with the then revolutionary idea of high-fidelity broadcasting. We talked about the station, known at the time as W2XR, and
debated whether it could be made commercially self-supporting. There
were already too many radio stations in New York City; we decided that
the only chance of success was to create a station that would emphasize the best in music. Both of us were lovers of good music, both felt that
the current standard of radio programs did not appeal to cultured listeners, and both saw a need to design a new form of on-the-air advertising,
one in keeping with intelligent programming.

That was the simple idea. On the spot we agreed to attempt to build this small 250-watt station into a commercial and cultural success—Hogan to contribute his great engineering knowledge and I to furnish the journalistic, advertising and business background acquired since my graduation from the School of Journalism in 1917.

It was not, of course, as simple as this might suggest. The idea had to be backed by money and work. The concept of a cultural commercial radio station was entirely new to advertisers. Long months passed before we found a first venturesome sponsor. The second advertiser came a little easier, however, and gradually we began to be recognized as a productive outlet for radio advertising. Nevertheless, it was seven years before our income caught up with our expenses, and there were many times during that period when we had cause to wonder whether the idea was truly as good as we had first believed.

Even after we persuaded advertisers that we were a useful medium, we had difficulty making them understand that our advertising policy was the only one which would influence our type of listener. We had rigid rules against singing jingles and raucous sound effects; we refused advertising for a variety of products. This was all part of the original assumption—that advertising had to be equal in importance with program content if we were to create something of significance to a special and influential segment of the listening public.

WQXR started business in Hogan's engineering offices at 41 Park Row, the building in which *The New York Times* was published until it moved to Times Square at the turn of the century. And when we applied to the Federal Communications Commission for permission to change from an experimental to a commercial station, we based our argument on the need to establish a radio station that in standards of content, news coverage, intellectual level and advertising would be to radio what *The Times* was to newspaper journalism. All this was purely happenstance—and yet, eight years later, in 1944, WQXR was purchased by *The New York Times* and has been a part of *The Times* operation ever since.

Even at our first meeting, Jack Hogan and I had decided to operate WQXR more like a newspaper or magazine than a radio station. Commercial radio stations were then primarily vehicles for carrying programs designed and produced by advertisers and advertising agencies. We believed this was wrong—indeed, that it alone would have prevented the creation of the kind of station we wanted. Therefore we would "edit" our station, supplying the program content in large measure and strictly controlling the advertising. The sponsor would simply associate his product with the editorial content of the station. And even today, WQXR is one of the few stations in the country that retain strict editorial control of sponsored programs; we accept a program brought to us by an advertiser only if it fits our over-all policy. This basic rule really meant that the advertiser's message would be placed within the content of the station, just as he would place his copy in a newspaper or magazine without control of the content of the adjacent columns of printed matter. In the very early days of the station, we could not afford the staff needed for news coverage. But as soon as it became possible we inaugurated five-minute news broadcasts "every hour on the hour," a policy that continued after we were acquired by *The Times,* and was enhanced by the unique facilities of the paper to supply and interpret the news.

The timing of the birth of WQXR was fortuitous. In the mid-Thirties the sale of phonograph records was at its nadir. People were listening to the radio and not to their phonographs. The classical record business was especially hard hit; some manufacturers feared that our broadcasting of good music would put them out of business completely. What we did, and what other good music broadcasters later did, had the opposite effect; an appetite for good music was created, and then and there the record business took off on its sky-rocketing career.

Today the American people are no longer regarded by Europeans as being musically uneducated. The United States has in fact grown so fast in its appreciation of good music that we are considered a nation of music lovers. Some statisticians claim that more people attend musical events in this country than go to professional baseball games. American orchestras are among the finest; American composers are listened to all over the western world; there are now many stations and networks that specialize in good music. Opera houses and concert halls are crowded—there is an increasing demand for the best in music.

Maybe some of this has happened as a result of the dinner Jack Hogan and I had back in 1935. Maybe some of it has happened because of concepts implanted at the Columbia School of Journalism.

Betsy Wade, who in 1961 wrote a paperback titled The Encyclopedia of Clothes Care, *describes here a very special kind of clothes problem she encountered as the first woman to sit on* The New York Times *copy desk.*

A 1952 Journalism School graduate, she arrived at The Times *by way of* The New York Herald Tribune *(where she wrote women's features) and Newspaper Enterprise Association, a syndicate for which she was a staff writer and columnist. She has also taught copyreading at Columbia. She is married to James R. Boylan and has two sons, Richard and Benjamin. Mr. Boylan, of the Class of 1951, is managing editor of the* Columbia Journalism Review. *Miss Wade's second book—a juvenile titled* Eugene, Why Don't You Paint?—*was published in late 1963.*

BETSY WADE:

Footnote

The challenges for Nellie Bly would be few these days. All that remains for women with a storm-the-barriers turn of mind is space exploration and McSorley's Wonderful Saloon.

My own part in reducing the number of frontiers closed to women was small. I was far from the first woman to work on a copy desk. However, I will tell how the copy desk of *The New York Times* fell—as quietly as a shoe, size 8½ C.

I had in mind no role for myself as a footnote to history; I just wanted a job. I equipped myself with a hat and a couple of good references and at the end of my job hunt, I stood in the boss's office.

"I have always been sure women would be good on the desk," he said, as I stared nervously at a map on the wall. "I've been waiting for you for 16 years." Pause. "You'd better be good."

And that was that. No more instructions or hints.

Since it clearly would have been folly to worry whether I was any good, I took up the normal worry—what to wear?

My previous experience with copyreaders had taught me that they considered all newspaper women to be blatherheads in basic black. So basic black was out. But how does one ask the lady at Saks: "Please, a suit in which I can sit in the middle of an ocean of men and not be noticed?" Saks functions by the opposite precept.

After agonies I expect only women to understand, I settled on one navy blue suit and one gray dress, both of which covered me from here to there. I wore the gray and the blue alternately until I looked like some schizoid Civil War belle.

I struggled doggedly with everything I got and the slotman, heaven rest him, corrected me just as doggedly, and just as Mr. Ochs advised—without fear or favor. I developed the first of my three calluses copying my errors into the back of my style book. They remain there to remind me, lest I grow vain, that I had to learn how to spell vichyssoise, and that a defendant is held in bail but is released on bail, and that attest is not followed by "to."

In the eyes of the rest of the desk, I was an amusing mascot, an amiable freak that, fortunately, would go away. My destiny at that time was reading copy in the women's department, and my colleagues hurriedly explained this to anyone who asked what a woman was doing editing the budget, a murder and a rape.

After four weeks of training (four weeks to learn a lexicon of unwritten law, *Times* style, and thousands of grim facts about the working of the city government) I disappeared into the women's department.

When I was returned to the city desk a year and a half, one confinement and one haircut later, things were decidedly different. This time I was there for good.

The men of the desk fell into three categories. One category thought the whole idea of a woman on the desk was poisonous. They mumbled, just loud enough to be heard—damn, hell, nonsense, place is getting to be a bloody tea party, not like the old days . . .

The second group, perhaps closer than it knew to the first, was kind, too kind. I could not struggle for twenty seconds with a headline before these gentlemen offered me one that was all counted and done up with banks and alternate word choices. This made things difficult. I had to think of something else, fast, and a good reason for liking my own better.

The third group just toiled away and ignored me. These men even sometimes told a clean joke to make me feel less like a temperance worker at a brewery picnic.

I think of the story of the woman who lost her panties on Fifth Avenue; a quick-witted, compassionate man cried, "Oh, look!"—while pointing to the sky. I have the same gratitude for these men: They looked to the sky while I sweated.

I began to feel the situation had eased on the night the make-up editor, a man who normally has little tolerance for profanity, came to the slotman to announce that some sons of bitches had lost the copy. Although he stood behind my chair, he gave no hint that I was there. No one on the desk looked around. The constant, knife-edged riposte, "Please, there are ladies present," was not spoken. I began to feel not so much in the way.

Now about the shoe that fell. When I was a student at the Graduate School of Journalism, I had not yet been shoe-broken. At the end of each lecture I had to grope under the desk for my pumps, like a matron at the movies. Several teachers noticed. For a time I was known as Shoeless Betsy.

When I went to *The Times*, I decided the hour had come to put away childish things. I decided to keep my shoes on. Corn plasters helped to remind me.

One night a clerk came over. "I heard something about you," he said, squatting to look at my feet. "Musta been somebody else," he said.

When I could get my eyes in focus again, I saw my former teacher, also a copyreader, trying so hard not to laugh that he looked apoplectic. A put-up job. Oh well. I took off my shoes and found, as I have found since, that A-heads compose more easily in stockinged feet.

Several nights later, I was granted a permanent lease, stocking feet and all. The man next to me brought me a fistful of proof sheets. "Keep your feet cleaner," he said, and put one on the floor.

At that point I began to see what I cannot yet explain—that someplace between fainting and giggling, and cursing and stomping, there is a demanding, yet comfortable job for a woman on the desk.

This is hardly a now-it-can-be-told story. Yet the little footnote is finished; the *Times* copy desks now have other women, and I hope we are not the last. The desk is a good place for a woman. And what could be nicer than being surrounded by men?

Henrietta Malkiel Poynter was a feature and drama editor for Vanity Fair *and* Vogue, *foreign editor of* Vogue, *a reporter and a literary agent before she and her husband, Nelson Poynter, founded* Congressional Quarterly *in 1945.*

Mrs. Poynter, who was graduated from the School of Journalism in 1922, is associate editor of The St. Petersburg (Fla.) Times *as well as editor of the* Quarterly. *During World War II she served with the Office of the Coordinator of Information and then with the Office of War Information.*

HENRIETTA POYNTER:

New Frontiers

This is the story of the way an idea developed into a national newspaper institution. I will tell it in some detail—not to boast, although I can't conceal our pride, but to illustrate that a new private journalistic enterprise can become viable and profitable without massive investments. I believe that other gaps exist in the journalistic spectrum, and that they afford opportunities for the young man or woman willing to contribute not cash but concentration and solid planning and an inordinate amount of hard work.

It all began, I suppose, with politics and in the Twenties. Interviewing Trotsky when I was still a teen-ager, and making what appeared then, while I was in school, to be so much money that I never will feel so rich again; sailing for Europe the day after the last examination, with a few odd assignments in music and the theatre, shunning the new tabloids and crime and scandal reporting. This was a time when fun was mixed with horror—living through a devastating inflation in Europe, the shock of the Fehme murders, hearing Hitler's rasping voice for the first time, covering the Salzburg Festival . . . and making the tour with George Gershwin through all the shops of the Boulevards, to find the right French taxi horns for "An American in Paris."

The London blackout spelled the end of covering leisure and the arts. The years of pounding a typewriter in Berlin, in Morocco and in Holly-

246

wood paved the way to Washington propaganda. And there came a day, a few short weeks after Pearl Harbor, when a handful of us—Jack Houseman, Bill Hale and a few refugee journalists—listened to our production of the first United States Government shortwave program, fifteen minutes in German, and named it "The Voice of America" because it could be translated into all the myriad languages we would use in the coming months and years.

When the war came to an end, we knew, my husband and I, that we could not give up public service—even though we had a newspaper in Florida to run, a thousand miles away. But we believed, too, that we could contribute more outside the Government than in it.

We were convinced that, with spot news largely preempted by radio (and eventually in turn by TV), newspapers could not survive unless they provided substance and background and perspective and facts for an increasingly aware public in an increasingly complicated world.

It was obvious that with the ending of hostilities, power would tend to move up Pennsylvania Avenue from the White House to Capitol Hill. And we had discovered, in trying to research our own stories, that despite hundreds of Washington sources it was impossible to follow the multiple activities of the Congress. Individual voting records were not available. We had to plow through millions of words of hearings and debate, and even hire professional researchers, to find out what really was going on. No method existed for measurement of party unity, or of a congressman's support of the President, or even of absenteeism.

So we started *Congressional Quarterly*—and it really was a quarterly —with weekly releases for newspapers on the key issues before Congress, and with a running record of all the bills, all the votes, all the actions of the Congress. We found a few alert editors, who, sharing our concern, bought the service. A half dozen dedicated staffers helped in the new private publishing venture.

The *Quarterly* soon turned into regular newspaper releases, a Weekly Report of facts and figures, and an annual hard-bound Almanac—Vol. XVIII, 1962, ran about 1,200 pages. The staff now numbers more than 50, which includes the people associated with *Editorial Research Reports,* a venerable newspaper service purchased by CQ in 1957. More than 400 daily newspapers, hundreds of schools and libraries, Government agencies, embassies and even members of Congress depend on CQ for accurate and unbiased information about Capitol Hill. We expected it to be profitable, without any illusions of a bonanza. We don't believe in subsidized journalism.

Since 1945, no congressman has been able to bury or dissemble his voting record—and if he tries, his opponent can lash back with, "Yes, you voted for that bill after you voted for all the crippling amendments and tried to kill it by sending it back to committee."

In the 1960 election, when the heads of both tickets had served in Congress, CQ spelled out, chapter and verse, their votes, their party unity, bipartisan support, agreement and disagreement with the President. We told how and how often they voted or failed to record their stands.

But this is not just an election year phenomenon. Week by week, CQ documents the record so that an editor in a small town, say, can have as much information about his congressmen as a paper with a large Washington bureau. For the second time in its history, CQ has spelled out the changes in districting caused by a decennial census, and pinpointed gerrymandering, doubtful districts, the background of candidates and the voting records of incumbents.

In every session, with each new Presidential program or domestic or international crisis, we have scurried to back volumes to compare the proposed changes in legislation. So many of the same problems presently before the Congress have been rewritten, strengthened or weakened during the years since World War II that CQ is now putting out a volume called "Congress and the Nation," tracing key bills and votes since 1945 by category, from Agriculture through Taxes.

When the facts went against them, a few politicians have attempted to challenge our integrity, our accuracy and even our patriotism. The attacks came from those who did not like to have their records made public, thus at the mercy of their opponents, in the pages of the local press, and, above all in the minds of the voters. Through it all, newspapers of every political persuasion, the national committees of both parties, and the White House continued to quote CQ as the one detached and authoritative voice on Congress.

We have reported secrecy in congressional committees, and regularly catalogue how much of their operation is behind closed doors. CQ follows, week by week, the registration, expenditures and campaigns of lobbyists in full detail. The law does not provide any means or appropriation for the Congress itself to monitor or analyze lobby reports. The editor of a weekly cannot do it; the paper with a one-man Washington "bureau" cannot do it; not even our finest dailies can do it day after day, week after week.

Perhaps we were most keenly conscious of the needs of local journalism because we were, and still are, running *The St. Petersburg Times* in Florida—the most liberal paper to be found south of the Potomac, yet published in one of the most conservative communities in the country. Moreover, it is one of the most competitive metropolitan newspaper areas in the United States, with half a dozen dailies competing for our immediate audience. If you question the rewards, excitement and even glamour that exist in local newspapering, look at our circulation; it was about 40,000 in 1950—it reached 150,000 in 1962.

Certainly it is no longer possible to start a daily newspaper with a few thousand dollars and a pocketful of type. Nor is it now possible to buy a paper for its debts, as a number of publishers did in the Thirties. But a need still exists for solid local coverage—and for a second paper— in many communities across the land.

The new "cold type" processes and offset presses are attaining practical use. They cost little, compared to present equipment which is rapidly becoming obsolescent. If a man and his wife are willing to challenge a million-dollar-plant giant with a paper offering saturated community coverage, ferreting out political misdemeanors and making a vigorous and honest attempt to better the area in which they live, there is still room for success and individual enterprise.

Indeed, the opportunities are greater today than they were in the Twenties. More papers existed then, but their staffs and coverage were limited. Radio commentators were, for the most part, actors who read bulletins with inflection. There was little demand for specialization in science, in military affairs, in the various arts, in the interpretation of events in faraway countries with exotic languages. If you had an aesthetic bent, you wrote about music and the theatre, art and books—and were grossly underpaid. If you wanted to be a foreign correspondent, you made your way overseas and picked up odd assignments and sent back space copy on spec until an editor thought you were costing more that way than if you were on a meager salary, and gave you a job—with no security and no severance or pension rights.

We envy the men and women coming into newspapering today, because their choice is so wide, their chance to specialize so vast, and the demand for truly dedicated talent so great. And moreover, journalism is beginning to pay what good journalism is worth. But we hope the newcomers won't all try to be science writers or foreign correspondents or TV stars. A rewarding career awaits many of them in responsible local journalism. And many of them, if they search, will find new frontiers.

William E. Giles, a 1951 School of Journalism graduate, was born in New Jersey, and his first newspaper job was as a reporter with his hometown paper, The Plainfield Courier-News.

Mr. Giles, who received his B. A. at Columbia College in 1950, became a reporter and regional editor with The Wall Street Journal, *and was then selected to serve as one of the founding members of the staff of the new Dow-Jones publication,* The National Observer. *He is editor of the weekly.*

Mr. Giles and his wife, Gloria, are the parents of five sons—William, Michael, Paul and Richard (twins) and Joseph.

WILLIAM GILES:

Birth of a Newspaper

When I walked into the executive conference room on that August morning in 1961, I could sense that something important was under way. Around the big oblong table sat many of the men with whom I had worked during my ten years as a reporter, rewriteman and regional editor for *The Wall Street Journal*. The executive editor, Bob Bottorff, was there; so were Vermont Royster and Warren Phillips, the editor and managing editor; and so were Bill Kerby and Buren McCormack, vice presidents of Dow Jones and Company.

I had been summoned to New York that day from Washington, D. C., where I'd been assigned two months earlier as a reporter in the *Journal* bureau. Warren's call made it seem that he wanted to do nothing more than chat routinely about the Washington assignment. But this was not going to be an ordinary kaffeeklatsch. The mystery was both intriguing and a little frightening.

Bob Bottorff got straight to the point.

"We're considering publishing a new newspaper, a weekly, to circulate nationally. It would be a family paper, aimed primarily at the home and the school. We're setting up a special projects group to get started, and we'd like you to be part of it . . ."

250

What the newspapermen who run Dow Jones wanted, essentially, was to produce a compact national newspaper designed to be read. To make it compact, the editors would have to select from the vast amounts of available information only the most significant and the most interesting stories. In making it readable, they wanted to give more than bloated headlines, more than straightaway reports on what had happened.

The task of translating this concept into a going newspaper fell on a nucleus of *Wall Street Journal* newsmen with diverse backgrounds. Don Carter, onetime city editor of *The Atlanta Journal* and, up to this time, executive director of The Newspaper Fund, was in on the initial planning. So was Jack Bridge, a longtime writer and associate editor on *The Wall Street Journal*.

In the beginning, there was the idea—but even that was subject to debate and change. We literally started from scratch; even the kind of type and newsprint we would use hadn't been decided. We had no name for the newspaper and no staff to produce it; all we had was a decision to set up a staff separate from that of the *Journal*.

Tucked away in a sixth-floor office in the *Journal's* building in lower Manhattan, we began assembling a crew. We were looking primarily for young newspapermen with fresh ideas and a talent for clean, uncluttered writing. Since we intended to challenge some fundamental concepts in newspapering, we wanted a group of spirited writers not content to follow old standards. We meant to innovate—we needed innovators.

By early September, with a six-man staff, we began experimenting in writing techniques. Our main aim was to devise ways of wrapping up the week's news and putting it into meaningful perspective. Most of us had been accustomed to dealing with events on a daily basis, but this would not do for the kind of newspaper we envisioned. We had to re-think the philosophy of news.

News, by its nature, is perishable. The train of events takes sudden and unexpected turns—a fact that makes reporting it ever interesting. But news today is highly complex too; it requires more than recounting. Elaboration and explanation is also needed, particularly in the volatile fields of space, medicine, diplomacy and government. At the same time, there are increasing demands on people's time; readers do not have unlimited hours in which to become well-informed about the world around them. So our byword was selectivity—a close, continuing search and evaluation of the news flow for material, and then a highly selective approach to the facts and backgrounding necessary to the telling of our story. In other words, we were determined to be editors, exercising editorial judgment.

There were other weaknesses in the current practice of daily journalism, it seemed to us, that might be overcome in a weekly news cycle. We found, for example, that significant stories which broke early in a week were often forgotten by the week's end, even though their importance had not diminished. They just seemed to flash up and then flash out again, with nobody's ever quite having the time or taking the trouble to spell out their lingering importance. Stories break piecemeal, too, over several days—and we saw that it was easy to lose a key section in a developing situation. Putting the pieces together at one time in one place, we decided, would be useful and informative.

News magazines, of course, had developed a style in the weekly field—a style of writing, a philosophy of coverage, distinctive methods of presentation—all tailored, quite naturally, to the requirements of a magazine format. We believed that a newspaper format offered several advantages. We could produce and distribute it faster, thus narrowing the gap between lock-up and delivery. The regular-sized news page offered an incomparable showcase for a variety of material that could be sampled quickly. The "news hole" of the *Observer,* set at 16 full pages, would be at least twice as big as the news magazine's, and this offered us the opportunity of running large and dramatic photographs as well as many articles that would not have to be actually compressed for the sake of space alone.

News magazines, too, have developed a way of reporting and writing peculiarly adapted to their needs and desires. It apparently works well for them, and we do not disparage it. But we felt from the beginning that another style of writing and editing would be more useful in achieving our aims: Clarity, preciseness, balance. We didn't want words to substitute for thoughts, nor felicitous phrases to distort facts, intentionally or unintentionally. So in our early days, we did a good deal of experimenting in writing techniques.

In our writing exercises, we tried scores of varying approaches. One man would write the same story in at least a half-dozen ways. Then we would let another fellow do the same thing on the same story. To get fresh viewpoints, we kept mixing assignments. Our science writer, for example, covered the World Series for a week. Our economics expert tried his hand on an airliner disaster story. We concluded from all this that specialization, though highly useful in some cases, could have a dampening effect on a good writer's urge to use his imagination. But drop him into an unfamiliar situation, and out come all kinds of interesting results.

"The conventional ways of saying things need to be examined," Barney Kilgore, president of Dow Jones, kept telling us. And the more we experimented with the news, the more convinced we became that there were entirely too many journalistic short-cuts in newswriting that led to imprecision and misunderstanding.

In September we began producing practice issues. At first we wrote only two or three stories for a single page, endeavoring to apply the journalistic techniques so useful in *The Wall Street Journal* to more general news situations. One of our first pieces, for example, was a complete rundown on the United States' position in Southeast Asia. In addition to telling what happened in the week under review, we fleshed out the article with geographical and diplomatic background.

In this process, however, we not only discovered gaps in our own information about the area, but we also drew some useful lessons. Among them: Many newsmen—and newspaper readers, as a consequence—assume they know a good deal more than they actually do. Under severe critical analysis, reports from abroad proved to lack much factual material—the sort of information that can throw needed light on a developing, complex situation. Too often, it seemed to us, writers substituted generalities and outmoded assumptions for facts, and this tended to distort and obscure the nature of the news. The distortion did not seem to be intentional; it was more the result of taking too much for granted.

Second, there was an abundance of sensationalism in news, notably in foreign coverage. "Crisis"—sometimes real but more often fanciful—appeared to be the hook for writing about most situations. We had "crises" in the Congo, in Angola, in Berlin, in Brazil, in Indonesia. "Rising tensions" everywhere, at least in the news dispatches. Thus the casual newspaper reader could easily get the impression that the whole world was coming apart tomorrow, or maybe the next day.

To be sure, there were and are and probably always will be tense situations in the world, but the end-of-the-world tone of many dispatches and their end-of-the-world treatment by headline writers seemed to us to jeopardize the very thing that newspapers aim to do—to clarify complicated situations and thereby make them understandable and subject to reason. What would happen, we wondered, when a genuine crisis occured? Would cries of "wolf! wolf!" someday be ignored?

Well, all of this suggested to us that we might perform a useful service in our new newspaper by taking a calmer, more analytical look at world news. In addition to dealing with the "crises," we determined to seek out and report other foreign news—economic, cultural, personal—

to add diversity to the vast outpouring of political matter. And we wanted to note the good things that were happening around the globe, not just the scary things.

As a national newspaper, we decided early that our prejudice would be toward newsworthy events that occurred in the United States. We felt then, and still do, that many important and interesting stories are given fairly good treatment by local and regional newspapers, but seldom receive a fair shake in the national press; again, "crisis" stories receive the most extensive coverage. But the subjcts that affect people most directly—school building, taxation, transportation and medicine, for instance—frequently get short shrift nationally.

Thus, an interesting approach to transportation problems in Detroit, we decided, might be of high interest, too, in such other places as Los Angeles, Dallas or Miami. Similarly, religious or cultural activities in the Northeast ought to be of sufficient interest to people in the Southwest or Northwest.

The handling of this kind of material, of course, had to be different in most cases from its treatment in local or regional newspapers. We would be telling our story to a diverse national audience. Our main task, therefore, was to devise methods of presentation that related local events to national trends.

As our staff began building up, we increased both the scope of coverage in the practice issues and the number of staff-produced pages. By early November, after we had shifted to our permanent headquarters in Washington, D. C., our staff of 15 writers was turning out a professional-looking paper of up to 12 pages a week. The post-mortem sessions on these practice issues, conducted by our own staff and by *Wall Street Journal* editors, were brutal, but they served to underscore the problems—and the potentials—of putting out a first-class newspaper.

About this time, we began setting up a network of correspondents around the country. Most of these "observers," as we came to call them, were active newsmen. In addition, we sought out specialists in various fields, in universities, in business, in government, who would contribute special articles. This material was to be supplemented by copy from three wire services—Associated Press, United Press International and Reuters—and through special reprint arrangements with *Atlas* magazine and *The London Telegraph*.

We wanted the typography and layout of our new newspaper to be dignified and attractive. We chose wide columns, easy-to-read body type, calm headline type. We stressed the need for quality printing and emphasized sharp reproduction of good pictures. As one critic, describing our publication in the *Saturday Review,* said, "It's surprising how new nowadays a good old-fashioned look can be."

Before settling on a name for the infant, Mr. Kilgore had compiled a list of the names of every newspaper that had ever been published in this country. We wanted something distinctive and descriptive. Though there was a good deal of judicious pondering, nearly everybody agreed from the start that "The National Observer" filled the bill. And so it was. Since the editors, hopefully, would be exercising the wisest of judgments, coolly and calmly, the owl became our symbol.

Looking back over the past months—the formative days before *The National Observer* began publishing on February 4, 1962, and since—it is impossible to fabricate even a momentary mood of detachment. For those of us fortunate enough to have been in at the beginning, it has been a fabulous experience, professionally and emotionally. We are very much like parents. Proud and somewhat awed by the miracle of creation. Secure in the feeling that we have given the utmost of our abilities. Anxious and sensitive about the development of our new child.

Robert M. Hall studied law at Northwestern University before becoming an advertising space salesman—during the worst years of the Depression—for his hometown newspaper, The Providence (R.I.) Journal. *In 1934 he completed his studies at Brown University, and then enrolled at the School of Journalism. He served as sales manager of United Feature Syndicate before forming his own organization.*

The Hall Syndicate distributes the work of, among others, Leonard Lyons, Ralph McGill, Dr. Norman Vincent Peale, Sylvia Porter, Victor Reisel, Eric Sevareid, Earl Wilson, Jack Nicklaus, Herblock, Jules Feiffer, Ed Dodd, and Walt Kelly.

ROBERT M. HALL:

"I've Got a Job For You"

I never planned to go into the syndicate business. It was, after all, a *business,* while journalism is a profession. If dollars, cents and circulation had been my chief interests, I'd never have left a good job in the advertising department of *The Providence Journal* to attend the School of Journalism at Columbia. Clearly, it was work as an editor that I wanted.

Carl Ackerman, dean of the School, made it one of his many duties to find jobs for the graduating students. In 1935, that was no easy assignment. The depression had not yet ended; retrenchment and economy drives were still the rule.

"I think I've got a job for you," said Dean Ackerman—and from the beginning it sounded good. Most of my classmates considered themselves lucky to be summoned to brief interviews at odd hours in deserted city rooms—but I was going to be interviewed over a luncheon table at Christ Cella's, a restaurant frequented by successful literati and heads of major advertising agencies.

My host and prospective employer was Monty Bourjaily of the United Feature Syndicate. He questioned me perfunctorily about my year at

256

Morningside Heights and then intensively about my record as a *Journal* space salesman in Rhode Island. Finally he began to discuss the unique role of the traveling syndicate representative. My small salary would be the least of it, he said. My true income would mount rapidly as I introduced such immensely popular comic strips as "Joe Jinks" and "Little Mary Mix-up" to attentive editors who were even now panting to buy more features. Enticing words floated across the table. "Commissions" . . . "entertainment" . . . "expense account."

While Monty spoke, another thought insinuated itself into my mind and played itself out, Hollywood style, on the screen of my youthful imagination. I saw myself in the office of a distinguished newspaper publisher. He had just bought "Ella Cinders," daily and Sunday. Now he turned to me and said, "Hall—you're a graduate of the Columbia School of Journalism. I'm in a jam! My managing editor retired this morning. Can you—*will you*—take over?"

Before the image faded, I accepted the job. But I've never left the syndicates.

Editor and Publisher issues a special syndicate supplement annually. The current edition lists hundreds of feature services. The materials available to editors on tape, in mat form, in manuscript, on glossy repro sheets, or in mimeographed bundles range in subject from astrology and graphology to veterans' affairs and women's page fillers. Some of the syndicates are one-man, one-feature operations conducted from an apartment or home; others are stables with scores of stalls. It's a big business. There isn't a general-interest newspaper in the nation, daily or weekly, that does not utilize some syndicated material.

While ours is a relatively new branch of journalism, its roots may be traced back in time to the "pigeon post" of the early 1840's. Daniel Craig and Arunah S. Abell of *The Baltimore Sun* trained homing pigeons to carry news summaries—first between ship and shore, then between Baltimore and Washington, and later to and from Philadelphia, New York and Boston. (Craig's first pigeon coops were housed in a building adjacent to the Maryland Hospital for the Insane. And so fierce was the competition to "get the news first" that bonuses of up to $500 an hour for each hour of early delivery were offered. And sometimes counter-measures were taken—including rifle fire—to prevent delivery to the opposition. But you can be sure that these beginnings had no influence on the later gentle and genteel operations of syndicates.)

By the late Twenties, the syndicates had created multi-million-reader audiences for an astonishing variety of men and women: Artists, writers, collectors of minutiae, pundits, caricaturists, snoops, snobs, versifiers, cartoonists, advisers, specialists, seven-day wonders, popularizers, uplifters and interpreters. New names shot to instant fame, power, wealth; new phrases became part of the American vocabulary. Even overseas the American feature found appreciative followers. Today you can read Ed Dodd's strip, "Mark Trail," in a score of languages, including Swahili. The information, humor and analysis sent out by American syndicates may be one of our most important exports.

The relationship between the newspaper and the individual whose syndicated work it purchases is an interesting one. The paper buys talent it otherwise could not afford. The artist or writer is given the opportunity to reach people whom he might otherwise never be able to address.

The syndicate's role, as I see it, is more than that of broker or agent. Ideally we should be able to find people with abilities that will be in demand tomorrow. Then we must help develop this talent and promote it. Before we can be salesmen we must first perform some of the functions of newspaper editors.

Today the newspaper is caught up in a whirl of rising production costs and conflicts over automation; one result we all acknowledge is the long list of mergers and failures. I think, though, that we're not far from the time when many of journalism's production problems will be solved by the inexorability of technological progress. Tomorrow, I believe, we can expect to see the trend reversed. Competition will be keen among urban and suburban papers, and in the big cities new publications will be founded. Tomorrow one will not need hundreds of thousands of dollars before one can start to publish a paper.

That's why I insist that newspaper journalism is neither moribund nor even chronically ill. It's as exciting today as it was when I was at the School. And—fortunately—so is the syndicate business.

Eight newspapers make up the unique All-Church
Press, described here by its founder and chairman
of the board, Douglas Tomlinson, who publishes
ChurchWeek, Dallas World, Fort Worth Tribune,
Houston Times, Memphis Mirror, Oklahoma City
Star, Tulsa Herald *and* Wichita Light.

Mr. Tomlinson, who lives in Fort Worth,
Texas, was a member of the Columbia School of
Journalism Class of 1914. He is chairman of the
board of Brite College of the Bible, Texas Chris-
tian University.

DOUGLAS TOMLINSON:
Life Assignment

There is one thing about my story. It is different. No one else who
ever attended the School of Journalism has had an experience like it.
There is nothing in America even remotely similar to the newspaper
organization I have built in these fifty years.

(And I am not going to be hampered in telling the story by shyness
or modesty. The pronoun "I" is going to be treated with the same
objectivity as are commas and semicolons. If anyone does not like
that "I" style, stop now. There is no other straightforward way; for a
long time I was the only person connected with our enterprise.)

When I began studying at the Columbia University School of Journalism in 1913, it was after seven years of purposeful scholastic preparation. I'd received my B.A. from Texas Christian University and a law
degree from the University of Texas. Columbia was to be the last educational stop prior to a journalistic-political career.

Then one classroom exercise changed all that. Our group was asked
to analyze the important classifications, by subject, of the newspapers
and magazines of the world. The class concluded, among other things,
that religious journalism was dying out.

To others in the class, this was merely another academic discovery.
But to me it was a terrific blow, an appalling portent. I believed that if
the influence of the churches did not reach out to the masses of people,

259

Christianity might not endure as the dominant factor in our civilization. And if it did not—then civilization itself, I feared, would be destroyed.

I sensed that the great and growing metropolitan centers would be the decisive battleground—that the churches would have to speak most directly and meaningfully to the people in our burgeoning cities. But this could not be done by one person, by one church, or by one denomination. It clearly would require the combined efforts of all denominations.

When I concluded my year as a journalism student at Columbia, I sailed to Europe on one of the last completed voyages of the *Lusitania*. My plan was to study at first hand the newspapers and magazines of the continent. In the course of this I met Lord Northcliffe, head of what was then the world's mightiest publishing enterprise. *The Daily Mail,* a newspaper he had established, had attained the largest circulation in the British Isles. He owned *The London Times,* known for three generations as "the voice of the British Empire." Trade papers reported that his 40 newspapers and magazines earned a profit of $25,000,000 a year, a colossal figure for those days.

Lord Northcliffe offered me a remarkable assignment; he would send me around the world as a special correspondent for these publications. It was an opportunity too glittering even for dreams.

And yet—there was the memory of the conclusion reached by our class at Columbia. Religious journalism was dying.

I declined Lord Northcliffe's offer. I returned to my home state, determined to attempt to carry out some revolutionary ideas that, I believed, might be able to reverse the trend. I knew that one man or one organization could not accomplish the miracle. But perhaps I could fashion a pattern; perhaps it would ultimately be adopted by dedicated men in other parts of the nation; perhaps a new and vital form of religious journalism could thus gradually extend across the United States.

During the first fifteen years of experimenting with what has become All-Church Press, Inc., there were times when I almost literally starved to death.

What was the condition of the religious press at this time?

Practically every religious journal represented just one denomination. Practically every journal had to be subsidized. They could not attract national advertisers—their circulation was much too small. They could not attract the advertising of local merchants; circulation was so scattered that the local advertiser had to pay for a thousand distant subscribers to reach a dozen local customers. They received occasional "donation" ads. The denominations made up the almost-inevitable deficits.

I have put this in terms of advertising revenue. The same problems afflicted the editorial content of these publications. Material was diffuse, not direct. It had to speak to people in rural areas and in vast cities; it had to speak to people in the South and in the Northeast. Thus the publications were either over-departmentalized or regrettably remote.

My fundamental idea was very simple—to establish *local* weekly church newspapers along lines parallel to the demonstrably-successful *local* daily press. Under this plan, we published one local newspaper in a city to serve *all* denominations. By drawing our subscriptions from many denominations, we were able to build up enough concentrated local circulation so that local merchants would find it worthwhile to schedule regular advertising. Our subscribers proved to be far above average in buying power and permanence.

Because we served local congregations in specific cities, our editorial material could be direct and of immediate interest. You are not indifferent to the activities of another denomination when those activities are related in terms of the family down the street or the church around the corner. The names you see are not the names of unknown individuals 3,000 miles away; they are the names of your neighbors, of fellow-members in your own local congregation.

It was a new idea, a simple one, and slowly it began to take hold. We went from Texas to Tennessee, from Tennessee to Oklahoma, from Oklahoma to Kansas. In the course of the years we developed new techniques, and each new and distinctive method strengthened the whole structure. Revenues from a greater volume of selected and appropriate advertising, sold strictly on the basis of commercial value to the advertiser, made it possible to keep subscription prices low enough to attract and hold many readers who would not have paid a much higher subscription price.

Instead of using the slow and expensive method of selling each individual subscriber one by one, we learned after a few years how to get an entire local congregation to subscribe as a group, thus quickly reducing our costs and multiplying our total circulation. Each paper was mailed directly into the home of each member family in that church, under the congregation-wide subscription plan. Within the last decade, the United States Congress has passed a special law still further simplifying our post office procedures.

Another long step forward came when we devised a system whereby

each local congregation could have its own separate edition of an
All-Church Press newspaper, with its own local congregational news
on the front page. This edition goes by mail into the homes of that
congregation—those most interested in it. The pastor is as free to express
himself in his own local church newspaper as he is in his own pulpit.
The church may use any part or all of its own front page, with additional pages if desired any week. The church pays only the cost of type
set up for its own local news each week. The remaining inside pages of
all denominations and all congregations remain the same. Mechanically,
we can make the change from one church edition to another by stopping
our high-speed rotary press for only 55 seconds. Again, this keeps
costs down tremendously.

In recent years we have gone even further in the general development of our structure. One by one we have been called upon to print
17 different denominational publications, owned not by our company
but by various denominational groups.

Here is the revolutionary feature of this arrangement. Any local
congregation which has its own news and announcements on the front
page may have its own denominational publication inserted as a supplement in the congregation's own local newspaper. The cost of reaching the masses of people in the cities with the influence of the churches
by this method is only a pittance compared to the cost by any other
process ever devised. Besides, it is much more effective than any other
plan. We believe our record shows that our entire revolutionary system
as a whole provides the most economical, powerful and effective religious journalism ever known. These methods already have added
several million subscribers to the religious journals of America.

All-Church Press is now directed by my son, Lambuth Tomlinson.
Our young managing editor, Robert L. Lynn, is a comparatively recent
graduate of Columbia's School of Journalism. All of us feel confident
that our greatest development lies ahead. Yet all this was only an un-
formed wish when I was stunned by that appraisal of my class at Columbia. It was only a dream when I carried the first edition of an All-
Church Press newspaper to the post office in a suitcase fifty years ago.

When journalists talk among themselves, they trade
memories---of the big or unforgettable stories,
of the problems of their craft, of the teachers who
guided them, of lessons learned.

They reflect, tell anecdotes, sum up. In moments
of frustration, some dream of getting out of the
big city. Some others determine from the start
to choose a small town, to edit a country weekly
or to write.

All speak of people they have met. They recall
new ventures, first jobs and turning points. They
discuss the widening scope of the profession---
in radio and television, in industry, internationally.

David Brown's career is proof of his thesis that a journalism education is a valuable background to careers in fields outside of newspapering. After a brief apprenticeship on Women's Wear Daily, *Mr. Brown—who was graduated from Columbia in 1937—went first into public relations and then, for many years, into magazine editing. His next stop was Hollywood, where he became executive story editor and a vice-president of Twentieth Century-Fox.*

Mr. Brown was recently elected editorial vice president of New American Library, where his special duties include the acquisition and publication of literary, scholarly and popular works in a variety of new formats. He is married and has one son.

DAVID BROWN:
"Former Newspaperman"

I don't know how many School of Journalism graduates are actually working on newspapers. I suspect and hope that the number is reasonably high. Why, after all, would anyone study journalism and then abandon it?

Why? There are several reasons. One is to be able to call oneself a former newspaperman. I am sure Sir Winston Churchill would have preferred "Former Newspaperman" to his famous wartime code designation of "Former Naval Person."

Vanity is not all, however. I have long wanted to speak for those who leave the newspaper business for advertising, public relations, magazines, motion pictures, television and other bizarre callings. The fact is that journalistic training sometimes fits a man better for other pursuits. A well-trained newspaperman can and frequently does become almost anything else. But not frequently enough. And that is my text for today.

Journalism is the art of communication, and the ability to com-

municate is one of man's most important skills. We are doing rather a
miserable job of it at present—from our personal lives (check divorce
statistics) to our international lives (check the headlines).

One need only listen to debates in Congress or in the United Nations,
or read most government and corporate directives, to realize how badly
needed are the skills of journalism *outside* journalism. Despite our
amazing scientific proficiency in communications, we are still in the
Stone Age so far as lucidity and clarity of expression in many important
areas are concerned. I sometimes think we did better when we were
writing on the walls of caves. Never before have so many people been
confused so swiftly, indeed instantaneously. We must be as precise in
writing and in speech as we are in our ability to bring a missile or space
capsule predictably on target. Perhaps more precise.

That is why I would like to see some of our best journalism school
graduates take their skills, after a sharpening-up period on newspapers, into government, industry, education, labor unions, the military
or even the clergy. The arts would also benefit from their infiltration.
When newspapermen became novelists and writers of short stories,
they brought a lean, clean-limbed style to literature. Hemingway was
a good example. Now lawyers and physicians are writing our best-
sellers, and our theatre is a shambles of mumbo-jumbo. What a joy it
would be to be able, once again, to *understand* a play! Such former
newspapermen as Ben Hecht, Charles MacArthur and Lawrence Stallings gave us no language difficulties.

Some people, including perhaps those at the School itself, may hold
that the goal of a school of journalism is to train men and women for
news work only. I agree that the press is entitled to a first refusal, so to
speak, on graduates of the School. However, I also believe that the
press must compete with other fields to hold the best of the graduates
in the news rooms. I see nothing inconsistent in my view that society
will benefit even more when competent news people are employed in
non-news fields. In law, for example, some of the most eminent graduates
of our law schools have never tried a case. They have become Presidents, ambassadors, leaders of mighty corporations. I believe journalism school graduates can and do render equally important service
when they do not limit themselves to their immediate field or specialty.

Happily, training in journalism can make a man or woman a jack
and master of many trades. This was a fortunate fact for those of us
who graduated from the Columbia School of Journalism in the thread-
bare Thirties. There were depressingly few jobs on newspapers then,
and none on *The New York Times,* an institution that many of us had

mistakenly believed to be an annex of the School. Since the faculty was composed of working newspapermen—many of them good, grey *Times* men—we students always hoped we might be tapped for jobs. When this did not happen, we were sent forth into a world where employment was the exception rather than the rule.

There was, nevertheless, something very exciting and hopeful about those days. Was it our age or The Age? In a little while we were to be clamped into uniform and shipped off to wherever strategic requirements dictated. For that little while, however, we were free, though poor and gloriously unprotected, in a world that had not yet learned to try to care for everyone. We would be the last generation to know the "before" as well as the "after" of a world soon to be forever changed.

I was one of the lucky ones who obtained a job on a New York newspaper just before the world changed forever. It was not *The New York Times* but *Women's Wear Daily,* a first-rate national business newspaper. I soon found I would not be reporting or editing news of the Civil War in Spain, not even as it affected Seventh Avenue. My first assignment was to change commodity prices on a paste-up clip of the previous day's prices. Style and syntax were unimportant. Only accuracy counted.

Later, on the copy desk of that paper, I learned much of what I know today about spelling, grammar, punctuation and word usage. My teacher was a former Latvian who had learned English when he was 23 years old. I doubt that he had ever heard it spoken correctly. Yet this man was a wizard of the written word, especially when it came to the word that had to be written in a hurry. When by some miracle I turned in an acceptable head, my reward was a grunt. No four-figure check from *Reader's Digest* ever pleased me more than this man's inarticulate praise.

While I did not stay with *Women's Wear* for long, the training there laid the groundwork for a successful career in many fields. Working on the copy desk was in itself a post-graduate course in Practically Everything. I learned labor relations, trade union practices, how to read a financial statement, libel law and a myriad of other subjects. Absorbing and compressing complex subject matter under pressure into a single-line head rapidly develops an executive point of view. Nowhere else does one have to decide more quickly and accurately what is important.

I have always believed that education is a late-blooming flower, nurtured by experience but with all the essential elements in the bulb. What was in the bulb (school) was the thing that took me to so many

places besides a newspaper office. I am glad it did. Perhaps a brief re-
cital of these adventures will inspire others to embark on their own
odyssey.

I went from the copy desk of *Women's Wear Daily* to a public relations job in the milk industry. Unable to report for work at nine
o'clock in the morning, I next became a theatrical and café reporter,
and for two years did not lay eyes on a glass of milk. From Broadway's
night life I went, in uneasy stages, to the editorship of *Liberty* Magazine
and then, as World War II closed in, to public relations and psychological warfare assignments in the Army. Four years after V-J day, I was a
professional lobbyist—editorial director of the American Medical Association's campaign against compulsory health insurance. Following
this I became managing director of Herbert Mayes' *Cosmopolitan* as
well as an editor of his *Good Housekeeping*. Here ends only the first
lap of the gamut of my many trades. Following a long magazine career,
I went to Hollywood and for 11 years was a top production executive
for Twentieth Century-Fox, supervising the purchase of many millions
of dollars of literary material at a time when Hollywood was the center
of the entertainment universe.

During this period of roughly twenty-five years, I also managed to
get my wife to write a best-selling book titled *Sex and The Single Girl*,
after her letters convinced me that she could write. Much earlier I myself earned a good livelihood writing for the magazines—but not until
I had written jokes for a radio comedian and horoscopes for vending
machines. There is no telling where journalism can take you!

Obviously I consider diversification a sound policy for individuals
as well as for companies. For one thing, a rolling stone gathers no boss,
except one's self. For another thing, diversification prevents technological unemployment. It is hard to displace a man whose skills are
so transferable as those of a former newspaperman. Print reporters,
for example, can, if caught in the contraction of the newspaper business, learn to write for the ear instead of the eye and find work in
radio or television. One former newspaperman I know teaches English
composition to scientists at the California Institute of Technology,
lest we develop scientists who are unable to make us understand what
they have learned. Another former newspaperman is mayor of a fair-
sized city. His speeches are notable for their brevity *and* wit. Any
number of ex-gentlemen of the press are working in public relations or
in its more explicit predecessor, press agentry. Several are playwrights,
literary agents, writers of short stories or of those shorter stories we
have come to know as advertising. At least one former classmate was,

at last report, profitably engaged in the manufacture of a paper too thin to write upon but nevertheless indispensable to all civilized peoples.

The point of this foray through my past is to illustrate just how far (and satisfactorily) afield training in journalism can take someone. I also hope to have made the point that journalism should not be solely the business of writing or editing news. It should be, I believe, communication of all sorts and in all places. A journalist should do more than carry a cane to distinguish him from a newspaperman.

Managing editors and newspaper publishers may accuse me of attempting to lure good people away from the business, or of causing them to seek a newspaper apprenticeship and then defect. I say that those who love the reporting and editing of news will stay aboard. Others will go elsewhere to the betterment of wherever they go. To those others, Good Hunting!

*Dublin-born George Allen was a syndicate editor
with North American Newspaper Alliance and
photo editor of the United Nations department
of public information before being named newsdesk supervisor for NBC News in Washington,
where he also teaches radio and television writing
at American University. He is the author of
"Undercover Teacher" and co-author of "Traitor
Within."*

*Mr. Allen is the winner of a number of im-
portant journalism prizes: The Heywood Broun
Award and a Sigma Delta Chi "Courage in
Journalism" Award, both given to him in 1958,
when he was a reporter for* The New York World-
Telegram & Sun. *The following year he received
two meritorious achievement awards, one from
the Columbia Journalism Alumni, the other from
the Columbia General Studies Alumni. He was
graduated from the School of Journalism in 1954.*

GEORGE ALLEN:

The Sound of a Semicolon

Radio and television networks draw many recruits from the ranks of
newspaper reporters, and for the newspaperman in the process of
switching from written to spoken journalism, there are helpful, practical
pointers in the textbooks on radio and television techniques. But the
books say little, if anything, about the derangements or satisfactions
likely to occur to one in the course of making the change. It's rather
like a marriage manual for bachelors leaving out the fact that while
marriage includes the delights of home cooking, it also includes bath-
rooms crowded with dripping nylons.

For a newspaper reporter with a few years of experience, the transi-
tion to a radio-television network can be disconcerting, perhaps even
shattering. Take me, for example—a champion speller since the fourth
grade. At *The New York World-Telegram & Sun* I had built up quite
a coterie of dictionary-shy reporters who depended on me to solve

their spelling problems. Things like that give a man a certain standing in his profession. But from the day I became a radio-television man, my carefully nurtured spelling ability wasn't worth a damn. In radio-television we don't spell. We pronounce. And pronouncing is an art that just doesn't have spelling's moxie. Who ever heard of a pronouncing bee?

Consider clippings. In radio-television there aren't any. For a reporter whose clipping book was a cherished possession, this can be a hard blow. There are, of course, your scripts, but a collection of second carbons (hard copy and first carbon to file for the FCC) just doesn't have the sex appeal of even a modest collection of inside-page clippings. Nor do audio tapes fill the bill. They are too expensive and take too long to listen to. The result is that for quite a while the former newspaper reporter turned electronic journalist (horrid phrase) feels like a man without a past. No clips; no journalistic history.

Another problem for the radio-television man is the matter of keeping tabs on the opposition. When you were a newspaper reporter the copy boys delivered great gobs of the opposition to your desk, where they quietly lay until you were ready to work them over. But in radio-television the opposition is most often broadcasting at the same moment as you, and so it's hellishly difficult to find out whether your side is holding its own. You must generally depend on second-hand opinions. Over a day or a week the network as a whole, of course, knows how it is doing. It has the ratings, many heads and lots of ears with which to keep tabs on the other fellow. But when you are the one who's covering a running story, all of this isn't much help in your minute-to-minute battle to keep ahead of the opposition reporters.

Eventually you discover that older and wiser heads have found a solution. They put science to work for them—in the form of miniature transistor radios. The next time you notice a chap with a vacant stare and a transistor set clapped to an ear, don't jump to conclusions too quickly. He might be a black-leather jacket type, but then again he might be a correspondent for one of the great networks.

Even on your day off, when you are at home in the bosom of your family, this need to know what your own network and network X are up to remains a problem. When you were a newspaper reporter you bought or had delivered early and late editions of your own paper and the opposition. You looked them over and gained a fairly clear picture of the way the news had developed during the day and who was ahead of whom. Not so in radio-television. The networks never stop. They are at it all day long. To know what they said in the morning, you must have listened in the morning; to know what they said in the afternoon, you had to listen in the afternoon, etc. This doesn't mean that you spend your day off glued to the radio. But it does mean that you must keep checking in.

In my house, this need to keep checking in—and my wife's desire to listen to an occasional music program—has led to a radio in every room, including the bathroom. I'm now trying to nerve myself up to buying a second television set. My wife objects to the idea; I've heard it said that it takes new radio-television wives about two years to get over the feeling that there is a tinge of the immoral about a second TV set.

All this is quite apart from the distresses created by learning to write for the ear instead of the eye. Dropping middle initials, using only last names, rounding out numbers, leaving out details—all this is in the textbooks, and is learned without much difficulty. But when I lost the semicolon I was upset for a week. As a semicolon connoisseur for many years, I played a little game with the *World-Telegram* copy desk. If I could slip at least one semicolon a week past the copy editors I would allow myself two martinis on Friday night. If they discovered and killed all my semicolons, I would have only one martini on Friday night. But in radio-television the lovely, complex semicolon is as dead as my handbook of demon spelling words. "Ya can't hear a semicolon," an NBC copy editor growled at me early in my first week of radio news-writing. That was the end of the semicolon game; it's no fun slipping in semicolons if they can't be heard.

Another dislocation for the newspaper reporter newly shifted to radio-television is the copydesk. Sometimes it isn't there. Many of us would shout hurrah! at the prospect of a copydeskless existence. But in our innermost hearts most of us admit that the copydesk—with its Experts on Everything and English Too—has been as a garment shielding our nakedness from the polite society of our readers. It was there to prevent us from laying bare our ignorance before the universe and the managing editor.

Until you work without the protection of a copydesk you just don't realize its value. In radio-television a reporter on a remote location must often operate too close to deadline for the copydesk to do him much good. His words go on the air the way he wrote them. And, let me tell you, the prospect of facing millions with an error of any magnitude in your script—and with no copy editor on whom to shift the blame—leads to the expenditure of considerable nervous energy. We sometimes can ameliorate the problem by copy-editing over the telephone—a method of operation which would give any sensible rim rider the screaming meemies. But it works.

Undoubtedly the greatest problem in changing from newspapering to radio-television is the new concept of deadline that you must absorb. Writers for the Sunday sections of newspapers have a once-weekly deadline, and reporters for the daily side sneer that the Sunday men don't know what a deadline is. Afternoon paper reporters tell the morning men *they* don't know what a deadline is. And wire service reporters claim to have a permanent deadline.

Let's get it straight! None of them knows what a deadline *really* is. In radio-television it's the word of the Lord, that's what it is. There is no ignoring it and no appeal from it. Your newspaper *can* be printed without your story in it. You may catch hell from your editor for missing an edition, but the paper hits the streets on time. Or if the top brass is so inclined, the newspaper deadline can even be put back a few minutes for a late story. Not so in radio-television. If you are not there with your story when the appointed moment arrives, nothing goes out on the air. You are involved in a catastrophe of major proportions. Facing such an inexorable, unforgiving deadline is like constantly being on call for the Last Judgment. Perhaps that's why what results when you miss your deadline is called "dead air."

In your early days in broadcasting the tension generated by facing this monstrous deadline leads to misreading clocks. They say 30 seconds past the hour instead of 30 seconds to the hour—with a consequent near-faint. You wake up sometimes in the middle of the night with a start because you dreamed that you had only five seconds to get to the microphone, that you rushed up to the broadcast booth—and found the door locked.

Such horrors actually do happen. Recently one of our Washington beat men was scheduled to make a broadcast from a booth overlooking the auditorium of one of the large government buildings. He was to go on the air about 10 minutes after a musical affair in the auditorium. Sitting before the microphone he received his cue and began to read. He had got through about two lines of the script when the building custodian walked into the auditorium, saw that it was empty, and snapped out the lights. All the lights. Our man was left in total darkness, dangling from the end of an open network line which reached from coast to coast and to ships at sea. Being psychologically prepared to face many mishaps while on the air—but not this particular one—he was too shocked for ad libbing. In any case, he couldn't read his watch to know when he should finish talking. Luck was with him, however. Hesitating only a startled moment, he reached into his pocket for his lighter. It was a gas lighter which lit on the first try, flaming long enough for our man to struggle through his script by its wavering light.

Such are some of the confusions which descend on one who makes the change from newspapers to radio-television. Along with them, however, go satisfactions unknown to the newspaper reporter. In network radio-television, for instance, you soon realize that there are no inside pages. Radio-television is all page one. When you are on the air, the listener is listening only to you. From you he gets the headline as well as the complete story. Only news of national interest can get on a nationwide network, so radio-television correspondents handle only page-one stories and top-level features. The radio-television correspondent has no truck with the niggling stories that beset every newspaper reporter—club meetings, minor sports, police news and a host of similar deadly stories.

Radio-television news coverage is never deadly. If anything it is *too* exciting. It also is nearly always a highly satisfying job. A story which contained a high degree of both was the Cuban crisis of October-November 1962. During the first week of the crisis the world was on the brink of nuclear war, and the world knew it. During that week the bulletins on NBC radio and television came thick and fast as the White House and the Kremlin exchanged threats, warnings and peace offers. The telephone inquiries that poured in made us at the NBC Washington newsdesk vividly aware that much of the nation that week was attending closely to radio and television. Our radio bulletins were hitting the air within 15 seconds of the end of Pierre Salinger's briefings. Because of electronic complexity, television took slightly longer. There is great satisfaction in getting the news out *that* fast.

One of the great pleasures in radio-television news is that—contrary to widespread opinion—we have no sacred cows. Every newspaper I know about has totems or taboos. Legitimate news about them is either not carried in the paper or is inflated all out of proportion. I have never seen this happen in radio-television. The size and diversity of the radio-television audience—being far greater than that of any single newspaper—probably precludes sacred cows. But while it is a great satisfaction, this lack of sacred cows also leads to some incertitude. Newspaper reporters making the switch to radio-television refuse at first to believe that there are no special orders about how the news concerning some particular people, places, things or ideas is to be handled. This lack of proscription applies equally as well to news involving NBC News itself or its parent company, RCA.

I have almost overlooked the most obvious satisfaction gained from working in radio-television news. The pay is better.

Two full-time occupations have somehow been carried out concurrently by Gerald Green. He is the author of many notable novels and the writer and producer of several of television's most distinguished programs.

Among Mr. Green's best-selling books are "The Last Angry Man," "The Portofino PTA," "The Lotus Eaters" and "His Majesty O'Keefe." And since he joined NBC Television News in 1950, he has been associated with such shows as "Today," "Wide, Wide World" and "Chet Huntley Reporting."

Mr. Green is a member of the Class of '47, is married to the former Marie Pomposelli, and is the father of three children.

GERALD GREEN:

What Does the Monkey Do?

The toughest assignment I ever had as a journalist involved a chimpanzee, a multi-million-dollar television program and a fair sampling of the hundred most distinguished people in the world.

The chimpanzee's name was (and is) J. Fred Muggs. He helped salvage television's great experiment in early morning news, information and culture, merely by being a chimpanzee, and an ill-tempered chimpanzee at that. A recounting of the travails of "Today," NBC Television's massive morning effort, starring Dave Garroway, would take a volume complete with glossary. In capsule, the program began disastrously—disorganized, beset with internal controversy as to *what* it should be, *whom* it should reach, *how* it should be presented. The critics hated it. The advertisers avoided it. The staff and the on-the-air talent began to lose faith in it. The show that would change the listening habits of America, upgrade people, bring vital news and information into every bathroom and kitchen in America from seven to nine every morning, Monday through Friday, appeared ready to give up the ghost.

Enter J. Fred Muggs. He was a child at that time (1952), a hairy

275

little fellow in a yellow trundle-bundle, owned by two young men who had once been NBC pages. One of the program's associate producers noticed him waiting for an elevator, sucking formula from a plastic bottle. He was introduced to the producer, who introduced him to the executive producer, who introduced him to Mr. Garroway. Possibly because he could not talk, and because the program, both on the air and in preparation, suffered from excess verbalizing, all agreed that he would be a happy addition, a leavening, a condiment.

Muggs made his debut. Few more successful debuts have been recorded in the annals of television. Where our tours of museums, our chats with novelists, our daily infusion of Senatorial wisdom had failed to hold an audience, attract the critics or titillate the sponsors—*Pan troglodytes* succeeded.

Women proposed to him; advertisers fought for the right to use his photo with their supermarket flyers; Chambers of Commerce sought his good offices; actresses posed with him; officers of newly-commissioned naval vessels demanded that he christen them. I am sure that Mr. Garroway, a humane and civilized man, would be the first to agree that when we took the "Today" show on the road, Muggs had to be given the final introduction, since he invariably got the biggest hand. In Ashland, Kentucky, he stopped traffic for a half hour. In Florida his strength was such that a restricted hotel opened its rooms to our entire staff of 50, without the usual preliminary screening about ancestry.

I suppose Muggs reached an apogee of some kind when he appeared in Central Park as guest of honor at "I Am An American Day." This has always puzzled me. Not only wasn't he an American (he was native to the British Cameroons), but he wasn't even human. Nonetheless he appeared on the Central Park Mall, beat time to the music of Edwin Franko Goldman, accepted the applause of the assembled and ignored an irate old lady in the front row who kept shouting at him: "Vishinsky, go home!"

The boy chimp grew older, and so did I. He became a national monument of sorts, and I advanced from news editor to managing editor to producer of the program. In this last job, I was required to be a kind of early morning *maitre d'*, greeting and putting at ease the guests who daily were interviewed by Mr. Garroway or one of the other performers.

And here is where the recurrent problem confronted me: At what point does one inform Dr. Robert Hutchins that he is to share the television air with a chimpanzee? Or should he be informed at all? And if he is informed, do you lie to him about the chimpanzee's importance?

Are there guests from whom the chimpanzee must be hidden? Are there guests for whom the chimpanzee must be *left at home?* I submit that Turner Catledge has never faced any such problem in editing *The New York Times.*

It is with pardonable pride that I report that in my tenure as producer, *not a single guest* ever walked off the program in indignation at the sight of Muggs. (This record, I imagine, is less a tribute to my diplomatic gifts than it is testimony to the vanity of famous persons.)

Probably the worst moment I ever had was with Ernest Gross, then the U.S. Ambassador to the United Nations. For some reason, I had always thought of him as *Sir* Ernest Gross, and, consequently, when I called for him at his Long Island home, to drive him to New York, I was all but tugging at my forelock.

Usually, I would avoid the subject of our ape. But I was tired and forgetful that morning and, in the course of our ride along the Long Island highways, I mentioned the chimpanzee.

"A chimpanzee?" asked Mr. Gross.

"Yes," I said weakly. "A big monkey."

"What does the monkey do?" Mr. Gross asked, his voice edged with the ice he reserved for Gromyko.

"Ah—he doesn't do much of anything. He's—ah—for the children."

"I see. You have invited me to be on a program with a chimpanzee."

Little more was said. It is probably my imagination, but I seem to recall Mr. Gross edging toward the door of the car. I began to speed recklessly. When we completed the crossing of the Queensboro Bridge, I expected him to order me to drive to the Long Island Rail Road Station. But he was a sport about it. We hid the chimpanzee that morning, and the interview went splendidly.

Some guests were anti-chimp at first, but pro-chimp the second time they visited us. In 1952, Adlai Stevenson coldly ignored Muggs. In 1956, possibly under the influence of those who wanted him to reach the average man, he shook hands with Muggs.

Henry Wallace had a particularly trying experience. I had asked him to come down from his chicken farm at South Salem to comment on the Eisenhower agricultural program—which seemed to be sheer plagiarizing of Mr. Wallace's farm proposals of the Thirties and Forties. Mr. Wallace agreed. As I went forth to meet him, he froze, anchored to our carpeted flooring, his hands grasping two stuffed briefcases, his eyes glazed.

"Is anything wrong, sir?"

He muttered something unintelligible and directed his gaze over my shoulder. I turned, to find not *one* chimpanzee but *three,* holding hands, trudging up the stairs. Muggs had invited two friends to the program that morning. They were dressed as flamenco dancers.

But Mr. Wallace, too, was decent about it. He gave us a fine interview.

The reactions of some people were predictable. Motion picture actors and entertainers generally were driven to hug, kiss, fondle and force themselves upon Muggs. Kim Novak had a picnic with him (in the studio) to plug a movie. Strangely, athletes were disdainful. Ball players and prize fighters did not find him especially amusing and tended to snub him.

Industrial and financial tycoons were the most unpredictable. They were either all out for Muggs, or they hated him—in the manner in which such persons are either High Tariff or Low Tariff, Rockefeller Republican or Goldwater Republican.

One industrial leader—a top-echelon man in one of our great corporations, the kind of white-haired, austere fellow who gives one confidence in free enterprise—reacted in particularly memorable fashion. Again, I had my usual morning crisis: Should I tell him about Muggs? Was he a man from whom Muggs must be hidden? He set my fears to rest by *asking* about the chimp. He wanted to be assured that he would meet him.

I was not prepared for the extravagant nature of their meeting. When the industrial giant had finished a dull interview with Mr. Garroway about the upsurge of the economy, he turned slyly in his seat, shook an admonishing "I see you, you bad boy" finger at our ape, and then walked tippy-toe across the studio to the spot where the chimp sat, dressed as a cub scout. They shook hands. Muggs threw an arm around the industrialist's blue-worsted shoulder and they looked deeply into each other's eyes. A professional photographer, in the employ of the tycoon's public relations firm, materialized. He began taking pictures. For many years I had one of the prints in my possession, and whenever I felt depressed about the state of the economy or the future of capitalism, I would study it and be reassured. There sits my steely-eyed executive, and there beside him sits Muggs. There is affection here, understanding, good will. In the fly-specked windows of barber shops in the Times Square area I have seen similar photos—the barber and a famous friend, arms around shoulders. *To my pal Ernie the best barber in New York—Rocky.* My tycoon is the barber, Muggs the celebrity.

There was a footnote to the incident of the industrialist and the ape.

The following morning, a tall, handsome woman in her fifties, in mink, black dress and pearls, approached me on the set.

"I am the wife of Mr. —————," she said, mentioning the executive's name. "May I also have my photo taken with Mr. Muggs?"

Generously, I accommodated her.

Such expressions of egalitarianism from the Power Elite must not go unrewarded. In a sense, J. Fred Muggs was the greatest leveler of his time.

Oliver Gramling joined the Associated Press in 1927 after his graduation from the School of Journalism, and became one of the key executives of the AP during its years of greatest growth. He began his newspaper career at the age of fifteen, writing for Southern newspapers, and did special correspondence for The New York Times *in 1925-26, the years he attended Columbia. His positions with the Associated Press have included those of reporter, bureau chief, executive assistant and assistant general manager.*

Mr. Gramling is the author of "AP, the Story of the News," published in 1940. A year later he was assigned to assist in the development of the AP radio news service, which he describes in this article. His account of the early years of World War II, "Free Men Are Fighting," was published in 1942.

OLIVER GRAMLING:

News by Wire

This is the story behind what was once known as "The News Wire to Nowhere."

Now that it's "The News Wire to Almost Everywhere," you may be interested in hearing how and why it all came about.

I'm referring to today's AP Broadcast News Wire—the longest single news circuit in the world, stretching across all 50 states like a gigantic but unseen spider web, and covering a total of almost 140,000 miles.

Over this sprawling skein of leased wire—reaching from the Canadian border on the north to Key West and the Mexican border on the south—the Associated Press now feeds world, national, state and regional news to 2,400 domestic radio and television station members. Additionally, the Canadian Press taps the wire at Detroit and relays much of its news content to virtually every radio and television station in Canada.

It is a Teletype circuit that delivers 60 words of news a minute, operating every hour of the day and every day of the week. Most of the AP's 125 domestic news gathering bureaus relay state and regional news on the wire day and night, transmitting it almost as soon as it happens in easily readable and easily understandable language written expressly for the ear. Not only are individual stories handled on that basis, but these stories are also rounded up into frequent summaries of the current news and delivered for hourly broadcast.

It was not always that way.

In 1940 the wire stretched only from end to end of a sixth-floor room in the Associated Press Building in New York. It was probably the shortest Teletype news circuit in the history of communications. At one end of the room was a sending keyboard; at the other, a receiving Teletype. Set up by AP technicians working under the supervision of the AP's wire expert, William J. McCambridge, this circuit was to be operated experimentally as a news wire—and, with some hyperbole, was named "The AP Radio Wire."

Banked against a wall at the sending end of the room were receiving Teletypes connected to all principal AP news circuits. They were there to deliver quickly all AP national and international news for fast rewrite into listenable language. Copy from these Teletypes went to the desk of newly-appointed Radio News Editor Tom O'Neil, fastest of rewrite men and the most miserly in the use of words in all AP history. He didn't read news copy; his eyes photographed it.

O'Neil quickly evaluated the news as it flooded across his desk and assigned it, story by story, to a nearby battery of carefully-selected rewrite experts. Their job was to convert each story into terse, easy, conversational English. From the rewrite desk the copy went back to O'Neil for fast, final editing—and then to a Teletype operator for transmission over the world's shortest news circuit.

Beyond the receiving Teletype at the other end of the room was an improvised "studio" with microphone equipment. There, with the rewrite men and others, a group of my associates and I assembled periodically each day to hear, study, criticize and frequently rewrite again what already had been rewritten. Polished announcers, raw announcers and uneasy amateurs took turns "broadcasting" the news for all assembled ears.

News experts from the networks and individual stations were invited to sit in, collaborate, criticize and suggest. Off-duty personnel from other AP departments—even pedestrians from the street—were asked to listen to the "broadcasts" and then to tell us bluntly if they had understood what they had heard. Had they found it interesting or dull? Could they repeat the details of any of the stories? Could they tell us *why* they remembered them?

And so it continued on the sixth floor, with news and traffic staffs working around the clock—writing, rewriting, receiving, "broadcasting," criticizing, correcting, trying new approaches with new opening sentences . . . rearranging the sequence of facts and subject matter in coordinated newscasts . . . trying for the most appealing words . . . experimenting with humor in the news and the most effective places to inject it in hourly summaries . . . studying human interest news, looking for proof of a theory that "wherever there are human beings, there is human interest" . . . experimenting with the idea that right words and imaginative phrases frequently can help make "heavy" but important news understandable and interesting without shunning the facts . . . *Always trying to make the news quickly comprehensible to an ear that has only one opportunity to hear it.*

This intensive study of the most effective way to write for the air—for the *ear*—continued for some months. We were intent on reaching a new level of skill in an area where little of value had yet been achieved.

AP news had been the first press association news ever broadcast. The occasion was the Harding-Cox election on November 2, 1920. Through their earphones, listeners heard the election returns as broadcast by the pioneer station, KDKA in Pittsburgh; the voting figures were supplied through arrangement with a local AP member newspaper.

From that time on, there never was a day when AP news was not being broadcast by one station or another in one place or another. And there probably was not a day for many years thereafter but that AP management received a complaint on this score from one member paper or another.

Competition between media for audience and advertising was frequently fierce. Some newspapers therefore bitterly opposed giving radio access to the news gathered by the press associations. Other papers favored the idea. Some broadcasters were willing to fight to get press-association service. Others couldn't have cared less.

History was moving dramatically and quickly in the Thirties. Increasingly, copy was taken off the newspaper wires and put on the air. A new agency, sponsored by some broadcasters, was created to develop a news service for radio. But the performance average was low. Stations mostly were broadcasting news that was meant to be read, not heard.

Late in the Thirties I was researching the history and development of news gathering for what, in 1940, became a book entitled "AP —The Story of News." Every signpost seemed to point toward new and significant changes in newspaper emphasis and reader interests. People generally wanted fast and ever-faster word on spot news, but they also wanted thorough analysis, background and interpretation. It seemed that the time was approaching when radio might well assume its natural place as a swift, economic purveyor of the latest spot news; that newspapers would provide the depth and the detail.

While some did not agree, these possibilities seemed to offer advantages both to the newspapers and to radio. The two media could complement each other instead of opposing each other.

I asked Kent Cooper, then General Manager of the AP, to let me assist in developing the AP's place in the broadcasting news field. Action by the AP Board of Directors enabled us to undertake the task.

On April 1, 1941, the experimental news wire that had reached from one end of a room to another became, officially, a new AP service. By that time our nucleus of nine carefully-selected writers had grown to 40. Today it runs into the hundreds.

The debut was by no means perfect. We didn't, for example, carry a single state or regional news story unless the news happened also to be of sufficient importance to qualify as national news. But neither did the wires of our competitors.

It was a beginning. And another meaningful chapter in the history and evolution of news—of journalism—had opened.

Dallas Townsend's career has been in the field of radio and television journalism. After his graduation from the School of Journalism in 1941, he spent a short period with radio station WQXR before joining the CBS news staff. Except for Army service in World War II (in New Guinea, the Philippines and Japan), he has been with CBS since.

Now a staff correspondent, Mr. Townsend was previously director of special events and manager of television news programs. He also conducted a course in radio newswriting at the School of Journalism in 1960-61. He is married to a former classmate, Lois Bradley. They live with their three daughters and a son in Montclair, New Jersey.

DALLAS S. TOWNSEND, JR.:

News on the Air

The other night I was strolling down West 45th Street toward the Fiasco Theatre in order to catch the opening (and closing) of the latest entry from the lunatic fringe. Its name, as I recall, was on the order of "Like Wow, Man." But I am straying from the point even before I make it. Two ladies passed me after pausing briefly at a newsstand to inspect the latest scare headlines, and one of them said to the other, "How about that Katanga! What is he, a Communist or something?"

I paid little heed to the remark at the time. But a few days later, much to my surprise, I heard it repeated practically verbatim by a woman who should have known better. She, too, was seriously wondering whether Katanga might be some sort of Communist.

The coincidence set me to thinking—something I seldom seem to have time for these days. I found myself proceeding from certain assumptions (possibly incorrect) to a rather disturbing conclusion (possibly unwarranted). I do not mean to imply that the conclusion sprang full-blown from the assumptions simply because two women had independently revealed a distressing lack of knowledge regarding Katanga;

rather, it resulted, to a great extent, from a nagging sense of uneasiness that has bothered me for some time—uneasiness about the way news is disseminated by this country's mass communications media. Particularly, I am worried about some news programs on radio and television.

I have an abiding distrust of sweeping generalizations, even though I resort to them more frequently than I should, and so I want to make it perfectly clear that I am not talking about *all* news programs. I know that many of them rank with the best products of American journalism. What I have in mind is a certain type of routine, run-of-the-mine program that can be seen and heard seven days a week, day in and day out—a type that makes up the great bulk of the output of both network and local news departments.

Here I cite my first assumption. It is that the overwhelming majority of the American people tune in to a news program at least once a day. Chances are that most of them tune in twice or more; there may even be some fanatics who listen every hour on the hour.

The second assumption is a corollary of the first. It is that most Americans get a large part of their information about current events, local and national as well as international, from radio or television news programs or both. Undoubtedly many of them increase this information with newspapers and news magazines as either primary or secondary sources; but it must also be true that many others do not, at least not regularly.

For purposes of this argument, at any rate, it can be hypothecated that most Americans learn much or most of what they know about current events and world affairs in general from what they see on those millions of little screens and hear on those many more millions of radio sets.

And what do they see and hear? Again emphasizing that I am not talking about all news programs, I must give this answer: A relatively small number of sentences, sometimes well-written, sometimes not, about a relatively small number of events, supplemented (in the case of television) with appropriate film or videotape and the use of such devices as rear projection. If the program runs ten or fifteen minutes, there will probably be a pause for a commercial every three or four minutes, sometimes oftener. There are some news programs, in fact, that seem to be built around commercials.

I am not going to be hypocritical and claim that I have anything against commercials. All of us have to eat. Networks and individual stations understandably want to show a profit, and a news operation of any size almost invariably runs in the red.

What I do object to, on professional grounds, is the way in which many news programs are being gimmicked up, and increasingly seem designed as vehicles for commercial messages. The effect of this on the actual news content is more serious than might be apparent to the casual listener.

It is all too easy to decide that the latest developments on Capitol Hill are "worth" only thirty seconds in a five-minute program, especially on a day when a great deal is happening elsewhere. But thirty seconds may not be enough time in which to deal with the legislative subject, except on a headline basis. And on this basis it may well be asked how much more the average listener really knows about the situation on Capitol Hill after the news program than he did before it.

I should emphasize that during 1963 the networks have all paid increasing attention to the improvement of their regular news programs. The action of both CBS and NBC in the fall of '63 in expanding their early evening television news broadcasts from fifteen minutes to half an hour was a prime case in point. This move was rightly applauded.

It also is a fact that many individual stations around the country have a superior news product by any standard.

Nevertheless, there can be no denying that the format of many news programs acts like a straitjacket and causes some baffling problems.

These problems can almost never be resolved satisfactorily. The most one can hope for is a workable compromise between the news and the format. The result is a constant process of cutting, revising, expanding and omitting in order to fit the format, all under the pressure of that fast-approaching and inflexible deadline. Occasionally I am reminded of the legend of Procrustes.

The consequence of this situation, and other situations as well, is that important and complicated events are all too often reported in a form that robs them of their significance. A minor ship-sinking in the Atlantic may be given a bigger play and more space than the fall of a government in Asia. A story that would be the automatic lead one day might get scarcely a mention on another day. Local news programs frequently play up local events out of all proportion to their importance. I have listened to many news programs around the country which gave me the impression that the news was being packaged and marketed like some commodity at a supermarket.

The conclusion is inevitable. The type of news program I have described is not doing what it should be doing. It may be adequate as a means of reporting late developments. (Flourish of trumpets. "And now—NEWS!!! Up to the second—when it happens, where it happens

. . . brought to you by . . .") But as a vehicle for putting those developments in perspective and giving them some meaning, it often falls flat.

I am afraid that these words may sound too harsh, and I may seem ungrateful in having written them about a business to which I owe a great deal, both personally and professionally. I have the utmost faith and confidence in this medium; I believe that its potentialities have only begun to be explored. When I say that we could do a better job of informing and explaining, I mean it in a constructive sense. The world situation has become so complicated in the past generation that the best job would still fall short. Even the most enlightened and best-informed among us have trouble keeping up with the frantic rush of events. Perhaps it is too much to expect that people who do not have a direct professional interest in the news will also make this effort. But I maintain that we can help them more than we do now.

Jules Bergman, peripatetic Science Editor for the American Broadcasting Company, is the author of "90 Seconds to Space" and of articles in the Reader's Digest *and* Science World. *He studied at the School of Journalism under a Sloan-Rockefeller Science Writer's Fellowship in 1960. Two years later he was named one of the ten outstanding young men of the year.*

Mr. Bergman, whose most recent book is "Anyone Can Fly," is a weekend pilot. He lives with his wife and three children in Rockland County, New York. Before attending Columbia, he studied at C. C. N. Y. and Indiana University.

JULES BERGMAN:

T-5 and Counting . . .

In the wind-blown, numbing cold at Edwards Air Force Base, on the high California desert, I watched the X-15 first fly; in the dank heat of Cape Canaveral, I've witnessed every U. S. astronaut and Atlas, Titan, Minuteman, Thor, Jupiter, Blue Scout, Pershing, Polaris, Mace, Saturn and Lord knows what else launched into space; in the snowy wastes of Montana and Colorado, I've shivered as Titan and Minuteman eerily came out of their underground silos; in a ten-below windstorm in New Mexico, I watched a nuclear blast go awry. In just about every state, in all kinds of weather—but almost always at 2 or 3 A.M.—I've watched America swiftly growing in the age of space and atom.

This is what I have to report: There is no single "most interesting experience." Rather there is the surging sense that the scientific might of a great nation is finally being harnessed and, most importantly, directed toward clear-cut goals. And as a newsman who devotes his life to science, this is my uppermost hope: That we will start launching rockets, spacecraft, test devices or what-have-you at 10 A.M. or noon.

There is seldom time for the science reporter to remember; in fact, there is hardly ever time for anything other than plunging on to the

288

next launch, to tomorrow's flight, to the new operation or to the new breakthrough. But out of the concentrated fervor of the scientific revolution, this is what I cannot ever forget:

The time: 9:47 A.M., February 20, 1962. *The place:* Cape Canaveral, a curious spit of land in the never-never land of Florida, rejected by pirates centuries ago as unfit for human habitation. Ah, but they didn't have DDT, bulldozers, millions of tons of cement, pumps or, strangely, rockets they had to launch. Result: The pirates cracked up on the shoals just south of here, while we persist, despite gnats, chiggers, mosquitoes, water mocassins and armadilloes, in launching missiles into space. *The event:* The first U. S. orbital flight. On Pad 14, 8,000 feet from our ABC News Center, Astronaut John Glenn has been cramped in the miniscule cockpit of Friendship 7 for nearly five hours.

The shot has been scrubbed so many times because of weather, leaky fuel diaphragms in the Atlas and numerous other mechanical hazards that we're all numbed. Three weeks earlier, we had almost made it. T-17 minutes, and then the weather and mechanicals had closed in.

I've been standing in the studio since 2 A.M., after a good one hour's sleep. We're all so dazed that the launch has assumed the unreality of Roger Bannister's trying to catch up with Stirling Moss in an Alfa.

"T minus five . . . four . . . three . . . two . . . one." At the count of two, the Atlas belches orangeish-black smoke, and begins to waver uncertainly on the pad. Suddenly adrenalin is pumping through me wildly. It's really going to happen, I tell myself. And there's a *man* in there, a crazy Marine pilot named Glenn, a guy you've eaten with, and talked with for hours on end, and run with on these beaches. The Atlas lifts off with agonizing slowness.

Now I'm speaking into a microphone, describing the launch, and distantly I hear the words. The Atlas blurs out for a second in the emotional moisture over my eyes. The characters shouting, "Go baby, go!" are a harsh intrusion on my own private prayer, "Godspeed, John Glenn!" Months later, the same phrase strangely turns up in a film on the Glenn flight and it produces the same emotional reaction. . . .

For every such storybook launch, there are half-a-dozen anti-climaxes when, after waiting the soggy night and dripping dawn, clouds roll in over the Cape ruining a perfect countdown. Or when the count dies at a frustrating T-9 minutes in a stuck valve or temperamental transistor. It ends then with an anonymous voice over a loudspeaker flatly intoning, "Test 6427 is scrubbed." But this will be remembered as the infancy of the rocketry era; in years to come, checkout, countdown and launch operations will be so improved and the reliability of equipment so perfected that the frustrations will be fewer even if the nights are just as long.

The time: 6 A.M., December 13, 1961. *The place:* The New Mexico desert, 20 miles from Carlsbad. *The event:* Project Gnome, America's first underground nuclear blast to test the peaceful uses of atomic energy, the first shot in Project Plowshare. A raw wind is pumping 10° air through the thin raincoat you brought because someone told you that it was warm and sunny in New Mexico. You've just finished a film interview with one of America's most famous physicists, who assured you that only a slight shock wave would be felt and that no radiation could possibly reach the surface.

Ground Zero is some two miles away. As the countdown reaches zero, nothing at all seems to have happened. The famed physicist is in a helicopter orbiting the blast area. The chopper turns tail at about the moment the shock wave lifts you, the camera and the ground about 12 inches into the air. Through your field glasses you watch the desert floor at ground zero heave about four feet into the air, then fall back abruptly. Just as you're about to tell the cameraman to turn off the camera, another physicist (somewhat less famous) taps you on the shoulder.

"Leave the camera on," he mutters quietly, "you'll get some interesting film." As you turn back to the blast site, a thin plume of steam thickens into a geyser-like flow out of the ground. "It's venting," somebody shouts. As usual, no official has any explanation. But many phones are picked up at once and suddenly there are warnings that we may either have to move out of here like lightning or not be allowed to leave at all.

The radioactive cloud (of a low order, it later turns out), moves in our general direction, then veers to the side. Just as you're about to pick up your film, state troopers close in from all directions. "No one leaves," the order goes out. And there isn't even a working phone so that you can call the story in for the ABC radio network. We make a few experimental sallies at the roadblocks, but the troopers heavily outnumber us. However, we do find that you *can* leave by the road to the north, and that it's only 100 miles back to Carlsbad that way. We also discover that if you're daring there is a dirt road across the desert.

And off you go with another reporter, one eye on the dirt road, the other on the radioactive cloud as it pushes steadily toward you. After two hours you're completely lost; a few Mexican farmers offer no help, and you're running out of gasoline. Desperately, you take the less likely of two drygulch trails and end up at an old potash mine shaft. It even has a phone, though no one in New York believes you when you call in. But

the story gets on. After borrowing some gas, you head off toward Carlsbad, clutching the can of "hot" film (hot indeed, possibly). Two more
roadblocks, but the troopers wave you on when you tell them you're
merely lost tourists. "Who, me? A *reporter?*"

Reaching Carlsbad, you find you have a "hot" car; you and the car
get a quick radioactive-count and you're passed. You *did* pass through
the radioactive cloud, but it had dissipated by then. Meanwhile, back at
the press site, everyone else is still trapped. After battling a snowstorm
through the mountains to get out (you battled a dust storm flying yourself in), you reach a jet at El Paso at 4 A.M. and get the film to New
York.

The moral of the story is roughly this: Scientists can be wrong, too,
and part of the adventure of the job is being there when experimental
tests do go awry. And even with the degree of failure, the shot—to see
if nuclear blasts deep in salt caverns can be harnessed to produce heat
and thus useful energy—was largely successful, though there are many
newsmen who still won't believe it.

No matter what the story, or where you are, editors will always be
editors. Covering the opening of our first underground Titan intercon-
tinental missile sites, in Colorado, south of Lowry Air Force Base, I
watched in awe as three Titans majestically rose out of their blastproof
pits at dawn. After shooting our film, I naturally had to call New York.
Trouble was, there were no phones. I made my way 200 feet down in
elevators, through snakelike caverns, past blast doors under guard and
through three checkpoints. Finally, the Launch Control Center, Top
Secret, loomed ahead. An obliging colonel okayed use of the phone.
I was plugged in from the missile site to the control point, to Lowry
AFB, to the phone company in Denver. And finally the phone rang in
our newsroom in New York. The assignment editor picked it up.

"Look," I cried, "I'm 250 feet underground in a missile silo . . ."

"Just hold on," he answered. "I'm busy on three phones, I'll put you
on hold or call you back." Click . . . click . . . went the phone. I smiled at
the colonel and the Air Police through the glass window and they smiled
back, trying to figure out what was going on. I never did tell them, because I'm sure they wouldn't have believed it.

For all the fatigue, the frustrations and the running for airplanes that
make up part of a reporter's life, there are also the moments of rare
satisfaction and human drama (moments that often go unreported, because the television news medium functions far differently from the
printed word; our 15-minute nightly news shows have, in effect, no page
two—only a fast-moving front page). Of all these moments of satisfaction, probably the most satisfying single event was witnessing a woman

regain her hearing in a stapedectomy performed at Polyclinic Hospital in New York. The operation wasn't brand new—the technique of using a miniature TV camera to show it and instruct other surgeons was. We shot our film story and, as the brief surgical procedure concluded, the chief surgeon leaned over his patient, testing to be sure that the tiny tube he'd placed in her ear to conduct sound waves had been properly positioned.

"Can you hear me?" he asked in a voice hardly above a whisper. The woman on the table, who hadn't heard in 20 years, grimaced in pain, and then responded: "Please, not so *loud*."

Without question, the most interesting single experience I've had, especially since I fly small planes and occasionally bigger ones, was going through the same physical qualification tests undergone by our first seven astronauts. Administered at Wright-Patterson Air Force Base after a rigorous general physical exam, these consisted of being whirled at up to 5 g's on a centrifuge; flying weightless in a transport plane and then in an F-100 jet fighter; enduring three hours in a 130° heat room as a test of mental and physical stamina; withstanding the cold pressor test—in which your feet, up to the ankles, are immersed in ice cubes; running for ten minutes on a treadmill; and flying "blind" on a violently oscillating "shake" table—a pilot's seat mounted on a gyroscopic motor. The finale was being tossed into a dark isolation chamber for several hours of meditation and then being exposed to head-rocking, screeching sound levels in a noise room.

The "reward" for passing all the tests, given to me by an Air Force friend, was a jet-fighter ride from New York to California—900 miles an hour at 50,000 feet. Over the Sierras, at 3 A.M., I looked down from the bubble canopy. America glistened. To the South, Mexico loomed clearly; and to the North, Utah . . . six or seven states in all.

In the cold (−65°) air outside our canopy, the stars shone with incredible brilliance. But for the crackling voice of traffic controllers on the radios, there *was* no Earth below, and we were as alone as humans can ever be on this planet. For three hundred miles we barrel-rolled through the stratosphere, cork-screwing within our wingspan as only jets really can—then loops, Immelmans and other fancy acrobatics.

It's the highest I've been over this earth, and the closest I've yet come to space. It primed me for the story I aim to cover: the first manned American launch for the moon.

There can be only one deeper experience for me—and that is when *I* launch for the moon, as one of the first newsmen, I hope, to do so. That flight hasn't been scheduled yet, but I'm waiting.

Some of the most distinguished television docu-
mentaries in recent years have been produced
by Reuven Frank, who was drafted out of the
Columbia Journalism Class of 1943, thrice at-
taining and twice losing the rank of private first
class before returning to graduate in 1947. Among
the NBC News programs he has produced are
"The Huntley-Brinkley Report," "Chet Huntley
Reporting," the 1956 and 1960 political conven-
tions and elections, "The Tunnel," "The Land,"
"The Problem with Water is People," "A Country
Called Europe" and "Our Man in the Mediter-
ranean."

Mr. Frank has twice won the Robert E. Sher-
wood Award, and has also received the Sigma
Delta Chi award, the Columbia Journalism alumni
award and the George Polk Award from Long
Island University.

REUVEN FRANK:

Life with Brinkley

[It may be interesting to consider what can happen, in this television
era, to two fortyish fellows who were lucky—one a North Carolinian
who progressed in a straight line from the UP bureau in Nashville to
stardom, the other a reporter from *The Newark Evening News* who
became a television producer. I use a record, somewhat bowdlerized,
made during the filming of an N.B.C. television program called "Our
Man in Hong Kong." It was December, 1960. David Brinkley of
Wilmington (N.C.) and I had gained some standing with our em-
ployers by our work at the political conventions that year, and we
used it to get as far from the United States as we could. We would
decide what to do when we got there.]

December 1. New York. Brinkley called from Washington, said we must
have yellow fever shots. Huntley, who was in Hong Kong in 1954, says
not so. Called Public Health Service, who also said not so. Called
Brinkley. He said you never can tell where we might run off to if we

293

have a day. Called Public Health Service. No time for yellow fever shots. Told Brinkley we had to be satisfied with typhoid, typhus and cholera, but I could buy pills. He said no need, he has large supply—sleeping pills, wake-up pills, cold pills, fever pills, salicylates, antibiotics, miracle drugs yet untested. I told him he'd be overweight. He reminded me about my tetanus booster.

December 2. Kravetz, director, called from Hong Kong. No film shot yet. Raining four days. Depressed. Whole project failure. Called Brinkley. He said it never rains in Hong Kong in December. Told him I'd advise Kravetz.

December 3. Met Brinkleys San Francisco Airport. Anne all excited; David depressed on account of baggage overweight, already tired anticipating long airplane ride. After midnight spent 90 minutes Honolulu airport. Hot, steamy place. Poor service in luncheonette. We agreed Hawaii overrated. Refueled at Guam. No one allowed off, but stewardess gave out folder of history of Guam. Not very exciting. Crossed International Date Line. Lost December 4. Very dull.

December 5 and 6. Tokyo. Too busy reporting news to see anything. Spent one evening recovering from airplane ride, second, at Brinkley's insistence, attending Israel Philharmonic instead of local wonders. Hall as cold as outside, which very cold. Tiny seats, made only for Japanese or Anne Brinkley. David and I cramped, chilled and surly. Didn't like concert. Brinkley said probably pickup band.

December 7. Hong Kong. Sunny, clear, warm, crisp, hilly, stunning, busy. Passports stamped forbidden to look for jobs. Local rates unskilled labor $1 a day. Met by our advance party, Kravetz, cameraman Priestley, unit manager Lynch. Also dozen local residents engaged for project. Two Americans. Rest Chinese including two coolies. First time in long career hired two coolies. Very Hollywood. Good for ego. Brinkley interviewed by Chinese reporter. Good for his ego.

Priestley, Kravetz, Lynch talk only cheap suits, slit skirts, watches, cameras, jade, brocade. Must watch expense accounts. Asked if any film shot. Told about Typhoon Phyllis. Brinkleys rode tram to Victoria Peak to gasp at view. I took crew to check film locations downtown. Remarked on beauty. Priestley said flatten it out, you've got Toledo. Kept losing one member of party after another who would return in half hour. Asked. Told they'd gone for fittings.

Went for fitting.

December 8. Brinkley touted me off my tailor to one he'd got on best authority. Much measuring then scribbling in Chinese. Eight tailors in small room. Boss tailor complained young people nowadays unwilling to work with hands. Used abroad as noun—want to go to abroad, what if no jobs in abroad. Nephews unhappy cannot afford abroad, wherefore studying medicine University of Hong Kong. Son studying physics M.I.T. No tailors. Too many physicists. Brinkley said too many tailors.

Took Brinkley to main downtown location, Peel Street off Hollywood Road, old Chinese section. Narrow streets. Step streets called ladders. Very hilly, crowded, people running with bamboo poles, shuffle, shuffle, shuffle, caroming off each other, selling in street, barbershops in street, carpenters and metal-workers in street, crouched, hammering, sawing, yelling, cooking, in street fourteen feet wide. Two blocks away World of Suzie Wong filmed, false front up for hotel. Many months' shooting, hundreds of people from Hollywood, New York, London, Tokyo, special power lines, generators. Said we'd substitute ingenuity. Drew looks askance.

Priestley went for fitting.

December 9. Hong Kong is many islands and one peninsula. Main island, also Hong Kong, extremely mountainous, peaks in clouds, where wealthy British live, some wealthy Chinese. Chinese excluded from peaks many years. Finally allowed, found damp mists cracked lacquer furniture and induced lumbago. Old ones moved back down. On island's north coast, facing mainland, the city, Victoria. On mainland, facing Victoria, another city, Kowloon, almost mirror image. Between them the harbor, full of freighters, warships, ferryboats, junks, launches, tugs, cruise ships, water taxis called walla walla. North of Kowloon stretch New Territories, several hundred square miles farms and villages. Across Kowloon mountains down into valley of terraced farms, stone bridges, pancake hats, farmer on bicycle carrying live 300-pound pig in wicker basket, reservoirs, water catchments, police posts. Near border Sheung Shui, walled farm village, last stand of ancient China. Scenes like watercolors, duck pond, line of harvesters, old men sitting, crouched families eating rice. Everywhere camera placed hundreds emerge from nowhere, children, old people, perfectly formed faces, laughing, jostling. Kravetz, Priestley in custom-made work pants measured, fitted and bought during Typhoon Phyllis. $2.50. Give coolies length of twine to hold back crowd. Coolies hold twine. Crowd holds back.

Missed fittings.

December 10. All stores sell watches. Newsstands, drugstores, radio shops, drygoods, all have watch counters. Crew compare Rolexes (Rolices?). Bellhop sports Tissot. Brinkley goes to reputable jewelers to buy Anne Christmas present, gold Swiss watch with gold Swiss bracelet, very reasonable. Feel left out. Buy watchband.

Courtesy call colony public information officer. Brinkley reluctant to go, stayed three hours. Large, rumpled Scot named Jock Murray. He and Brinkley talked Scot to Scot. Much reference by government fellows to H. E. Eventually learned it meant Governor—His Excellency. Jock advised against filming H.E. at police parade Sunday, suggested instead filming H.E. in plumed hat leaving Government House for parade. No retakes on H.E. Showed us some movies he made. Scripts full of gems: "Hong Kong—land of contrasts—the old and the new—where East meets West," etc.

December 11. Government House. Large white colonial building with columns and portico. Aide-de-camp in civilian clothes, young, English, curly blond, rosy cheeks, starched. Stands on steps facing camera crew setting up on lawn. Snaps fingers, extends right hand, faces straight ahead. Large orange juice appears in hand. Figure in white coat melts back into the house.

Five-man Government House guard presents arms as H.E.'s car leaves. One extra turn around driveway but no retakes. Bugler fluffs. Brinkley speculates on problems of being bugler with hangover.

By car to Aberdeen, opposite side Hong Kong Island from Victoria. Shipyard about size of three-car garage making hand-carved teakwood junks as pleasure boats. About 60 a year. Half to local residents, half to Americans. Americans insist on good luck symbols, Chinese names, and cute English names in wedge-shaped letters. Filmed sampan people, tiny boat home for entire family, where they live and die. Shrine to ancestors in stern, incense burner, sticks with red ribbons. Filmed wedding. Dozens, hundreds, thousands boats in coves, along shores, washed up on salt flats. Children, women, old people walking through mud to land. Brinkley beginning to get mad. These people exploited.

December 12. Hillside squatters. There are half million mostly refugees from China. Very clean. Always washing. Board and tar paper and sheet-metal shacks in colonies of thousands above, below and even down among fanciest modern apartment buildings and houses. Cooking and frying odors but no sick or rotten smells like Casbahs. Whenever we move them around they smile. They sit for medium shots, closeups. They move when we ask, they walk, they cook, they eat. Can't understand why they don't throw us off hillside. Some ask for money—cumshaw. Local allies handle these matters. Then they go instinctively to Priestley who gives them more, upsetting local scales. He yells at them and they follow him everywhere. The cumshaw king of Hong Kong. Old man kept him from giving some Hong Kong dollars (18 cents each) to small children. They have not learned begging yet, he said.

Most hillside squatters wear blue denim pajamas—sam foo—dress with pants. (Cheongsam, long dress.) Barefoot woman in sam foo carrying bamboo pole with two buckets of water from tap at bottom to home up top. Up top means recent arrival. Closer to water better. Her hair attractively waved. Lipstick. Unusual. Young fellow apparently on way to work. Green sweater, gray slacks, sparkling clean white shirt, shiny shoes, carrying paper bag. Lunch? How do they press shirts in those shacks? Everywhere steps cut out of rock. Tried to ask what social organization, who arranges public works, who punishes petty evildoers. Local allies stumped. Chinese vocabulary of Americans among them and English of Chinese among them insufficient for sociology.

We develop technique for crowds. Whenever too many for film or for coolies holding twine, we send local ally with extra tripod running up and down, clapping hands, shouting orders to nobody, making racket. Crowd always follows.

Third fitting.

December 13. Increasing worry about opening sequence, Brinkley walking through crowds near Hollywood Road. Kravetz, Priestley advise strong December sun in narrow streets very bad for color film. Too much contrast. Must wait for hazy day. As time grows short decide to scrim two blocks. (Scrim stage term for screening or reducing or diffusing light.) Investigate how much for sixteen coolies to stand on rooftops and how much for two blocks' length, one street width of cheesecloth to be held on rooftop level to diffuse sunlight over length of scene. About 300 dollars. Anywhere else thousands. Approve project. Feel like Darryl Zanuck.

Time magazine reporter calls for interview.

December 14. Newsweek reporter calls for interview. Anne Brinkley buys gown for Inaugural Ball. Back to Government House for changing of the guard. Royal Artillery, huge Englishmen, going off guard. Seventh Gurkha Rifles, tiny brown men in pillbox bellhop hats, coming on guard. Five each plus Gurkha piper in tartan playing "Over the Seas to Skye."

December 15. Construction. Roads. Hotels. Resettlement blocks. Government aims to resettle 100,000 refugees and other squatters a year. Big and modern looking like Perez Jimenez' Caracas. Tiny rooms. One running water facility per floor. Better than hillsides. Almost all labor by hand. Cheaper than machines. Men, women carrying dirt, rocks at ends of bamboo poles. Construction labor known as earth coolies. Brinkley recoils at term.

Filmed Chinese funeral. Two bands. One played "Tramp, tramp, tramp, the boys are marching."

Brinkley stopped at vegetable booth to listen to radio. Chinese words to "Sixteen Tons." Bought record to go with construction sequence. Later learned Chinese words are love song. Who'll know?

Fittings.

December 16. Overcast morning. Changed all plans and raced to Hollywood Road to film Brinkley walking through crowd. No need to scrim two blocks. Letdown.

Time reporter called to cancel interview. Ordered to Vientiane.

Suggested Brinkley talk into camera on location instead of in studio. He thought maybe background of busy Chinese. Should be easy in Hong Kong. Spent half day finding right spot. Hills, narrow streets, color film make lighting conditions almost impossible. Found one just perfect from 12:30 to 1 p.m. Balcony over snake butcher shop. As we negotiate, clerks selling and slaughtering live snakes. Organs used as medicine. Didn't film.

December 17. Newsweek reporter called. Cancelled interview. Ordered to Vientiane.

Filmed Billy Tingle, small banty Englishman formerly featherweight champion Far East, physical instructor, teaches calisthenics and cricket Saturday mornings to hundreds of small boys and girls on grounds of Hong Kong Cricket Club—heart of downtown, property more valuable than midtown Manhattan. Tingle says things like, "Building character through discipline . . . White men go soft in this climate . . ." Amahs gossip while waiting for children. Chauffeurs deliver and pick up. Billy and boys wear white sweaters, ducks, round red caps. The playing fields of Hong Kong.

Filmed Billy's classes until noon. Filmed Billy at noon. Club cricketers began to emerge on field to be bowled at by Chinese ball boys. Boys very good. Get one chance a year to play real game. Hong Kong Club boys versus Kowloon Club boys. Boys 20 to 60 years old. Cricket coolies?

December 18. Maritime police take us out in two launches—70-footer and 50-footer—to look for illegal immigrants. Brinkley afraid we'll stop junk, find hold full of CIA agents. Sub-inspector Li only man aboard speaking some English. Not much. Heads for Aberdeen, almost an hour by water. Water calmer there. Sub-inspector Li says better for camera work. Everybody now film expert.

Stop sampan; inspect credentials. Stop junk. Kravetz and number two cameraman on other boat shooting cover shots. Three sails reefed, junk hove to. Fisherman, wife, five children, dog. Much smiling. Priestley grinds away on larger boat as policemen in sailor suits go aboard. Priestley boards with policeman who goes below. Priestley makes him go

below again for closer shot. He emerges with two sticks gelignite.
Highly illegal. For dynamiting fish. Fisherman summoned aboard launch.
Woman spanks baby to make it cry. Brinkley feels like a heel. Our
launch takes off. Kravetz and his cameraman covering departure. Woman
must hoist sails herself. Very awkward. One sail falls down. Brinkley
feels worse. Into cabin to make closeups culprit. Across left knee large
patch, clearly visible word "FLOUR." Brinkley wants to pay fine, but
fisherman gets two months in jail. Help stamp out fish dynamiters!
December 19. Filmed rooftop squatters. Hundred thousand live on rooftops of tenements. Up and down many tenements looking for right one.
Most don't look like rooftops except when filmed from other rooftops.

Sent crew racing ahead to Brinkley balcony location (above snake
store). Arrived there to find street empty. Everybody standing below
balcony watching camera being set up. Twenty minutes left of proper
light. Once again, sent local ally out with tripod to run up and down
street. It worked again. Filmed Brinkley against background busy
Chinese street.

Fittings not going well.
December 20. Anne Brinkley shopping for furniture. Running out of
things to shop for.

To border to film McIntosh Cathedrals. These Beau-Geste-like ob-
servation towers placed along border hilltops by one-time Police Commissioner named McIntosh. Red China stretching vastly away in sunlight.
Barely visible dam and pipeline under construction to sell Communist
water to Hong Kong, will end restricted bathing hours in hotels. From
one side of tower see wonderful picture. Yellow Coca-Cola truck driving
within six feet of border of Communist China. Priestley can't get equipment over in time. Wait extra hour for return. In vain. Brinkley thinks
it was captured.

To Mankamto, border village where Red Chinese food comes into
Hong Kong. Bailey bridge. Chinese half of bridge red, British half green.
Chinese can walk in any time. Locals always ask why should they? Same
question asked about Japanese in 1941. Brinkley and I return by train,
what is left of Kowloon-to-Canton Railway. Once you could go from
Hong Kong to London by train. Mess-boy sells beer. Brinkley feels like
commuter to Westport. Wants to equip farmers with attaché cases.
December 21. Last minute rush. Not enough clichés. Send crew out to
film clichés. Sequence of slit skirts. Even knobby, dumpy legs look al-
luring, even though less shown than on any beach. Difference between
verb display and verb reveal. Very difficult to film. Finally hire four
dance hall girls who do as told, into and out of rickshaw, up and down

streets for different angles. Girl in cheogsam getting out of sports car
—best of both civilizations. Tea for dance hall girls. How to list on
expense accounts?

Suit doesn't fit. Brinkley's do. Learn too late he has sneaked off to
another tailor. His tailor has no son at M.I.T.

December 22. Elevator man asks, You leave today? How did he know?
I off twelve o'clock. Room boys also ask. Also doorman. Also bellhops.
Have finally found real Hong Kong underground. Tip everybody. Clear,
sunny, warm, busy airport. Brinkley still overweight. Most pills intact.
Tokyo airport newsstand closed. Cross international dateline.

December 22. San Francisco. Unshaven. Red-eyed. Short-tempered.
Waiting to make telephone calls. Brinkley asks stranger is today Thursday or Friday? Stranger says Thursday. Later I hear him ask, Is that
really David Brinkley?

Plan to have suit altered.

HONORS LIST
Graduate School of Journalism, Columbia University
1913-1963

These alumni of the Graduate School of Journalism were cited for professional accomplishment in journalism or related fields as part of the School's semi-centennial celebration. They received bronze medallions bearing the School's anniversary motto, "That the People Shall Know." The following list, representative rather than inclusive, records those honored up to August 15, 1963. Nominations for the list were made by graduates of the School.

ELIE ABEL '42, commentator, National Broadcasting Company

CARL W. ACKERMAN '13, dean emeritus, Graduate School of Journalism, Columbia University

PHELPS ADAMS '24, vice president, public relations, United States Steel Corporation; former chief, New York Sun, Washington Bureau, and president of the Gridiron Club

RICHARD T. BAKER '37, associate dean, Graduate School of Journalism, Columbia University

LINCOLN BARNETT '31, freelance writer, author

EVERETT A. BAUMAN '41, public relations manager, Creole Petroleum Corporation, Caracas; former United Press correspondent

ELLIOTT V. BELL '25, editor and publisher, Business Week

JULES BERGMAN, Advanced Science Writing Program 1959-1960, science editor, American Broadcasting Company

THEODORE M. BERNSTEIN '25, assistant managing editor, The New York Times

MURRAY TEIGH BLOOM '38, freelance writer, founder and president, Society of Magazine Writers

F. FRASER BOND '21, author and former professor of journalism

HAL BORLAND '23, author and outdoor editorial essayist, The New York Times

MILTON BRACKER '31, general assignment reporter, The New York Times; Maria Moors Cabot Prize, Columbia University, 1949

HERBERT BRUCKER '24, editor, Hartford Courant; president, American Society of Newspaper Editors, 1963-1964

ROGER BUTTERFIELD '28, author and former national affairs editor, Life

HODDING CARTER '29, author; editor and publisher, Greenville (Miss.) Delta Democrat-Times; Pulitzer Prize for editorials, 1946

BENNETT CERF '20, president, Random House, book publishers; author and television panelist

LENOIR CHAMBERS '18, retired editor, Norfolk Virginian-Pilot; Pulitzer Prize for editorials, 1960

HARDING S. CHRIST '29, managing editor, Cleveland Press

GRADY CLAY '39, editor, Landscape Architecture; real estate editor, Louisville Courier-Journal

JOHN CRIDER '28, information officer, Committee for Economic Development; former editor-in-chief, Boston Herald; Pulitzer Prize for editorials, 1949

JUDITH CRIST '45, film critic and associate drama critic, New York Herald-Tribune

SAMUEL DAWSON '23, financial columnist, Associated Press

SANCHE DE GRAMONT '55, foreign correspondent, New York Herald Tribune, Rome; Pulitzer Prize for local reporting, 1961

PIERRE J. M. DENOYER '27, editor, Selection du Reader's Digest, Paris

EVEREST P. DERTHICK '23, member of the faculty, School of Journalism, Ohio State University; former managing editor, Cleveland Plain Dealer

HOWARD DIETZ '17, lyricist and publicist

MARCUS DUFFIELD '26, former editor of "History in the Making" section, New York Herald Tribune

WILLIAM DWIGHT '26, publisher, Holyoke Mass. Transcript-Telegram and other newspapers; former president, American Newspaper Publishers Association

DANIEL J. EDELMAN '41, president, Daniel J. Edelman Associates, Inc., Chicago; former newswriter, Columbia Broadcasting System

WALTER EVERETT '33, associate director, American Press Institute, Columbia University

STERLING W. FISHER '22, public relations director, Reader's Digest, and director of the Reader's Digest Foundation; formerly Director of Public Affairs, National Broadcasting Company

REUVEN FRANK '47, television producer, National Broadcasting Company

EMANUEL R. FREEDMAN '32, foreign news editor, The New York Times

ROBERT E. GARST '24, assistant managing editor, The New York Times

MAXWELL M. GEFFEN '16, publisher of Medical World News and chairman of the board of Arrow Press and other publishing enterprises; former editor, Omnibook

EMILY GENAUER '30, art critic, New York Herald Tribune

WILLIAM GILES '51, editor, National Observer, Washington, D.C.

MATTHEW GORDON '32, director of information, Communications Satellite Corporation; former director of press services, United Nations

BEATRICE BLACKMAR GOULD '24, former co-editor, Ladies Home Journal

OLIVER GRAMLING '27, former assistant general manager, The Associated Press

GERALD GREEN '47, novelist; television producer, National Broadcasting Company

GEORGE GRIM '34, columnist, Minneapolis Tribune; television commentator

LEONARD GROSS '50, senior editor, Look

ROBERT M. HALL '35, president, The Hall Syndicate, Inc.

WILLIAM E. HALL '50, director, School of Journalism, University of Nebraska

PHILIP HAMBURGER '38, author and staff writer, The New Yorker

GUY HENLE '42, executive editor, House Beautiful

MARGUERITE HIGGINS '42, diplomatic correspondent, New York Herald Tribune; Pulitzer Prize for international reporting, 1951

JOHN HOHENBERG '27, professor, Graduate School of Journalism, Columbia University, and secretary of the advisory board on the Pulitzer Prizes

GEORGE HORNE '27, transport news editor, The New York Times

GEORGE A. HOUGH JR. '17, editor and publisher, Falmouth Mass. Enterprise

CLARA SHARPE HOUGH '18, co-editor and co-publisher, Falmouth Mass. Enterprise; novelist

HENRY BEETLE HOUGH '18, author; co-editor and co-publisher, The Vineyard Gazette, Edgartown, Mass.

ELIZABETH BOWIE HOUGH '19, co-editor and co-publisher, The Vineyard Gazette, Edgartown, Mass.

MARIA CONSTANZA HUERGO '39, London

correspondent, La Prensa, Buenos Aires; Maria Moors Cabot Prize, 1950

JOHN L. HULTENG '47, dean, School of Journalism, University of Oregon

ROBERT L. JINKS '56, executive city editor, Miami Herald

HOWARD P. JONES '21, United States ambassador to Indonesia

JOSEPH L. JONES '22, vice president for international operations, United Press International

FRANK J. JORDAN '50, manager of election planning and former chief, midwest bureau, National Broadcasting Company

ALLAN KELLER '26, staff writer, New York World-Telegram & Sun; author

ARDIS M. KENNEDY '17, retired Sunday editor and day managing editor, Chicago Tribune

GEORGE R. LAMADE '17, president and general manager, Grit, Williamsport, Pa.

MYRICK LAND '46, senior editor, Look; author

JOHN E. LEARD '46, managing editor, Richmond Va. Times-Dispatch

IRVING R. LEVINE '47, Mediterranean director, National Broadcasting Company; author

FLORA LEWIS '42, London correspondent, Washington Post and Times-Herald; author

A. J. LIEBLING '25, staff writer, New Yorker; author

JOSEPH A. LOFTUS '31, Washington bureau, The New York Times

STUART H. LOORY '58, science writer, New York Herald Tribune

SAMUEL LUBELL '33, political analyst and syndicated columnist

JOHN MAGOR '37, publisher, Cowichan Leader (Duncan, British Columbia) and other newspapers

LESTER MARKEL '14, Sunday editor, The New York Times

ROBERT P. MARTIN '38, Far Eastern editor, U. S. News & World Report

BURTON W. MARVIN '37, dean, William Allen White School of Journalism and Public Information, University of Kansas

WILLIAM MCGAFFIN '35, Washington correspondent, Chicago Daily News

FOYE F. MCNAUGHTON '15, publisher, Pekin Ill. Daily Times and other newspapers

JOHN A. MCWETHY '36, managing editor, midwest edition, Wall Street Journal

GEORGE R. METCALF '37, New York state senator from Auburn and columnist for the Auburn Citizen-Advertiser

DAVID MILLER '58, Moscow correspondent, New York Herald Tribune

EUGENE MILLER '48, vice president and director of public affairs and communications, McGraw-Hill Publishing Company

HARRY S. MILLIGAN '51, general manager and co-publisher, Binghamton N. Y. Sun-Bulletin

ARTHUR F. MONROE '37, vice president and director of public affairs for J. M. Mathes, Inc.; former foreign correspondent, United Press International; and former staff member of Time

PAT MUNROE '41, chief, Munroe News Bureau, Washington, D.C.; Washington correspondent, Editor & Publisher

ROBERT NEVILLE '29, author; former Near East correspondent, Time and Life

MARSHALL E. NEWTON '24, assistant city editor, The New York Times

ROBERT C. NOTSON '26, managing editor, Portland Oregonian

MICHAEL J. OGDEN '32, executive editor, Providence R. I. Journal and Bulletin

ALLAN L. OTTEN '42, White House correspondent, Wall Street Journal

VANCE PACKARD '37, author, magazine writer, lecturer

WAYNE W. PARRISH '29, editor and publisher, American Aviation Publications, Washington, D.C.

BUEL W. PATCH '23, associate editor, Editorial Research Reports, Washington, D.C.

DAVID PERLMAN '40, science editor, San Francisco Chronicle

JOSEPH B. PHILLIPS '22, public affairs officer, U. S. Embassy, Rome; former foreign editor, Newsweek

WAYNE PHILLIPS '49, special assistant to the administrator, United States Housing and Home Finance Agency; former reporter, The New York Times

ALICE FOX PITTS '17, former executive secretary, American Society of Newspaper Editors

FREDERIC G. PITTS '17, former editor, American Society of Newspaper Editors Bulletin

HENRIETTA MALKIEL POYNTER '22, editor, Congressional Quarterly Services, Washington, D.C.; associate editor and vice president, St. Petersburg Fla. Times

GABE PRESSMAN '47, radio and television reporter, National Broadcasting Company

HUGH W. ROBERTSON '15, vice president, Westchester County Publishers, Inc.

DAVID B. ROGERS '23, editor-in-chief, Regina Saskatchewan Leader-Post; former president, Canadian Press

ABRAHAM D. ROTHMAN '17, former American representative of the Sydney, Australia, Morning Herald and associated newspapers

MERRYLE S. RUKEYSER '17, syndicated financial columnist

JAMES B. L. RUSH '37, executive news editor, Winston-Salem N. C. Journal and Sentinel

MORRIE RYSKIND '17, columnist, Los Angeles Times; film writer and playwright; Pulitzer Prize for "Of Thee I Sing," 1932

ELLIOTT M. SANGER '17, vice president and general manager, radio station WQXR

MARIE F. SAUER '35, women's editor, Washington Post and Times Herald

RICHARD J. SCHAAP '56, senior editor, Newsweek

LEWIS L. SCHELLBACH '27, vice president and managing editor, Standard & Poor's Corporation

DANA ADAMS SCHMIDT '38, foreign correspondent, The New York Times, Beirut

M. LINCOLN SCHUSTER '17, president and editor-in-chief, Simon & Schuster, Inc., book publishers

FRANK SCULLY '17, humorist, author, columnist

JOHN H. SECONDARI '40, executive producer for special projects, American Broadcasting Company; author

ROBERT SHAPLEN '38, staff writer, New Yorker; author

LEROY E. SMITH '47, editorial writer, Buffalo Evening News

RALPH B. SMITH '17, former vice president and editorial director, publications division, McGraw-Hill Publishing Company

ROBERT W. SOUTHAM '37, publisher, Ottawa Citizen; former president, Canadian Daily Newspaper Publishers Association

ROBERT M. SPEIDEL '41, former editor and publisher, Visalia Calif. Times-Delta

SAMUEL SPEWACK '20, playwright

RICHARD SPONG '41, associate editor, Editorial Research Reports, Washington, D.C.

JACK STEELE '37, chief, Washington bureau, Scripps-Howard Newspapers

JOHN E. STEMPEL '28, chairman, Department of Journalism, Indiana University

MORT STERN '49, editor of the editorial page, Denver Post

KENNETH N. STEWART '30, professor, Department of Journalism, University of California, Berkeley; former president, Association for Education in Journalism

MARVIN L. STONE '49, national staff, U. S. News & World Report

JOHN STROHMEYER '48, editor and vice president, Bethlehem Pa. Globe-Times

ANSEL E. TALBERT '35, vice president and executive editor, Flight Safety Foundation; former military and aviation editor, New York Herald Tribune

JOHN TEBBEL '37, chairman, Department of Journalism, New York University; author

KATHLEEN TELTSCH '44, United Nations correspondent, The New York Times

ALAN H. TEMPLE '17, retired vice chairman, First National City Bank of New York

OTTO D. TOLISCHUS '16, editorial writer, The New York Times; Pulitzer Prize for foreign correspondence, 1940

DOUGLAS TOMLINSON '14, founder and chairman of the board, All-Church Press

HOLLINGTON K. TONG '13, former ambassador of the Republic of China to the United States

DALLAS S. TOWNSEND JR. '41, staff correspondent, Columbia Broadcasting System

GLENN TUCKER '15, historian and author

FREDERIC F. VAN DE WATER '14, novelist and historian

A. GAYLE WALDROP '22, professor and former director, College of Journalism, University of Colorado

R. LYLE WEBSTER '29, director of information, United States Department of Agriculture

RICHARD WITKIN '40, aviation-aerospace editor, The New York Times

IRA WOLFERT '30, staff writer, Reader's Digest; Pulitzer Prize for international reporting, 1943

WILLIAM J. WOESTENDIEK '48, editorial director, Newsday, Garden City, Long Island

AHMED E. YALMAN '13, former editor, Daily Vatan, Istanbul

MORTON YARMON '35, associate managing editor, Parade